Working Together to Safeguard Children

A guide to inter-agency working to safeguard and promote the welfare of children

HM Government

2006

London: TSO

Published by TSO (The Stationery Office) and available from:

Online
www.tsoshop.co.uk

Mail, Telephone, Fax and E-mail
TSO
PO Box 29, Norwich, NR3 1GN
Telephone orders/General enquiries: 0870 600 5522
Fax orders: 0870 600 5533
E-mail: customer.services@tso.co.uk
Textphone 0870 240 3701

TSO Shops
123 Kingsway, London, WC2B 6PQ
020 7242 6393 Fax 020 7242 6394
68-69 Bull Street, Birmingham B4 6AD
0121 236 9696 Fax 0121 236 9699
9-21 Princess Street, Manchester M60 8AS
0161 834 7201 Fax 0161 833 0634
16 Arthur Street, Belfast BT1 4GD
028 9023 8451 Fax 028 9023 5401
18-19 High Street, Cardiff CF10 1PT
029 2039 5548 Fax 029 2038 4347
71 Lothian Road, Edinburgh EH3 9AZ
0870 606 5566 Fax 0870 606 5588

TSO Accredited Agents
(see Yellow Pages)

and through good booksellers

Published with the permission of the Department for Education and Skills
on behalf of the Controller of Her Majesty's Stationery Office

ISBN-13: 978 0 11 271187 2
ISBN-10: 0 11 271187 1

Printed in the United Kingdom for The Stationery Office
N188401 09/06 C1500

Contents

Part 2: Non-statutory practice guidance

Working Together to Safeguard Children: Executive Summary

This document sets out how organisations and individuals should work together to safeguard and promote the welfare of children.

It is addressed to practitioners and front-line managers who have particular responsibilities for safeguarding and promoting the welfare of children, and to senior and operational managers, in:

- organisations that are responsible for commissioning or providing services to children, young people, and adults who are parents/carers, and
- organisations that have a particular responsibility for safeguarding and promoting the welfare of children.

Part 1 of the document comprises Chapters 1 to 8, which are issued as statutory guidance. Practitioners and agencies will have different responsibilities that apply to different areas of the guidance and should look in the preface for a fuller explanation of their statutory duties. Part 2 of the document incorporates Chapters 9 to 12 and is issued as non-statutory practice guidance.

This executive summary is not guidance in itself. It is included to help readers gain an overview of the document.

Part 1: Statutory guidance

Chapter 1 – Introduction: working together to safeguard and promote the welfare of children and families

Chapter 1 sets the context for the revised guidance by discussing the reasons for the changes in safeguarding policy and practice since 1999. It also outlines the key definitions and concepts used in the guidance.

The statutory inquiry into the death of Victoria Climbié (2003), and the first joint Chief Inspectors' Report on safeguarding children (2002), highlighted the lack of priority status given to safeguarding. The Government's responses to these findings included the Green

Paper *Every Child Matters* and the provisions in the Children Act 2004. Three of the most important in this context are:

- the creation of children's trusts under the duty to co-operate
- the setting up of Local Safeguarding Children Boards (LSCBs)
- the duty on all agencies to make arrangements to safeguard and promote the welfare of children.

A shared responsibility and the need for effective joint working between agencies and professionals that have different roles and expertise are required if children are to be protected from harm and their welfare promoted. In order to achieve this joint working, there must be constructive relationships between individual practitioners, promoted and supported by:

- the commitment of senior managers to safeguard and promote the welfare of children; and
- clear lines of accountability.

Chapter 2 – Roles and responsibilities

Chapter 2 explains the roles, responsibilities and duties of the different people and organisations that work directly with, and whose work affects, children and young people. It states that all organisations that provide services or work with children and young people should:

- have senior managers who are committed to children's and young people's wellbeing and safety
- be clear about people's responsibilities to safeguard and promote children's and young people's welfare
- have effective recruitment and human resources procedures, including checking all new staff and volunteers to make sure they are safe to work with children and young people
- have procedures for dealing with allegations of abuse against members of staff and volunteers
- make sure staff get training that helps them do their job well
- have procedures about how to safeguard and promote the welfare of young people
- have agreements about working with other organisations.

Section 11 of the Children Act 2004 and s175 of the Education Act 2002 place duties on organisations and individuals to ensure that their functions are discharged with regard to the need to safeguard and promote the welfare of children. An overview of these duties and the structure of children's services under the Children Act 2004 are set out in the preface to this guidance and Appendix 1.

Safeguarding and promoting the welfare of children is the responsibility of the local authority (LA), working in partnership with other public organisations, the voluntary sector, children and young people, parents and carers, and the wider community. A key objective for LAs is to ensure that children are protected from harm. Other functions in LAs that play an important role in safeguarding are housing, sport, culture and leisure services, and youth services.

Health professionals and organisations have a key role to play in safeguarding and promoting the welfare of children. The general principles they should apply are:

- aim to ensure that all affected children receive appropriate and timely therapeutic and preventative interventions
- those professionals who work directly with children should ensure that safeguarding and promoting their welfare forms an integral part of all stages of care they offer
- those professionals who come into contact with children, parents and carers in the course of their work also need to be aware of their safeguarding responsibilities
- ensure that all health professionals can recognise risk factors and contribute to reviews, enquiries and child protection plans, as well as planning support for children and providing ongoing promotional and preventative support through proactive work.

Standard 5 of the *National Service Framework for Children, Young People and Maternity Services* sets the standards for health and social care agencies' work to prevent children suffering harm and to promote their welfare.

The police recognise the fundamental importance of inter-agency working in combating child abuse, as illustrated by well-established arrangements for joint training involving police and social work colleagues. All forces have child abuse investigation units (CAIU) and while they normally take responsibility for investigating such cases, safeguarding children is a fundamental part of the duties of all police officers. The police are committed to sharing information and intelligence with other organisations and should be notified as soon as possible where a criminal offence has been, or is suspected of, being committed.

LSCBs should have in place a protocol agreed between the LA and the police, to guide both organisations in deciding how child protection enquiries should be conducted, and in which circumstances joint enquiries are appropriate.

Probation services supervise offenders with the aim of reducing re-offending and protecting the public. By working with offenders who are parents/carers, Offender Managers can safeguard and promote the welfare of children. Probation areas will also:

- supervise 16- and 17-year-olds on Community Punishment

- second staff to Youth Offending Teams
- provide a service to child victims of serious sexual or violent offences.

Offender Managers should also ensure there is clarity and communication between risk management processes; these are described in greater detail in Chapter 12.

Governors/Directors of all prison establishments must have in place arrangements that protect the public from prisoners in their care. All prisoners who have been identified as presenting a risk to children will not be allowed contact with them unless a favourable risk assessment has been undertaken by the police, probation, prison and social care services. Governors/Directors of women's establishments with Mother and Baby Units need to ensure that staff working on duty are prioritised for child protection training.

Governors/Directors of juvenile Young Offenders' Institutions are required to adhere to the policies, agreed by the Prison Service and the Youth Justice Board, for safeguarding and promoting the welfare of children held in custody.

Secure Training Centres (STCs) house vulnerable, sentenced and remanded juveniles aged between 12 and 17. Each STC has a duty to safeguard and promote the welfare of the children in its custody.

Youth Offending Teams (Yots) are responsible for the supervision of children and young people subject to pre-court interventions and statutory court disposals. Yots have a duty to make arrangements to ensure that their functions are discharged with regard to the need to safeguard and promote the welfare of children.

Schools (including independent and non-maintained schools) and further education institutions have a duty to safeguard and promote the welfare of pupils under the Education Act 2002. They should create and maintain a safe learning environment for children and young people, and identify where there are child welfare concerns and take action to address them, in partnership with other organisations where appropriate.

Childminders and everyone working in day care services should know how to recognise and respond to the possible abuse and neglect of a child. All organisations providing day care must have a designated person who liaises with local child protection agencies and Ofsted on child protection issues.

In care and related proceedings under the Children Act 1989, the responsibility of the Children and Family Court Advisory and Support Service (CAFCASS) is to safeguard and promote the interests of individual children who are the subject of family proceedings by providing independent social work advice to the court.

Looking after under-18s in the armed forces comes under the MoD's comprehensive welfare arrangements, which apply to all members of the armed forces. There is already a responsibility on social care services to monitor the wellbeing of care leavers, and those joining the armed forces have unrestricted access to LA social services workers.

The voluntary sector is active in working to safeguard the children and young people with whom they work, and provides a key role in providing information and resources to the wider public about the needs of children.

Faith communities provide a wide range of activities for children and, as such, should have appropriate arrangements in place to safeguard and promote their welfare.

Chapter 3 – Local Safeguarding Children Boards

Chapter 3 explains the role, functions, governance and operation of Local Safeguarding Children Boards (LSCBs).

The LSCB is the key statutory mechanism for agreeing how the relevant organisations in each local area will co-operate to safeguard and promote the welfare of children, and for ensuring the effectiveness of what they do.

The scope of the LSCB role falls into three categories: firstly, they will engage in activities that safeguard all children and aim to identify and prevent maltreatment, or impairment of health or development, and ensure that children are growing up in circumstances consistent with safe and effective care; secondly, they will lead and co-ordinate proactive work that aims to target particular groups; and thirdly, they will lead and co-ordinate arrangements for responsive work to protect children who are suffering, or at risk of suffering, maltreatment.

The core functions of an LSCB are set out in Regulations and are:

- policies and procedures including those on:
    - action taken where there are concerns, including thresholds for intervention
    - training of people who work with children or in services affecting the safety and welfare of children
    - recruitment and supervision of people who work with children
    - investigation of allegations concerning people who work with children
    - safety and welfare of children who are privately fostered
    - co-operation with neighbouring children's services authorities (i.e. LAs) and their LSCB partners
- communicating and raising awareness
- monitoring and evaluation
- participating in planning and commissioning
- reviewing the deaths of children
- serious case reviews.

County-level and unitary LAs are responsible for establishing an LSCB in their area and ensuring that it is run effectively. LSCBs should have a clear and distinct identity within local children's trust governance arrangements. It is the responsibility of the LA to appoint the Chair.

Membership of the LSCB is made up of senior managers from different services and agencies in a local area, including the independent and voluntary sector. In addition, the Board receives input from experts – e.g. the designated nurse or doctor.

To function effectively, LSCBs need to be supported by their member organisations with adequate and reliable resources. The budget for each LSCB and the contribution made by each member organisation should be agreed locally.

LSCB work should be effectively planned and is usually part of the Children and Young People's Plan.

The LSCBs' work to ensure the effectiveness of work by member organisations will be a peer review process, based on self-evaluation, performance indicators and joint audit.

Chapter 4 – Inter-agency training and development

Chapter 4 is about training and development. Training for multi- and inter-agency working means training that will equip people to work effectively with those from other agencies.

Employers are responsible for ensuring their employees are confident and competent in carrying out their responsibilities, and for ensuring employees are aware of how to recognise and respond to safeguarding concerns. Employers should also identify adequate resources and support for inter-agency training.

LAs and their partners are responsible for ensuring that workforce strategies are developed in the local area, including making sure that the training opportunities to meet the needs of the workforce are identified and met by LSCBs. The LSCBs should work within the workforce strategy to manage the identification of training needs; use the information to inform the planning and commissioning of training; and check and evaluate single- and inter-agency training.

All training in safeguarding and promoting the welfare of children should create an ethos that:

- values working collaboratively
- respects diversity
- promotes equality
- is child-centred
- promotes the participation of children and families in the processes.

It should also work within *The Common Core of Skills and Knowledge* (2005) for the Children's Workforce. This sets out the six areas of expertise that everyone working with children, young people and families should be able to demonstrate. It can be found at: www.everychildmatters.gov.uk/deliveringservices/commoncore/.

Training and development for inter-agency work at the appropriate level should be targeted at practitioners in voluntary, statutory and independent agencies who:

- are in regular contact with children and young people
- work regularly with children and young people, and with adults who are parents or carers, and who may be asked to contribute to assessments of children in need
- have particular responsibility for safeguarding children.

Training and development are also relevant to operational managers and those with strategic responsibility for services.

Chapter 5 – Managing individual cases

Chapter 5 provides guidance on what should happen if somebody has concerns about the welfare of a child (including those living away from home) and, in particular, concerns that a child may be suffering, or may be at risk of suffering, significant harm. It also sets out the principles that underpin work to safeguard and promote the welfare of children.

The chapter is structured according to the four key processes that underpin work with children and families: assessment, planning, intervention and reviewing, as set out in the *Integrated Children's System* (2002). The *Framework for The Assessment of Children in Need and their Families* (2000) should be followed when undertaking assessments on children in need and their families.

The chapter sets out in detail the processes to be followed when safeguarding and promoting the welfare of children. These include:

- responding to concerns about the welfare of a child and making a referral to a statutory organisation (children's social care, the police or the NSPCC) that can take action to safeguard and promote the welfare of children
- undertaking an initial assessment of the child's situation and deciding what to do next
- taking urgent action to protect the child from harm, if necessary
- holding a strategy discussion where there are concerns that a child may be suffering significant harm and, where appropriate, convening a child protection conference
- deciding whether a child is at continuing risk of significant harm and therefore should be the subject of a child protection plan, implementing the plan and reviewing it at regular intervals.

Effective supervision is important in promoting good standards of practice, and supervisors should be available to practitioners as an important source of advice and expertise.

Chapter 6 – Supplementary guidance on safeguarding and promoting the welfare of children

Chapter 6 summarises the supplementary guidance to *Working Together to Safeguard Children*.

The following guidance is available:

- Department of Health, Home Office (2000). *Safeguarding Children Involved in Prostitution*
- Department of Health, Home Office, Department for Education and Skills, Welsh Assembly Government (2002). *Safeguarding Children in whom Illness is Fabricated or Induced*
- Home Office, Department of Health (2002). *Complex Child Abuse Investigations: Inter-agency issues*
- Home Office. *Female Circumcision Act* (1985). *Female Genital Mutilation Act* (2003). Home Office Circular 10/2004
- Association of Directors of Social Services, Department of Education and Skills, Department of Heath, Home Office, Foreign and Commonwealth Office (2004). *Young People and Vulnerable Adults Facing Forced Marriage.* Practice Guidance for Social Workers; and
- Guidance on allegations of abuse made against a person who works with children, which can be found in Appendix 5 of this document.

Chapter 7 – Child death review processes

Chapter 7 sets out the procedures to be followed when a child dies in the LSCB area(s) covered by a Child Death Overview Panel.

There are two inter-related processes for reviewing child deaths:

- a rapid response by a group of key professionals who come together for the purpose of enquiring into and evaluating each unexpected death of a child
- an overview of all child deaths in the area, undertaken by a panel.

Either of these processes can identify cases requiring a Serious Case Review (covered in Chapter 8).

As stated in Chapter 3, the LSCB Regulations mean that the functions to which Chapter 7 relates will come into force on 1 April 2008, but can be carried out by any LSCB from 1 April 2006. When an LSCB commences this function before that date, it should follow the guidance in this chapter.

Chapter 8 – Serious case reviews

Chapter 8 sets out the procedures LSCBs should follow when undertaking a serious case review.

When a child dies, and abuse or neglect are known or suspected to be a factor in the death, the LSCB should always conduct a serious case review. This should look at the involvement with the child and family of organisations and professionals to consider whether there are any lessons to be learned about the ways in which they work together to safeguard and promote the welfare of children. Additionally, LSCBs should always consider whether a serious case review should be conducted in other circumstances where a child has been harmed. These circumstances are set out in the guidance.

Following the serious case review, an action plan should be drawn up and implemented. Reviews are of little value unless lessons are learned from them. At least as much effort should be spent on acting on recommendations as conducting the review.

Part 2: Non-statutory practice guidance

Chapter 9 – Lessons from research and inspection

Chapter 9 summarises the impact of maltreatment on children's health and developmental progress, and goes on to set out some of the key messages from research and inspection that have informed this guidance.

The sustained maltreatment of children – physically, emotionally, sexually or through neglect – can have major long-term effects on all aspects of a child's health, development and wellbeing.

Professionals must take special care to help safeguard and promote the welfare of children and young people who may be living in particularly stressful circumstances. These include families:

- living in poverty
- where there is domestic violence
- where a parent has a mental illness
- where a parent is misusing drugs or alcohol
- where a parent has a learning disability
- that face racism and other forms of social isolation
- living in areas with a lot of crime, poor housing and high unemployment.

Chapter 10 – Implementing the principles on working with children and their families

Chapter 10 sets out in more detail specific aspects of working with children, young people and families.

Family Group Conferences (FGCs) may be appropriate in a number of contexts where there is a plan or decision to be made. The family is the primary planning group in the process. Where there are plans to use FGCs in situations where there are concerns about possible harm to a child, they should be developed and implemented under the LSCB. FGCs should not replace or remove the need for child protection conferences.

Children and families may be supported through their involvement in safeguarding processes by advice and advocacy services, and they should always be informed of services that exist locally and nationally.

LAs have a responsibility to children and adults to understand the processes that will be followed when there are concerns about the child. Information should be available in the family's preferred language.

Children from all cultures are subject to abuse and neglect, and while professionals should be sensitive to differing family patterns and lifestyles, they must be clear that child abuse cannot be condoned for religious or cultural reasons.

Chapter 11 – Safeguarding and promoting the welfare of children who may be particularly vulnerable

Chapter 11 outlines the circumstances of children who may be particularly vulnerable. The purpose of this chapter is to help inform rather than substitute the procedures in Chapter 5, which sets out the basic framework within which action should be taken when a parent, professional or any other person has concerns about the welfare of a child.

It gives advice to organisations and individuals on safeguarding in the context of:

- children living away from home
- the abuse of disabled children
- abuse by children and young people
- bullying
- children whose behaviour indicates a lack of parental control
- race and racism
- domestic violence
- children of drug-misusing parents
- child abuse linked to belief in 'possession' or 'witchcraft', or in other ways related to spiritual or religious beliefs
- child abuse and information communication technology (ICT)
- children and families who go missing

- children of families living in temporary accommodation
- migrant children
- child victims of trafficking
- unaccompanied asylum-seeking children (UASC).

Chapter 12 – Managing individuals who pose a risk of harm to children

Chapter 12 provides practice guidance and information about a range of mechanisms that are available when managing people who have been identified as presenting a risk, or potential risk, of harm to children.

The Children Act 1989 recognised that the identification and investigation of child abuse, together with the protection and support of victims and their families, requires multi-agency collaboration. As part of that protection, action has been taken, usually by the police and social services, to prosecute known offenders or control their access to vulnerable children. The Sexual Offences Act 2003 introduced a number of new offences to deal with those who abuse and exploit children in this way. Both Acts can be found at: www.opsi.gov.uk.

The term 'Schedule One offender' should no longer be used for anyone convicted of a crime against a child. The focus should be on whether the individual poses a 'risk of harm to children'. Interim guidance has been issued explaining how these people who present a potential risk of harm to children should be identified. This can be found at: www.knowledgenetwork.gov.uk. Practitioners should use the new list of offences as a 'trigger' to further assessments.

Where the offender is given a community sentence, Offender Managers monitor their risk to others and liaise with partner agencies. Prison establishments undertake a similar responsibility where the offender has been sentenced to a period of custody.

The Multi Agency Public Protection Arrangements (MAPPA) provide a national framework for the assessment and management of risks posed by serious and violent offenders. The Responsible Authorities need to ensure that strategies to address risk are identified, and plans developed, implemented and reviewed on a regular basis. The MAPPA framework identifies three separate but connected levels at which risk is managed:

- ordinary risk management
- local inter-agency risk management
- Multi Agency Public Protection Panels (MAPPP).

There are other processes and mechanisms for working with and monitoring people who may present a risk to children. For example, the Protection of Children Act 1999 gives the Secretary of State power to keep a list of people who are unsuitable to work with children in childcare positions. DfES List 99 is a confidential list of people whom the Secretary of State has directed may not be employed by LAs, schools and further education institutions as a teacher, or in work involving regular contact with children under 18 years of age.[1] As another example, people placed on the sex offender list are served with a notification that ensures the police are informed of their whereabouts in the community.

1 The Safeguarding Vulnerable Groups Bill, the legislation necessary to implement the Government's response to Recommendation 19 of the Bichard Inquiry, to set up a vetting and barring scheme, was introduced to Parliament on 28 February 2006. www.parliament.gov.uk

Preface

Background and how to read the document

Working Together to Safeguard Children has evolved through several revisions, to try to provide a clear and detailed procedural guide. It is a lengthy document containing a good deal of material on how to safeguard children in different situations. Some parts of the document are statutory guidance for particular organisations and this is set out below. However, it is not necessary for all practitioners to read every part of *Working Together* to understand the principles and perform their roles effectively. Table 1 sets out for reference which parts of the document are particularly relevant to different roles. The rest of the document contains information that may also be useful.

Purpose of the document and who should read it

This document sets out how organisations and individuals should work together to safeguard and promote the welfare of children.

It is addressed to practitioners and front-line managers who have particular responsibilities for safeguarding and promoting the welfare of children, and to senior and operational managers, in organisations that:

- are responsible for commissioning or providing services to children, young people, and adults who are parents/carers
- have a particular responsibility for safeguarding and promoting the welfare of children.

Table 1 can be used as a guide to navigate the document. All practitioners and managers may be required to read chapters that are not listed as necessary under their job function in particular circumstances.

Table 1: How to use this document

Practitioners	**Chapters it is necessary to read**	**Chapters it is advisable to read**
Those with a strategic and managerial responsibility for commissioning and delivering services for children and families	1, 2, 3, 4, 5	6, 9, 10
Operational managers within organisations employing staff to work with children and families, or with responsibility for commissioning and delivering services	1, 2 (relevant section), 5	3, 4, 6, 9, 10, 11, 12
Those with a particular responsibility for safeguarding children, such as designated health and education professionals, police, social workers	1, 2, 3, 4, 5, 7, 8, 10, 11	6, 9, 12
Those who work regularly with children and young people and adults who are carers and who may be asked to contribute to assessments of children in need	1, 2 (relevant section), 5, 11	6, 8, 9, 10, 12
Others in contact with children and young people and parents who are carers	It is not necessary for others to read this document. Instead read the summary guide *What To Do If You're Worried A Child Is Being Abused*	1, 2 (relevant section), 5, 10

For more detail on which practitioners come under which group, see paragraphs 4.19–4.20.

Content of this guidance

This guidance reflects the principles contained within the United Nations Convention on the Rights of the Child, ratified by the UK Government in 1991. It takes into account the European Convention of Human Rights, in particular Articles 6 and 8. It also takes account of other relevant legislation at the time of publication. It is particularly informed by the requirements of the Children Act 1989, which provides a comprehensive framework for the care and protection of children, and the Children Act 2004, which underpins the *Every Child Matters: Change for Children* programme and includes the provisions for the establishment of Local Safeguarding Children Boards.

Other related guidance

This document is one of a suite of five that gives guidance on children's trust governance and strategic planning, and on the cross-cutting issue of safeguarding and promoting the welfare of children. All documents referred to are accessible at: www.everychildmatters.gov.uk.

The five documents support provisions in the Children Act 2004, which underpin Every Child Matters: Change for Children. These include the creation of duties on local agencies in relation to children's and young people's 'wellbeing' and 'welfare'.

- (1) *Inter-Agency Co-operation to Improve Wellbeing of Children: Children's Trusts* describes the duties placed on local authorities (LAs) and other key partners to co-operate to improve the wellbeing of children and young people. The guidance sets out the features of co-operation through children's trusts and provides a strategic framework within which all children's services in an area will operate.
- 'Wellbeing' is based on five outcomes; their achievement of these is, in part, dependent upon the effective safeguarding and promotion of children's welfare. Statutory guidance on the (2) *Duty to Make arrangements to Safeguard and Promote the Welfare of Children* sets out the key arrangements agencies should make to safeguard and promote the welfare of children in the course of discharging their normal functions.
- Where an agency has both co-operation and safeguarding and promoting welfare duties, this is because it is both a strategic body with a significant impact on children's services within the LA area, and also an agency with direct responsibility for the provision of services to children and young people. Certain agencies are included within only one of these duties.
- Guidance on the (3) *Children and Young People's Plan* supports the fulfilment of both the co-operation and safeguarding and promoting welfare duties. The Regulations to which this guidance refers require LAs to work with partners to produce a strategic plan describing the actions and provisions by which they will achieve the five outcomes for children and young people. The removal of 19 other planning requirements will help to reduce the overall planning burden.

- Guidance on the governance, leadership and structures required within the new strategic framework is provided by (4) *The Role and Responsibilities of the Director of Children's Services and the Lead Member for Children's Services* and (5) the chapter on Local Safeguarding Children's Boards within this revised version of *Working Together to Safeguard Children*.

These five core documents should be used alongside other key policy and planning documents relating to Every Child Matters. These include:

- *The National Service Framework for Children, Young People and Maternity Services*, which sets out a 10-year programme to stimulate long-term and sustained improvement in children's health and wellbeing. This guidance will help health and social care organisations to meet Standard Five on safeguarding and promoting the welfare of children and young people
- *Every Child Matters: Change for Children – Young People and Drugs*, which gives guidance on co-operation and joint planning to counter drug misuse
- *Duty on Local Authorities to Promote the Educational Achievement of Looked After children*, which sets out the implications of the new duty in the Children Act 2004 for LAs' strategic planning, joint area reviews and day-to-day working practices
- *The Framework for the Inspection of Children's Services*, which sets out the principles to be applied by an inspectorate or commission assessing any children's service, and defines the key judgements which, where appropriate and practical, inspections will seek to make. It is available from: www.ofsted.gov.uk
- *Sharing Information: Practitioner's Guide* and the supporting materials, which are for everyone who works with children and young people, and explain when and how information can be shared legally and professionally.

A number of other documents focus directly on integrated front-line delivery and the processes that support it. These can be found at: www.everychildmatters.gov.uk

Appendix 1 sets out the statutory framework for safeguarding and promoting children's welfare.

Status of the document as statutory guidance

This document is intended to provide a national framework within which agencies and professionals at local level – individually and jointly – draw up and agree on their own ways of working together to safeguard and promote the welfare of children. It applies to England.

This guidance replaces the previous version of *Working Together to Safeguard Children*, which was published in 1999. The supplementary guidance documents issued under that version, *Safeguarding Children Involved in Prostitution* (2000), and *Safeguarding Children in*

Whom Illness is Fabricated or Induced (2002) remain in force and now become supplements to this guidance. Both documents can be found at: www.dh.gov.uk/PublicationsAndStatistics/Publications/Publications/fs/en.

Part 1 of this document is statutory guidance. Part 2 is non-statutory practice guidance.

The whole of Part 1 is issued as guidance under **s7 of the Local Authority Social Services Act 1970**, which requires LAs in their social services functions to act under the general guidance of the Secretary of State. It should be complied with by LAs carrying out their social services functions, unless local circumstances indicate exceptional reasons that justify a variation.

Chapters 3, 4, 7 and 8 are issued under **s16 of the Children Act 2004**, which states that Children's Services Authorities (county-level and unitary LAs – see Glossary) and each of the statutory partners must, in exercising their functions relating to a Local Safeguarding Children Board (LSCB), have regard to any guidance given to them for the purpose by the Secretary of State. This means that they must take the guidance into account and, if they decide to depart from it, have clear reasons for doing so. A full list of statutory LSCB partners is given in Chapter 3 and summarised in Table A in Appendix 1.

Where this document is not statutory guidance for a particular organisation, it still represents a standard of good practice and will help organisations fulfil other duties in co-operation with partners. For example, managers and staff with a particular responsibility in the organisations covered by the duty to safeguard and promote the welfare of children in s11 of the Children Act 2004 (found at: www.everychildmatters.gov.uk/socialcare/safeguarding/) are encouraged to read this document and follow it in conjunction with the guidance on that duty. The same principle applies to educational institutions with duties in this area under the Education Act 2002, s157 and s175.

When does the guidance apply?

The requirement to have LSCBs in place applies from 1 April 2006 and the guidance in Chapter 3 should be followed from that date. The chapter was published in December 2005 to facilitate this.

The requirement for LSCBs to undertake the functions relating to child deaths will not apply until 1 April 2008. The requirements set out in Chapter 7 apply to all LSCBs from 1 April 2008. However, where an LSCB decides to undertake these functions before that date, the guidance in Chapter 7 will apply and should be followed.

Chapter 5 sets out the processes for recording that a child is the subject of a child protection plan, principally in paragraphs 5.141 to 5.143. This replaces the requirement in the previous version of Working Together to have in place a child protection register and will apply from 1 April 2008. This is to give LAs time to put in place the necessary IT systems before discontinuing their child protection registers. Authorities may move from the child protection register to the new mechanism at any point before 1 April 2008.

All other parts of the guidance will apply from 1 October 2006 to provide a transitional period in which LSCBs can update their policies and procedures.

Glossary

Terminology in this area is complex, and changes as services are reshaped. This glossary sets out what is meant in the document by some key terms.

Term used in this document	Meaning
Abuse and neglect	Forms of maltreatment of a child – see paragraphs 1.29–1.33 for details
Child	Anyone who has not yet reached their 18th birthday – see paragraph 1.17
Child protection	Process of protecting individual children identified as either suffering, or at risk of suffering, significant harm as a result of abuse or neglect – see paragraphs 1.20, 1.21 and Chapter 5
'Children's social care' or 'local authority (LA) children's social care'	The work of LAs exercising their social services functions with regard to children. This is not meant to imply a separate 'children's social services' department
Local authorities (LAs)	In this guidance, this generally means LAs that are children's services authorities – effectively, LAs that are responsible for social services and education. Section 63 of the Children Act 2004 defines a children's services authority in England as: a county council in England; a metropolitan district council; a non-metropolitan district council for an area where there is no county council; a London borough council; the Common Council of the City of London and the Council of the Isles of Scilly
Safeguarding and promoting the welfare of children	The process of protecting children from abuse or neglect, preventing impairment of their health and development, and ensuring they are growing up in circumstances consistent with the provision of safe and effective care that enables children to have optimum life chances and enter adulthood successfully. See paragraphs 1.18 and 1.19
Wellbeing	Section 10 of the Children Act 2004 requires LAs and other specified agencies to co-operate with a view to improving the wellbeing of children in relation to the five outcomes first set out in *Every Child Matters* – see paragraph 1.1

Part 1: Statutory guidance

Chapter 1 – Introduction: working together to safeguard and promote the welfare of children and families

Supporting children and families

1.1 All children deserve the opportunity to achieve their full potential. We set this out in five outcomes that are key to children and young people's wellbeing:

- stay safe
- be healthy
- enjoy and achieve
- make a positive contribution
- achieve economic wellbeing.

1.2 To achieve this, children need to feel loved and valued, and be supported by a network of reliable and affectionate relationships. If they are denied the opportunity and support they need to achieve these outcomes, children are at increased risk not only of an impoverished childhood, but also of disadvantage and social exclusion in adulthood. Abuse and neglect pose particular problems.

Parenting, family life and services

1.3 Patterns of family life vary and there is no one, perfect way to bring up children. Good parenting involves caring for children's basic needs, keeping them safe, showing them warmth and love, and providing the stimulation needed for their development and to help them achieve their potential, within a stable environment where they experience consistent guidance and boundaries.

1.4 Parenting can be challenging. Parents themselves require and deserve support. Asking for help should be seen as a sign of responsibility rather than as a parenting failure.

1.5 A wide range of services and professionals provide support to families in bringing up children. In the great majority of cases, it should be the decision of parents when to ask for help and advice on their children's care and upbringing. However, professionals do also need to engage parents early when to do so may prevent problems or difficulties becoming worse. Only in exceptional cases should there be compulsory intervention in family life – e.g. where this is necessary to safeguard a child from significant harm. Such intervention should – provided this is consistent with the safety and welfare of the child – support families in making their own plans for the welfare and protection of their children.

The inquiry into the death of Victoria Climbié, and the Chief Inspectors' safeguarding reports

1.6 Shortcomings when working to safeguard and promote children's welfare were brought into the spotlight once again with the death of Victoria Climbié and the subsequent inquiry. The inquiry revealed themes identified by past inquiries that resulted in a failure to intervene early enough. These included:

> *poor co-ordination; a failure to share information; the absence of anyone with a strong sense of accountability; and frontline workers trying to cope with staff vacancies, poor management and a lack of effective training (Cm 5860, p.5).*

1.7 The examination of the legislative framework for safeguarding and promoting the welfare of children set out in the Children Act 1989 found it to be basically sound: the difficulties lay not in relation to the law but in its interpretation, resources and implementation. The recommendations from the inquiry upheld the principles of the Children Act 1989 and made it clear that support services for children and families cannot be separated from services designed to investigate and protect children from deliberate harm.

1.8 In 2002, eight inspectorates published their report, *Safeguarding Children*, following joint inspections of children's safeguards. The inspectorates found that the priority given to safeguarding was not reflected firmly, coherently or consistently enough in service planning and resource allocation.

1.9 A second joint Chief Inspectors' Report on *Safeguarding Children* was published in July 2005. This report showed that since 2002, the priority given to safeguarding children across agencies has increased, and children are listened to and consulted better. Agencies are also working better together to identify and act on welfare concerns. However, the report identified some specific concerns about the priority given to safeguarding in practice and the safeguarding arrangements for particular groups of children, including disabled children and children living away from home.

The Government's response

1.10 The Government's response to the Victoria Climbié inquiry report and the first joint Chief Inspectors' Report (Cm 5861) identified the key features of an effective system to safeguard children. These informed the Green Paper *Every Child Matters* (Cm 5860) and the Children Act 2004, in particular the plans for integration of services around the needs of children through the creation of children's trusts, the requirement for local authorities (LAs) to set up Local Safeguarding Children Boards (LSCBs) and the new duty on agencies to make arrangements to safeguard and promote the welfare of children.

1.11 As part of its response to the Victoria Climbié inquiry, the Government published practice guidance to assist practitioners to work together to safeguard and promote the welfare of children and safeguard them from harm (Department of Health *et al.* (2003) *What To Do If You're Worried A Child Is Being Abused*). The document summarises the key processes set out in Chapter 5 of this guidance.

An integrated approach

1.12 Children have varying needs that change over time. Judgements on how best to intervene when there are concerns about harm to a child will often, and unavoidably, entail an element of risk – at the extreme, of leaving a child for too long in a dangerous situation or of removing a child unnecessarily from his or her family. The way to proceed in the face of uncertainty is through competent professional judgements, based on a sound assessment of the child's needs, the parents' capacity to respond to those needs – including their capacity to keep the child safe from significant harm – and the wider family circumstances.

1.13 Effective measures to safeguard children are those that also promote their welfare. They should not be seen in isolation from the wider range of support and services already provided and available to meet the needs of children and families:

- enquiries under s47 of the Children Act 1989 may reveal significant unmet needs for support and services among children and families. These should always be explicitly considered, even where concerns are not substantiated about significant harm to a child, if the family so wishes
- if processes for managing concerns about individual children are to result in improved outcomes for children, then effective plans for safeguarding and promoting children's welfare should be based on a wide-ranging assessment of the needs of the child, parental capacity and their family circumstances.

A shared responsibility

1.14 Safeguarding and promoting the welfare of children – and in particular protecting them from significant harm – depends on effective joint working between agencies and professionals that have different roles and expertise. Individual children, especially some of the most vulnerable children and those at greatest risk of social exclusion, will need co-ordinated help from health, education, children's social care, and quite possibly the voluntary sector and other agencies, including youth justice services.

1.15 In order to achieve this joint working, there need to be constructive relationships between individual workers, promoted and supported by:

- a strong lead from elected or appointed authority members, and the commitment of chief officers in all agencies – in particular, the LA's Director of Children's Services and Lead Member for Children's Services[2]
- effective local co-ordination by the LSCB in each area.

1.16 For those children who are suffering, or at risk of suffering, significant harm, joint working is essential, to safeguard and promote welfare of the child(ren) and, where necessary, to help bring to justice the perpetrators of crimes against children. All agencies and professionals should:

- be alert to potential indicators of abuse or neglect
- be alert to the risks that individual abusers, or potential abusers, may pose to children
- share and help to analyse information so that an assessment can be made of the child's needs and circumstances
- contribute to whatever actions are needed to safeguard and promote the child's welfare
- take part in regularly reviewing the outcomes for the child against specific plans
- work co-operatively with parents, unless this is inconsistent with ensuring the child's safety.

Key definitions and concepts

Children

1.17 In this document, as in the Children Acts 1989 and 2004, **a child** is anyone who has not yet reached their 18th birthday. 'Children' therefore means 'children and young people' throughout. The fact that a child has reached 16 years of age, is living independently or is in further education, is a member of the armed forces, is in hospital, in prison or in a Young Offenders' Institution, does not change his or her status or entitlement to services or protection under the Children Act 1989.

Safeguarding and promoting welfare, and child protection

1.18 **Safeguarding and promoting the welfare of children** is defined for the purposes of this guidance as:

- protecting children from maltreatment
- preventing impairment of children's health or development

2 Guidance on the roles and responsibilities of the Director of Children's Services and Lead Member for children's services, published in April 2005, can be downloaded from www.everychildmatters.gov.uk/keydocuments.

- ensuring that children are growing up in circumstances consistent with the provision of safe and effective care

and undertaking that role so as to enable those children to have optimum life chances and to enter adulthood successfully.

1.19 Protecting children from maltreatment is important in preventing the impairment of health or development. Protecting children from maltreatment and preventing impairment of children's health and development are necessary, but not sufficient to ensure that children are growing up in circumstances consistent with the provision of safe and effective care. These aspects of safeguarding and promoting welfare are cumulative, and all contribute to the outcomes set out in paragraph 1.1.

1.20 **Child protection** is a part of safeguarding and promoting welfare. This refers to the activity that is undertaken to protect specific children who are suffering, or are at risk of suffering, significant harm.

1.21 Effective child protection is essential as part of wider work to safeguard and promote the welfare of children. However, all agencies and individuals should aim proactively to safeguard and promote the welfare of children so that the need for action to protect children from harm is reduced.

Children in need

1.22 Children who are defined as being 'in need', under s17 of the Children Act 1989, are those whose vulnerability is such that they are unlikely to reach or maintain a satisfactory level of health or development, or their health and development will be significantly impaired, without the provision of services (s17(10) of the Children Act 1989), plus those who are disabled. The critical factors to be taken into account in deciding whether a child is in need under the Children Act 1989 are:

- what will happen to a child's health or development without services being provided; and
- the likely effect the services will have on the child's standard of health and development.

LAs have a duty to safeguard and promote the welfare of children in need.

The concept of significant harm

1.23 Some children are in need because they are suffering, or likely to suffer, significant harm. The Children Act 1989 introduced the concept of significant harm as the threshold that justifies compulsory intervention in family life in the best interests of children, and gives LAs a duty to make enquiries to decide whether they should take action to safeguard or promote the welfare of a child who is suffering, or likely to suffer, significant harm.

1.24 A court may make a care order (committing the child to the care of the LA) or supervision order (putting the child under the supervision of a social worker or a probation officer) in respect of a child if it is satisfied that:

- the child is suffering, or is likely to suffer, significant harm; and
- the harm, or likelihood of harm, is attributable to a lack of adequate parental care or control (s31).

1.25 There are no absolute criteria on which to rely when judging what constitutes significant harm. Consideration of the severity of ill-treatment may include the degree and the extent of physical harm, the duration and frequency of abuse and neglect, the extent of premeditation, and the presence or degree of threat, coercion, sadism and bizarre or unusual elements. Each of these elements has been associated with more severe effects on the child, and/or relatively greater difficulty in helping the child overcome the adverse impact of the maltreatment. Sometimes, a single traumatic event may constitute significant harm, e.g. a violent assault, suffocation or poisoning. More often, significant harm is a compilation of significant events, both acute and long-standing, which interrupt, change or damage the child's physical and psychological development. Some children live in family and social circumstances where their health and development are neglected. For them, it is the corrosiveness of long-term emotional, physical or sexual abuse that causes impairment to the extent of constituting significant harm. In each case, it is necessary to consider any maltreatment alongside the family's strengths and supports.[3]

Under s31(9) of the Children Act 1989 as amended by the Adoption and Children Act 2002:

'harm' means ill-treatment or the impairment of health or development, including, for example, impairment suffered from seeing or hearing the ill-treatment of another;

'development' means physical, intellectual, emotional, social or behavioural development;

'health' means physical or mental health; and

'ill-treatment' includes sexual abuse and forms of ill-treatment which are not physical.

Under s31(10) of the Act:

Where the question of whether harm suffered by a child is significant turns on the child's health and development, his health or development shall be compared with that which could reasonably be expected of a similar child.

3 For more details see Adcock, M. and White, R. (1998). *Significant Harm: its management and outcome.* Surrey: Significant Publications.

1.26 To understand and identify significant harm, it is necessary to consider:

- the nature of harm, in terms of maltreatment or failure to provide adequate care
- the impact on the child's health and development
- the child's development within the context of their family and wider environment
- any special needs, such as a medical condition, communication impairment or disability, that may affect the child's development and care within the family
- the capacity of parents to meet adequately the child's needs
- the wider and environmental family context.

1.27 The child's reactions, his or her perceptions, and wishes and feelings should be ascertained and taken account of according to the child's age and understanding.[4]

1.28 To do this depends on communicating effectively with children and young people, including those who find it difficult to do so because of their age, an impairment, or their particular psychological or social situation. It is essential that any accounts of adverse experiences coming from children are as accurate and complete as possible. 'Accuracy is key, for without it effective decisions cannot be made and, equally, inaccurate accounts can lead to children remaining unsafe, or to the possibility of wrongful actions being taken that affect children and adults.'[5]

What is abuse and neglect?

1.29 Abuse and neglect are forms of maltreatment of a child. Somebody may abuse or neglect a child by inflicting harm, or by failing to act to prevent harm. Children may be abused in a family or in an institutional or community setting, by those known to them or, more rarely, by a stranger. They may be abused by an adult or adults, or another child or children.

Physical abuse

1.30 Physical abuse may involve hitting, shaking, throwing, poisoning, burning or scalding, drowning, suffocating, or otherwise causing physical harm to a child. Physical harm may also be caused when a parent or carer fabricates the symptoms of, or deliberately induces, illness in a child.

4 Section 53 of the Children Act 2004 amended s17 and s47 of the Children Act 1989, so that before determining what, if any, services to provide to a child in need under s17, or action to take with respect to a child under s47, the wishes and feelings of the child should be ascertained as far as is reasonable and given due consideration.

5 Jones, D. P. H. (2003). *Communicating with Vulnerable Children: a Guide for Practitioners*, pp.1-2. London: Gaskell.

Emotional abuse

1.31 Emotional abuse is the persistent emotional maltreatment of a child such as to cause severe and persistent adverse effects on the child's emotional development. It may involve conveying to children that they are worthless or unloved, inadequate, or valued only insofar as they meet the needs of another person. It may feature age or developmentally inappropriate expectations being imposed on children. These may include interactions that are beyond the child's developmental capability, as well as overprotection and limitation of exploration and learning, or preventing the child participating in normal social interaction. It may involve seeing or hearing the ill-treatment of another. It may involve serious bullying, causing children frequently to feel frightened or in danger, or the exploitation or corruption of children. Some level of emotional abuse is involved in all types of maltreatment of a child, though it may occur alone.

Sexual abuse

1.32 Sexual abuse involves forcing or enticing a child or young person to take part in sexual activities, including prostitution, whether or not the child is aware of what is happening. The activities may involve physical contact, including penetrative (e.g. rape, buggery or oral sex) or non-penetrative acts. They may include non-contact activities, such as involving children in looking at, or in the production of, sexual online images, watching sexual activities, or encouraging children to behave in sexually inappropriate ways.

Neglect

1.33 Neglect is the persistent failure to meet a child's basic physical and/or psychological needs, likely to result in the serious impairment of the child's health or development. Neglect may occur during pregnancy as a result of maternal substance abuse. Once a child is born, neglect may involve a parent or carer failing to:

- provide adequate food, clothing and shelter (including exclusion from home or abandonment)
- protect a child from physical and emotional harm or danger
- ensure adequate supervision (including the use of inadequate care-givers)
- ensure access to appropriate medical care or treatment.

It may also include neglect of, or unresponsiveness to, a child's basic emotional needs.

Chapter 2 – Roles and responsibilities

Introduction

2.1 An awareness and appreciation of the role of others is essential for effective collaboration between organisations and their practitioners. This chapter outlines the main roles and responsibilities of statutory organisations, professionals and the voluntary sector in safeguarding and promoting the welfare of children.

2.2 At the same time, it is important to emphasise that we all share a responsibility for safeguarding and promoting the welfare of children and young people. All members of the community can help to safeguard and promote the welfare of children and young people, if they are mindful of children's needs and are willing and able to act if they have concerns about a child's welfare.

Statutory duties

2.3 All organisations that work with children share a commitment to safeguard and promote their welfare, and for many organisations that is underpinned by a statutory duty or duties. Local authorities (LAs) that are children's services authorities[6] have a number of specific duties to organise and plan services and to safeguard and promote the welfare of children.

2.4 County-level LAs, unitary authorities, district councils, NHS bodies (Strategic Health Authorities, designated Special Health Authorities, Primary Care Trusts, NHS Trusts and NHS Foundation Trusts), the police (including the British Transport Police), probation and prison services (under the National Offender Management structure), Youth Offending Teams, Secure Training Centres and Connexions have a duty under s11 of the Children Act 2004 to ensure that their functions are discharged with regard to the need to safeguard and promote the welfare of children. Guidance for these organisations about their duty under s11 is contained in *Making Arrangements to Safeguard and Promote the Welfare of Children*, published by DfES in August 2005 (www.everychildmatters.gov.uk/resources-and-practice/IG00042/)

6 County-level or unitary authorities are defined as children's services authorities in the Children Act 2004. Section 63 of the Act sets out the full definition. See Glossary.

2.5 LAs also have a duty to carry out their functions under the Education Acts, with a view to safeguarding and promoting the welfare of children under s175 of the Education Act 2002. In addition, maintained (state) schools and further education (FE) institutions, including sixth-form colleges, also have a duty under s175 to exercise their functions with a view to safeguarding and promoting the welfare of their pupils (students under 18 years of age in the case of FE institutions). The same duty is put on independent schools, including academies and technology colleges, by Regulations made under s157 of the Education Act 2002. Guidance to LAs, schools and FE institutions about these duties is in *Safeguarding Children in Education*, published by DfES in September 2004. In addition, under s87 of the Children Act 1989, independent schools that provide accommodation for children also have a duty to safeguard and promote the welfare of those pupils. Boarding schools, residential special schools, and further education institutions that provide accommodation for children under 18 must have regard to the respective National Minimum Standards for their establishment. These can be found at:

www.csci.org.uk/information_for_service_providers/national_minimum_standards/default.htm

2.6 The Children and Family Court Advisory and Support Service (CAFCASS) also has a duty under s12(1) of the Criminal Justice and Court Services Act 2000 to safeguard and promote the welfare of children involved in family proceedings in which their welfare is, or may be, in question.

2.7 An overview of the duties mentioned above, and of the structure of children's services under the Children Act 2004, is set out in the Preface to this guidance and in Appendix 1.

Common features

2.8 To fulfil their commitment to safeguard and promote the welfare of children, all organisations that provide services for, or work with, children must have:

- clear priorities for safeguarding and promoting the welfare of children, explicitly stated in strategic policy documents
- a clear commitment by senior management to the importance of safeguarding and promoting children's welfare
- a clear line of accountability within the organisation for work on safeguarding and promoting the welfare of children
- recruitment and human resources management procedures that take account of the need to safeguard and promote the welfare of children and young people, including arrangements for appropriate checks on new staff and volunteers
- procedures for dealing with allegations of abuse against members of staff and volunteers (see paragraphs 6.20 to 6.30)

- arrangements to ensure that all staff undertake appropriate training to equip them to carry out their responsibilities effectively, and keep this up-to-date by refresher training at regular intervals; and that all staff, including temporary staff and volunteers who work with children, are made aware of the establishment's arrangements for safeguarding and promoting the welfare of children and their responsibilities for that
- policies for safeguarding and promoting the welfare of children (e.g. pupils/students), including a child protection policy, and procedures that are in accordance with guidance and locally agreed inter-agency procedures
- arrangements to work effectively with other organisations to safeguard and promote the welfare of children, including arrangements for sharing information
- a culture of listening to, and engaging in dialogue with, children – seeking children's views in ways that are appropriate to their age and understanding, and taking account of those views in individual decisions and in the establishment or development of services
- appropriate whistle-blowing procedures, and a culture that enables issues about safeguarding and promoting the welfare of children to be addressed.

Local authorities that are children's services authorities [7]

2.9 The safety and welfare of children is the responsibility of the LA, working in partnership with other public organisations, the voluntary sector and service users and carers. All LA services have an impact on the lives of children and families, and LAs have a particular responsibility towards those children and families most at risk of social exclusion.

2.10 These LAs also have responsibility for safeguarding and promoting the welfare of children who are excluded from school, or who have not obtained a school place – e.g. children in pupil referral units or being educated by the LA's home tutor service. They also ensure that maintained schools give effect to their responsibilities for safeguarding – make available appropriate training, model policies and procedures; provide advice and support; and facilitate links and cooperation with other organisations. LAs normally extend these functions to any non-maintained special schools in their area.

2.11 A key objective for these local authorities is to ensure that children are protected from harm. They provide a wide range of care and support for:

- adults
- children and families – including children at risk of harm, disabled children, unaccompanied asylum-seeking or refugee children

7 County-level or unitary authorities are defined as children's services authorities in the Children Act 2004. Section 63 of the Act sets out the full definition. See Glossary.

- older people
- people with physical or learning disabilities
- people with mental health or substance misuse problems
- ex-offenders and young offenders
- families where children have special needs, and/or where children are growing up in special circumstances, as set out in the *National Service Framework for Children, Young People and Maternity Services*
- children who need to be accommodated or looked after by the LA, through fostering or residential care
- children who are placed for adoption.

LAs also have a duty under s17 of the Crime and Disorder Act 1998 to do all they reasonably can to prevent crime and disorder in the exercise of their functions.

2.12 These authorities have specific duties in respect of children under the Children Acts 1989 and 2004. They have a general duty to safeguard and promote the welfare of children in need in their area and – provided this is consistent with the child's safety and welfare – to promote the upbringing of such children by their families, by providing services appropriate to the child's needs. They should do this in partnership with parents, in a way that is sensitive to the child's race, religion, culture and language and that, where practicable, takes account of the child's wishes and feelings. Services might include day care for young children, after-school care for school children, counselling, respite care, family centres or practical help in the home.

2.13 Within those authorities, children's social care staff act as the principal point of contact for children about whom there are welfare concerns. They may be contacted directly by children, parents or family members seeking help, by concerned friends and neighbours, or by professionals and others from statutory and voluntary organisations. The need for support should be considered at the first sign of difficulties, as early support can prevent more serious problems developing. Contact details need to be clearly signposted, including on LA websites and in telephone directories.

2.14 Children's social care staff and LSCBs should offer the same level of support and advice to independent schools and further education colleges, in relation to safeguarding and promoting the welfare of pupils and child protection, as they do to maintained (state) schools. It is particularly important that children's social care staff and LSCBs establish channels of communication with local independent schools (including independent special schools), so that children requiring support receive prompt attention, and any allegations of abuse can be properly investigated.

2.15 Under Part X of the Children Act 1989, as amended by the Care Standards Act 2000, LAs are required to ensure that information and advice about day care and childminding are made available, and that training is provided for day care providers and childminders. LAs' training programmes for early-years staff, in the private and voluntary sectors as well as in the maintained sector, should include training in child protection procedures.

2.16 LAs, with the help of other organisations as appropriate, also have a duty to make enquiries if they have reason to suspect that a child in their area is suffering, or likely to suffer, significant harm, to enable them to decide whether they should take any action to safeguard or promote the child's welfare (see Chapter 5).

2.17 Where a child is at risk of significant harm, children's social care staff are responsible for co-ordinating an assessment of the child's needs, of the parents' capacity to keep the child safe and promote his or her welfare, and of the wider family circumstances.

Secure Children's Homes

2.18 LA Secure Children's Homes provide care and accommodation for young people placed under a secure welfare order for the protection of themselves or others, and for those placed under criminal justice legislation by the Youth Justice Board. Secure Children's Homes, like all children's homes, are registered and inspected, and must comply with the Children's Homes Regulations 2001 and meet the Children's Homes National Minimum Standards, both of which cover a range of issues including child protection. (See also paragraph 2.112, The Secure Estate for children and young people.)

Other local authority roles

Housing authorities and registered social landlords

2.19 Housing and homelessness staff in LAs can play an important role in safeguarding and promoting the welfare of children as part of their day-to-day work – recognising child welfare issues, sharing information, making referrals and subsequently managing or reducing risks. Housing managers, whether working in a LA or for a registered social landlord (RSL), and others with a front-line role such as environmental health officers, also have an important role. For instance:

- housing staff, in their day-to-day contact with families and tenants, may become aware of needs or welfare issues that they can either tackle directly (for instance, by making repairs or adaptations to homes) or by assisting the family in accessing help through other organisations
- housing authorities are key to the assessment of the needs of families with disabled children, who may require housing adaptations in order to participate fully in family life and reach their maximum potential

- housing authorities have a front-line emergency role – for instance, managing re-housing or repossession when adults and children become homeless, or at risk of homelessness, as a result of domestic violence

- housing staff, through their day-to-day contact with members of the public and with families, may become aware of concerns about the welfare of particular children. Also, housing authorities and RSLs may hold important information that could assist LA children's social care to carry out assessments under s17 or s47 of the Children Act 1989. Conversely, children's social care staff and other organisations working with children can have information that will make assessments of the need for certain types of housing more effective. Authorities and RSLs should develop joint protocols to share information with other organisations – e.g. children's social care or health professionals in appropriate cases

- environmental health officers inspecting conditions in private rented housing may become aware of conditions that impact adversely on children. Under Part 1 of the Housing Act 2004, authorities will take account of the impact of health and safety hazards in housing on vulnerable occupants, including children, when deciding on the action to be taken by landlords to improve conditions.

2.20 In many areas, LAs do not directly own and manage housing, having transferred these responsibilities to one or more RSLs. Housing authorities remain responsible for assessing the needs of families, under homelessness legislation, and for managing nominations to registered social landlords who provide housing in their area. They continue to have an important role in safeguarding children because of their contact with families as part of the assessment of need, and because of the influence they have designing and managing prioritisation, assessment and allocation of housing.

2.21 RSLs are independent organisations, regulated by the Housing Corporation under its regulatory code, and are not public bodies. RSLs are not under the same duties to safeguard and promote the welfare of children as are LAs. However, the Housing Corporation supports the principle of RSLs working in partnership with a range of organisations to promote social inclusion. Its regulatory code states that housing associations must work with LAs to enable the latter to fulfil their duties to the vulnerable and to those covered by the Government's Supporting People policy.

2.22 There are a number of RSLs across the country who provide specialist supported housing schemes specifically for young people at risk and/or young people leaving care and pregnant teenagers. These schemes cater for 16- and 17-year-olds.

Sport, culture and leisure services

2.23 Sport and cultural services designed for children and families – such as libraries, play schemes and play facilities, parks and gardens, sport and leisure centres, events and attractions, museums and arts centres – are directly provided, purchased or grant-aided by

LAs, the commercial sector, and by community and voluntary organisations. Many such activities take place in premises managed by authorities or their agents.

2.24 Staff, volunteers and contractors who provide these services have various degrees of contact with children who use them, and appropriate arrangements need to be in place. These should include:

- procedures for staff and others to report concerns they may have, about the children they meet, which are in line with *What To Do If You're Worried A Child Is Being Abused* and LSCB procedures, as well as arrangements such as those described above
- appropriate codes of practice for staff, particularly sports coaches, such as the codes of practice issued by national governing bodies of sport, the Health and Safety Executive or the LA. Sports organisations can also seek advice on child protection issues from the Child Protection in Sport Unit (CPSU), which has been established as a partnership between the NSPCC and Sport England.

Youth services

2.25 Youth and community workers (YCWs) have close contact with children and young people and should be alert to signs of abuse and neglect, and know how to act on concerns about a child's welfare. LA youth services (LAYS) should give written instructions, consistent with *What To Do If You're Worried a Child Is Being Abused* and LSCB procedures, on when YCWs should consult colleagues, line managers and other statutory authorities about concerns they may have about a child or young person. The LAYS instructions should emphasise the importance of safeguarding the welfare of children and young people, and should assist the YCW in balancing the desire to maintain confidentiality between the young person and the YCW and the duty to safeguard and promote the welfare of the young person and others. Volunteers within the youth service are subject to the same requirement.

2.26 Where the LA funds local voluntary youth organisations or other providers through grant or contract arrangements, the authority should ensure that proper arrangements to safeguard children and young people are in place. (For example, this might form part of the agreement for the grant or contract.) The organisations might get advice on how to do so from their national bodies or the LSCB.

Health services

The impact that abuse and neglect have on children's development

2.27 The *National Service Framework for Children, Young People and Maternity Services* (NSF) highlights the serious impact that physical, emotional or sexual abuse, neglect and domestic violence (and parental mental ill health, substance misuse problems) can have on all aspects of a child's health, development and wellbeing. This impact can last throughout adulthood. The high cost of this, both to individuals and to society, underpins the statutory responsibility of all health organisations to make arrangements to safeguard and promote the welfare of children.[8] This is defined[9] as:

- protecting children from maltreatment
- preventing impairment of children's health or development
- ensuring that children are growing up in circumstances consistent with the provision of safe and effective care

and undertaking that role so as to enable those children to have optimum life chances and to enter adulthood successfully.

2.28 The NSF sets out a 10-year programme for improving the quality of services for children, young people and pregnant women. Safeguarding children is a theme running through the NSF, and Standard 5 deals specifically with safeguarding and promoting the welfare of children. The NSF is an integral part of the *Every Child Matters: Change for Children* programme.

2.29 Health professionals and organisations have a key role to play in actively promoting the health and wellbeing of children. Section 11 of the Children Act 2004[10] places a duty on Strategic Health Authorities, designated Special Hospitals, Primary Care Trusts, NHS Trusts and NHS Foundation Trusts have a duty to make arrangements to ensure that, in discharging their functions, they have regard to the need to safeguard and promote the welfare of children.

2.30 The Public Health White Paper and Delivery Plan sets out the issues of safeguarding and promoting the welfare of children in a public health policy and prevention context.

General principles

2.31 The aim is to ensure that all affected children receive appropriate and timely therapeutic and preventative interventions. These principles apply to all health services and health service providers in both the NHS and independent healthcare settings.

2.32 The safety and the health of a child are intertwined aspects of their wellbeing. Many 'health' interventions also equip a child to 'stay safe'.[11]

2.33 All health professionals working directly with children should ensure that safeguarding and promoting their welfare forms an integral part of all stages of the care they offer. Other health professionals who come into contact with children, parents and carers in the course of their work also need to be aware of their responsibility to safeguard

8 Guidance on s11 of the Children Act 2004

9 Statutory guidance on making arrangements to safeguard and promote the welfare of children under s11 of the Children Act 2004

10 s11 of the Children Act 2004 came into force on 1 October 2005

11 'Staying safe' is a key outcome of *Every Child Matters*

and promote the welfare of children and young people. This is important even when the health professionals do not work directly with a child, but may be seeing their parent, carer or other significant adult.

2.34 All health professionals who work with children and families should be able to:

- understand the risk factors and recognise children in need of support and/or safeguarding
- recognise the needs of parents who may need extra help in bringing up their children, and know where to refer for help
- recognise the risks of abuse to an unborn child
- contribute to enquiries from other professionals about children and their family or carers
- liaise closely with other agencies, including other health professionals
- assess the needs of children and the capacity of parents/carers to meet their children's needs, including the needs of children who display sexually harmful behaviour
- plan and respond to the needs of children and their families, particularly those who are vulnerable
- contribute to child protection conferences, family group conferences and strategy discussions
- contribute to planning support for children at risk of significant harm, e.g. children living in households with domestic violence or parental substance misuse
- help ensure that children who have been abused and parents under stress (e.g. those who have mental health problems) have access to services to support them
- play an active part, through the child protection plan, in safeguarding children from significant harm
- as part of generally safeguarding children and young people, provide ongoing promotional and preventative support, through proactive work with children, families and expectant parents
- contribute to serious case reviews and their implementation.

2.35 The above should all be undertaken with reference to the core processes set out in this document (summarised in *What To Do If You're Worried A Child Is Being Abused* (Department of Health, 2003)), *Responding to domestic abuse: A handbook for health professionals* (Department of Health, 2006) and LSCB procedures. It is essential that all health professionals and their teams have access to advice and support from named and designated child safeguarding professionals, and undertake regular safeguarding training and updating.

Standards and healthcare

2.36 *National Standards, Local Action* (Department of Health, 2004)[12] incorporates *Standards for Better Health* (Department of Health, 2004), which describes the level of quality that healthcare organisations, including NHS Foundation Trusts and private and voluntary providers of NHS care, are expected to meet. It sets out core standards, which are not optional, and developmental standards – such as National Service Frameworks – which the Healthcare Commission uses to assess continuous improvement. Core Standard C2, within the 'safety' domain, states that 'Health care organisations protect children by following national child protection guidance within their own activities and in their dealings with other organisations'.

2.37 The NSF, especially in Standard 5, 'Safeguarding and promoting the welfare of children and young people', gives additional detail and markers of good practice in achieving this. In discharging their roles and responsibilities, NHS organisations therefore need to meet Core Standard C2 and take account of the NSF.

2.38 The Healthcare Commission is responsible for assessing and reporting on the performance of the NHS and independent health organisations, to ensure that they are providing a high standard of care. The Healthcare Commission is required to pay particular attention to 'the rights and welfare' of the child, and to safeguard the public by acting swiftly and appropriately on concerns about healthcare. The Healthcare Commission is also responsible for regulating the independent healthcare sector.

2.39 All health organisations, whether in the NHS or the independent health sector, should ensure safeguarding children is an integral part of their governance systems.

Recruitment

2.40 All healthcare organisations must ensure they have in place safe recruitment policies and practices, including enhanced Criminal Record Bureau (CRB) checks, for all staff – including agency staff, students and volunteers – who work with children.

Training

2.41 All staff involved in working with children should attend training in safeguarding and promoting the welfare of children, and should have regular updates as part of any post-registration educational programme.

12 The NHS is increasingly assessed through core and developmental standards. The Health and Social Care (Community Health and Standards) Act 2003 includes a duty on each NHS body 'to put and keep in place arrangements for the purpose of monitoring and improving the quality of healthcare provided by and for that body' (s45) and gives the Secretary of State the power to set out standards to be taken into account by every English NHS body in discharging that duty (s46).

2.42 Employers have a responsibility to ensure that all staff, including administrative staff, are given opportunities to attend local courses in safeguarding and promoting the welfare of children, or to ensure that safeguarding training is provided within the team. See Chapter 4 for details of inter-agency training.

Health organisations

Strategic Health Authorities

2.43 The Strategic Health Authority's (SHA's) role is to performance manage and support the development of NHS and Primary Care Trusts' arrangements to safeguard and promote the welfare of children and young people.[13] SHAs need to manage performance against the core and developmental standards and Trusts' implementation of child protection serious case review action plans. They can draw on the findings of a number of inspection processes:

- the Joint Area Review and Youth Offending Teams inspections, undertaken by a number of inspectorates working in partnership, including the Healthcare Commission
- the annual health checks, improvement reviews and investigations undertaken by the Healthcare Commission.

SHAs' membership of the LSCBs enables them to oversee the health contribution to safeguarding children at local level. The Department of Health holds SHAs to account for this role.

Primary Care Trusts

2.44 Primary Care Trusts (PCTs) are under a duty to make arrangements to ensure that, in discharging their functions, they have regard to the need to safeguard and promote the welfare of children. PCTs should work with LAs to commission and provide co-ordinated and, wherever possible, integrated services. PCTs should identify a senior lead for children and young people[14] to ensure that their needs are at the forefront of local planning and service delivery. There should be a named public health professional who addresses issues related to children in need as well as children in need of protection.

2.45 PCT Chief Executives have responsibility for ensuring that the health contribution to safeguarding and promoting the welfare of children is discharged effectively across the whole local health economy through the PCTs' commissioning arrangements. The PCTs' role is not only about specific clinical services, but also about exercising a public health responsibility for a whole population, and a key task is ensuring the health and wellbeing of children in need in their area. Where practice-based commissioners undertake commissioning of services, this should be done in partnership with PCTs, who need to ensure their safeguarding duties are fulfilled.

13 Foundation Trusts are accountable to an independent corporate body called Monitor, which is responsible for authorising, monitoring and regulating NHS Foundation Trusts.

2.46 PCTs must co-operate with the LA in the establishment and operation of the LSCB and, as partners, must share responsibility for the effective discharge of its functions in safeguarding and promoting the welfare of children. Representation on the Board should be at an appropriate level of seniority. PCTs are also responsible for providing and/or ensuring the availability of appropriate expertise and advice and support to the LSCB, in respect of a range of specialist health functions – e.g. primary care, mental health (adult, adolescent and child) and sexual health – and for co-ordinating the health component of serious case reviews (see Chapter 8). PCTs should notify the SHA of all serious case reviews. The PCT must also ensure that all health organisations, including the independent healthcare sector with whom they have commissioning arrangements, have links with a specific LSCB, and that health agencies work in partnership in accordance with their agreed LSCB plan. This is particularly important where Trusts' boundaries/catchment areas are different from those of LSCBs. This includes Ambulance Trusts and NHS Direct services.

2.47 PCTs should ensure that all health providers from whom they commission services – both public and independent sector – have comprehensive single- and multi-agency policies and procedures to safeguard and promote the welfare of children. These policies and procedures should be in line with, and informed by, LSCB procedures, and easily accessible for staff at all levels within each organisation.

2.48 Each PCT is responsible for identifying:

- a senior paediatrician and senior nurse to undertake the role of designated professionals for safeguarding children across the health economy
- a named doctor and a named nurse (or midwife) who will take a professional lead within the PCT on safeguarding children matters.

(For more detail on designated and named professionals, see paragraphs 2.58 to 2.65.) Designated professionals should be performance-managed in relation to their designated functions at the level of Board level Director who has executive responsibility for safeguarding children as part of their portfolio of responsibilities. If this person is not the Board level lead for clinical governance and clinical professional leadership, the designated professional also needs to work closely with this lead person. PCTs should ensure that all their staff are alert to the need to safeguard and promote the welfare of children, have knowledge of local procedures and know how to contact the named and designated professionals.

2.49 PCTs are expected to ensure that safeguarding and promoting the welfare of children are integral to clinical governance and audit arrangements. Service specifications drawn up by PCT commissioners should include clear service standards for safeguarding and promoting the welfare of children, consistent with LSCB procedures. By monitoring the service standards of NHS Foundation Trusts and contracted service providers, PCTs will assure themselves that service providers are meeting the required safeguarding standards.

2.50 PCTs should ensure that all primary care teams have easy access to paediatricians trained in examining, identifying and assessing children and young people who may be experiencing abuse or neglect, and that local arrangements include having all the necessary equipment and staff expertise for undertaking forensic medical examinations. These arrangements should avoid repeated examinations.

2.51 PCTs, with the police and voluntary sector organisations, jointly commission services of Sexual Assault Referral Centres (SARCs) for victims of rape and sexual assault, including services for children and young people. SARCs provide forensic, medical and counselling services, involving specialist sexual health input. This is a target in the Public Health White Paper Delivery Plan, and joint Department of Health, National Institute for Mental Health in England and Home Office national service guidelines have been published on Developing Sexual Assault Referral Centres (2005).

NHS Trusts and NHS Foundation Trusts

2.52 NHS Trusts, Mental Health Trusts and NHS Foundation Trusts are responsible for providing health services in hospital and community settings. They must co-operate with the LA in the establishment and operation of the LSCB and, as statutory partners, must share responsibility for the effective discharge of the LSCB's functions in safeguarding and promoting the welfare of children. Representation on the Board should be at an appropriate level of seniority. A wide range of Trusts' staff will come into contact with children and parents in the course of their normal duties. All these staff should be trained in how to safeguard and promote the welfare of children, be alert to potential indicators of abuse or neglect in children, and know how to act on their concerns in line with LSCB procedures.

2.53 All NHS Trusts and NHS Foundation Trusts should identify a named doctor and a named nurse/midwife for child protection (see paragraphs 2.62–2.65 for more detail).

2.54 Staff working in Accident and Emergency (A&E) departments, ambulatory care units, walk-in centres and minor injury units should be able to recognise abuse and be familiar with local procedures for making enquiries to find out whether a child is subject to a child protection plan. Staff in A&E departments should also be alert to the need to safeguard the welfare of children when treating parents or carers of children. They should be alert to parents and carers who seek medical care from a number of sources in order to conceal the repeated nature of a child's injuries. Specialist paediatric advice should be available at all times to A&E departments and all units where children receive care. If a child – or children from the same household – presents repeatedly, even with slight injuries, in a way that doctors, nurses or other staff find worrying, staff should act on their concerns in accordance with Chapter 5 of this guidance. (The key processes are summarised in *What To Do If You're Worried A Child Is Being Abused.*) Children and families should be actively and appropriately involved in these processes, unless this would result in harm to the child.

2.55 The relevant child's GP should be notified of visits by children to an A&E department, ambulatory care unit, walk-in centre or minor injury unit. Where the child is not registered with a GP, the appropriate contact in the Primary Care Trust should be notified to arrange registration. Consent should be sought from a competent child or young person for the PCT, health visitor and school nurse or other health professional to be notified where such professionals have a role in relation to the child. This requires careful discussion and explanation, but overriding a refusal to provide consent should only take place when there is a public interest of sufficient force. Where there is a clear risk of significant harm to a child, or serious harm to an adult, the public interest test will almost certainly be satisfied.[15] In such circumstances, the reasons for taking such action should be carefully documented and an explanation given to the child or young person.

Ambulance Trusts and NHS Direct sites

2.56 The staff working in these health services will have access (by phone or in person) to family homes and be involved with individuals in a time of crisis. They may therefore be in a position to identify initial concerns regarding a child's welfare. Each of these organisations should have a named professional for child safeguarding. (See paragraphs 2.62–2.65 for more detail.) All staff should be aware of local procedures in line with LSCB policies.

Independent sector

2.57 PCTs should ensure that, through their contracting arrangements, independent sector providers deliver services that are in line with PCTs' obligations with respect to safeguarding and promoting the welfare of children, and their duty to notify the LA of children who are, or are likely to be, accommodated for at least three months.[16] Should the Healthcare Commission be obliged at any time to consider deregistration of the independent healthcare provider, there is a need to ensure measures are in place to make arrangements to re-provide relevant services for children as quickly and safely as possible. PCTs should ensure that they apply the same standards and requirements as for NHS providers (as set out in paragraphs 2.36–2.39) when contracting with the independent sector. PCTs need to ensure that appropriate links are established between independent providers and LSCBs, and that the providers are aware of LSCB policies and procedures. Employers should have access to regular safeguarding training and supervision. Where PCTs have commissioning arrangements with independent providers, providers should have a named professional on site, and access to designated professionals for complex issues or where concerns may have to be escalated and involve social services. Clinical networks[17] can provide a further opportunity for sharing highly specialised resources across teams and geographical areas.

15 *Information Sharing: Practitioner's Guide* provides advice on these issues – see www.everychildmatters.gov.uk

16 s85, Children Act 1989

17 *A Guide to Promote a Shared Understanding of the Benefits of Managed Local Networks* (Department of Health, 2005)

Health professionals

Designated and named professionals

2.58 The terms 'designated professionals' and 'named professionals' denote professionals with specific roles and responsibilities for safeguarding children. All PCTs should have a designated doctor and nurse to take a strategic, professional lead on all aspects of the health service contribution to safeguarding children across the PCT area, which includes all providers. PCTs should ensure establishment levels of designated and named professionals are proportionate to the local resident populations, following any mergers, and to the complexity of provider arrangements. For large PCTs, NHS Trusts and Foundation Trusts that may have a number of sites, a team approach can enhance the ability to provide 24-hour advice and provide mutual support for those carrying out the designated and named professional role. If this approach is taken, it is important to ensure that the leadership and accountability arrangements are clear.

2.59 Designated and named professional roles should always be explicitly defined in job descriptions, and sufficient time and funding should be allowed to fulfil their child safeguarding responsibilities effectively. The Royal Colleges have produced and published a set of safeguarding competencies and job descriptions for these roles.

Designated professionals

2.60 Appointment as a designated professional does not, in itself, signify personal responsibility for providing a full clinical service for child protection. This is usually done by a team of professionals. Designated professionals provide advice and support to the named professionals in each provider Trust. Designated professionals are a vital source of professional advice on matters relating to safeguarding children for other professionals, the PCT, LA children's services departments and the LSCB.

2.61 Designated professionals play an important role in promoting, influencing and developing relevant training – on both a single- and inter-agency basis – to ensure that the training needs of health staff are addressed. They also provide skilled professional involvement in child safeguarding processes, in line with LSCB procedures, and in serious case reviews. As part of serious case reviews, designated professionals should review and evaluate the practice and learning from all involved health professionals and providers who are involved within the PCT area. For more details see paragraph 8.18.

Named professionals

2.62 All NHS Trusts, NHS Foundation Trusts, and PCTs providing services for children should identify a named doctor and a named nurse/midwife for safeguarding. In the case of NHS Direct, Ambulance Trusts and independent providers, this should be a named professional. The focus for the named professional's role is safeguarding children within their own organisation.

2.63 Named professionals have a key role in promoting good professional practice within the Trust, and provide advice and expertise for fellow professionals. They should have specific expertise in children's health and development, child maltreatment and local arrangements for safeguarding and promoting the welfare of children.

2.64 Named professionals should support the Trust in its clinical governance role, by ensuring that audits on safeguarding are undertaken and that safeguarding issues are part of the Trust's clinical governance system.

2.65 Named professionals are usually responsible for conducting the Trust's internal case reviews – except when they have had personal involvement in the case, when it will be more appropriate for the designated professional to conduct the review. Named professionals are able to ensure that the resulting action plan is followed up. They also have a key role in ensuring a safeguarding training strategy is in place and is delivered within their organisation.

Paediatricians

2.66 Paediatricians, wherever they work, come into contact with child abuse in the course of their work. All paediatricians need to maintain their skills in the recognition of abuse, and be familiar with the procedures to be followed if abuse and neglect is suspected. Consultant paediatricians, in particular, may be involved in difficult diagnostic situations, differentiating those where abnormalities may have been caused by abuse from those that have a medical cause. In their contacts with children and families, paediatricians should be sensitive to clues suggesting the need for additional support or enquiries.

2.67 Where paediatricians undertake forensic medical examination, they must ensure they are competent to do so, or must work together with a colleague, such as a forensic medical examiner, who has the necessary complementary skills.[18]

2.68 Paediatricians are sometimes required to provide reports for child protection investigations, civil and criminal proceedings, and to appear as witnesses to give oral evidence. They must always act in accordance with guidance from the General Medical Council and professional bodies, ensuring their evidence is accurate.

2.69 Some paediatricians act as independent expert witnesses in legal proceedings. The Academy of Royal Colleges issued guidance for those undertaking expert witness work in 2005.[19]

[18] The core and case-dependent skills required are outlined in detail in *Guidance on Paediatric Forensic Examinations in Relation to Possible Child Sexual Abuse* (2004), produced by the Royal College of Paediatrics and Child Health and the Association of Forensic Physicians.

[19] *Medical Expert Witness: Guidance from the Academy of Medical Royal Colleges* (2005) www.aomrc.org.uk

Dental practitioners and dental care professionals (DCPs)

2.70 Dental practitioners and dental care professionals (dental therapists, dental hygienists, dental nurses, etc.) work in a variety of settings as salaried staff of PCTs, as providers of PCT commissioned services and as independent practitioners. They may see vulnerable children, both within healthcare settings and when undertaking domiciliary visits. They are likely to identify injuries to the head, neck, face, mouth and teeth, as well as potentially identifying other child welfare concerns.

2.71 The dental team, irrespective of the healthcare setting in which they work, should therefore be included within the child protection systems and training within the local trust. Guidance for all dental practice staff, *Child protection and the Dental Team – an introduction to safeguarding children in dental practice* was published in 2006. Dentists should have access to a copy of the LSCB's procedures.

2.72 The dental team should have the knowledge and skills to identify concerns regarding a child's welfare. They should know how to refer to children's social care and who to contact for further advice, including the named professionals in the local health trust.

Other health professionals

2.73 All other health professionals and staff who provide help and support to promote children's health and development should have knowledge of the LSCB procedures and how to contact named professionals for advice and support. They should receive the training and supervision they need to recognise and act on child welfare concerns and to respond to the needs of children. Such staff include those covered in the preceding sections as well as:

- clinical psychologists
- staff in genito-urinary medicine services
- obstetric and gynaecological staff
- occupational therapists
- physiotherapists
- staff in sexual health services
- speech and language therapists
- optometrists
- pharmacists
- other professionals allied to medicine.

This list is not exhaustive.

Roles of different health services

Universal services – general practitioner, the primary healthcare team, practice-employed staff and school nurses

2.74 General practitioners (GPs), other members of the primary healthcare team (PHCT) and practice-employed staff have key roles to play in the identification of children who may have been abused and of those who are at risk of abuse, and in subsequent intervention and protection. Surgery consultations, home visits, treatment room sessions, child health clinic attendance, drop-in centres and information from staff such as health visitors, midwives, school nurses and practice nurses may all help to build up a picture of the child's situation, and can alert the team if there is some concern.

2.75 All PHCT members and practice-employed staff should know when it is appropriate to refer a child to children's social care for help as a 'child in need', and know how to act on concerns that a child may be at risk of significant harm through abuse or neglect. In addition, the child's GP should be informed at the earliest opportunity, if he or she is not making the referral.

2.76 The GP, practice-employed staff and the PHCT are also well placed to recognise when a parent or other adult has problems that may affect their capacity as a parent or carer, or that may mean they pose a risk of harm to a child. While GPs have responsibilities to all their patients, children may be particularly vulnerable and their welfare is paramount. If the PHCT has concerns that an adult's illness or behaviour may be causing, or putting a child at risk of, significant harm, they should follow the procedures set out in Chapter 5 of this guidance (summarised in *What To Do If You're Worried A Child Is Being Abused)*.

2.77 Because of their knowledge of children and families, GPs, together with other practice staff and PHCT members, have an important role in all stages of child protection processes. This includes appropriate information sharing (subject to normal confidentiality requirements) with children's social care when enquiries are being made about a child, contributing to assessments, and involvement in a child protection plan to protect a child from harm. GPs, practice staff and other PHCT practitioners should make available to child protection conferences relevant information about a child and family, whether or not they – or a member of the PHCT – are able to attend.

2.78 All GPs have a duty to maintain their skills in the recognition of abuse, and to be familiar with the procedures to be followed if abuse is suspected. GPs should take part in training about safeguarding and promoting the welfare of children, and should have regular updates as part of their post-graduate educational programme. As employers, they should ensure that practice nurses, practice managers, receptionists and any other staff whom they employ are given the opportunity to attend local courses in safeguarding and promoting the welfare of children, or ensure that safeguarding training is provided within the team.

2.79 PHCTs should have a clear means of identifying, in records, those children (together with their parents and siblings) who are the subject of a child protection plan. This enables the children to be recognised by the partners of the practice, and by any other doctor, practice nurse or health visitor who may be involved in their care. There should be good communication between GPs, health visitors, school nurses, practice nurses and midwives in respect of all children about whom there are concerns.

2.80 Standard 1 of the NSF outlines the new universal child health promotion programme. This provides a framework to ensure the promotion of the health and wellbeing of individual children and young people. The child health promotion programme is being delivered by multi-agency support services involved with children and young people, including GPs, midwives, health visitors, dentists, early-years workers, school nurses and teachers working together. The programme addresses the needs of children from pre-conception to adulthood, and integrates pre-school and school-aged health promotion and assessment. All professionals need to be alert to concerns and to the requirements to safeguard children. More support should be targeted to children and families who are vulnerable or to those with complex needs.

2.81 The NSF recognises that many children have contact with a variety of professionals beyond those described in the child health promotion programme. If, during an assessment, concerns arise that may require support from another agency, it is important for the professionals involved to work in partnership and to share relevant information, as required, in accordance with confidentiality obligations.

2.82 PCTs are responsible for planning integrated GP out-of-hours services in their local area. Staff working within these services should know how to access advice from designated and named professionals within the PCT and from local LSCBs. Each GP and member of the PHCT should have access to a copy of the local LSCB's procedures.

2.83 School nurses have regular contact with school-age children and spend a significant proportion of their time in school. Their skills and knowledge of child health and development mean that, in their work with children in promoting, assessing and monitoring health and development, they have an important role in all stages of safeguarding children and child safeguarding processes.

Maternity services

2.84 Midwives are the primary health professionals likely to be working with and supporting women and their families throughout pregnancy. However, other health professionals – including maternity support workers, health visitors and, where applicable, specialist key workers – may also be directly engaged in providing support. The close relationship they foster with their clients provides an opportunity to observe attitudes towards the developing baby and identify potential problems during pregnancy, birth and the child's early care.

2.85 It is estimated that one-third of domestic violence starts or escalates during pregnancy (see paragraphs 11.45–11.50). All health professionals working with pregnant women should understand that vulnerable women are more likely to delay seeking care, to fail to attend antenatal clinics regularly and to deny and minimise abuse. Recognising the prevalence of abuse across all socio-economic groups, it is important to provide a supportive and enabling environment, where the issue of abuse is raised with every pregnant woman, with the provision of information about specialist agencies, enabling a woman to disclose abuse should she so choose (Maternity Section Children's NSF, 2004). The Department of Health issued revised guidance, *Responding to Domestic Violence: a Handbook for Health Professionals*, in January 2006.

2.86 Women and their families are increasingly choosing to access midwifery-led maternity services. These are provided primarily outside hospitals in community-based settings, including in children's centres. Where midwives and other maternity support staff are employed directly by NHS Primary Care or Hospital Trusts, they are integrated in that Trust's safeguarding arrangements. In the future, new commissioning arrangements may provide more flexible employment options. Contracting processes must explicitly specify and monitor that health professionals working in this way are fully integrated into the local safeguarding arrangements applicable to all other relevant healthcare providers.

2.87 Nurses and other health professionals working with children and families in a variety of environments need to be alert to the strong links between adult domestic abuse and child abuse. They are well placed to recognise when a child is in need of help or services, or is at potential risk of significant harm.

Child and adolescent mental health services

2.88 Standard 9 of the NSF is devoted to the 'Mental Health and Psychological Wellbeing of Children and Young People'. The importance of effective partnership working is emphasised, and this is especially applicable to children and young people who have mental health problems as a result of abuse and/or neglect.

2.89 As part of assessment and care planning, child and adolescent mental health professionals should identify whether child abuse or neglect, or domestic violence, are factors in a child's mental health problems, and should ensure that this is addressed appropriately in the child's treatment and care. If mental health professionals think a child is currently affected, they should follow the child protection procedures laid down for their services within their area. Consultation, supervision and training resources should be available and accessible in each service.

2.90 Child and adolescent mental health professionals have a role in the initial assessment process in circumstances where their specific skills and knowledge are helpful. Examples include:

- children and young people with severe behavioural and emotional disturbance, eating disorders or self-harming behaviour
- cases where there is a perceived high risk of danger
- families with very young children, or where the abused child or abuser has severe communication problems
- cases where the parent or carer fabricates or induces illness
- cases where multiple victims are involved.

In addition, assessment and treatment services may need to be provided to young people with mental health problems who offend. The assessment of children with significant learning difficulties, a disability or sensory and communication difficulties may require the expertise of a specialist learning disability service or child and adolescent mental health service.

2.91 Child and adolescent mental health services also have a role in the provision of a range of psychiatric and psychological assessment and treatment services for children and families. Services that may be provided, in liaison with social services, include the provision of reports for court, and direct work with children, parents and families. Services may be provided either within general or specialist multi-disciplinary teams, depending on the severity and complexity of the problem. In addition, consultation and training may be offered to services in the community – including, for example, social services, schools, primary healthcare teams and nurseries.

Adult mental health services

2.92 Adult mental health services – including those providing general adult and community, forensic, psychotherapy, alcohol and substance misuse and learning disability services – have a responsibility in safeguarding children when they become aware of, or identify, a child at risk of harm. This may be as a result of a service's direct work with those who may be mentally ill, a parent, a parent-to-be, or a non-related abuser, or in response to a request for the assessment of an adult perceived to represent a potential or actual risk to a child or young person. These staff need to be especially aware of the risk of neglect, emotional abuse and domestic abuse. They should follow the child protection procedures laid down for their services within their area. Consultation, supervision and training resources should be available and accessible in each service.

2.93 To safeguard children of patients, mental health practitioners should routinely record details of patients' responsibilities in relation to children, and consider the support needs of patients who are parents and of their children, in all aspects of their work, using the Care Programme Approach. Mental health practitioners should refer to Royal College of Psychiatrists policy documents, including *Patients as Parents and Child Abuse and Neglect: the Role of Mental Health Services*.

2.94 Close collaboration and liaison between adult mental health services and children's social services are essential in the interests of children. This may require sharing information to safeguard and promote the welfare of children or to protect a child from significant harm. The expertise of substance misuse services and learning disability services may also be required. The assessment of parents with significant learning difficulties, a disability, or sensory and communication difficulties, may require the expertise of a specialist psychiatrist or clinical psychologist from a learning disability service or adult mental health service.

Visiting of psychiatric patients by children

2.95 All inpatient mental health services must have policies and procedures relating to children visiting inpatients, as set out in the *Guidance on the Visiting of Psychiatric Patients by Children* (HSC, 1999/222: LAC (99)32) to NHS Trusts. Additional guidance has been provided for high-security hospitals. Mental health practitioners must consider the needs of children whose parent or relative is an inpatient – whether formal or informal – in a mental health unit, and make appropriate arrangements for them to visit if this is in the child's best interests.

Alcohol and drug services

2.96 A range of services is provided, in particular by health and voluntary organisations, to respond to the needs of both adults (with parental responsibilities) and children who misuse drugs. These services are linked to the relevant agencies at local level through Drug Action Teams, which comprise, as a minimum, health, social services, education and police representatives. It is important that arrangements are in place to enable child protection services and substance misuse (including alcohol) services referrals to be made in relevant cases. Where children may be suffering significant harm because of their own substance misuse, or where parental substance misuse may be causing such harm, referrals need to be made by Drug Action Teams or alcohol services, in accordance with LSCB procedures. Where children are not suffering significant harm, referral arrangements also need to be in place to enable children's broader needs to be assessed and responded to.

Criminal justice organisations

The police

2.97 The main roles of the police are to uphold the law, prevent crime and disorder and protect citizens. Children, like all citizens, have the right to the full protection offered by the criminal law. The police have a duty and responsibility to investigate all criminal offences and, as Lord Laming pointed out in his report into the circumstances leading to the death of Victoria Climbié (2003), 'the investigation of crimes against children is as important as the investigation of any other serious crime and any suggestions that child protection policing is of lower status than any other form of policing should be eradicated'. Offences committed against children can be particularly sensitive, and often require the police to work with other organisations, such as children's social care, in the conduct of any investigation.

2.98 The police recognise the fundamental importance of inter-agency working in combating child abuse, as illustrated by well-established arrangements for joint training involving police and social care colleagues. The police have invested a great deal in both training and resources to enhance their ability to offer the best possible service to child victims of crime.

2.99 All police forces have child abuse investigation units (CAIUs) and, despite variations in their structures and staffing levels, they normally take primary responsibility for investigating child abuse cases. From December 2005, all CAIUs have IT capability under the national IMPACT Nominal Index (INI) quickly to check which forces (broadly, UK-wide) hold information on a particular individual. This has greatly enhanced the police's ability to contribute swiftly to inter-agency requests in addressing perceived risks. The INI capability draws on a number of police databases, including child protection, domestic violence, crime, custody and intelligence. As an investigation tool, it enables access to information that may not be on the police national computer. An important guidance document, *Investigating Child Abuse and Safeguarding Children*, was published by the Association of Chief Police Officers (ACPO) in 2005. This sets out the suggested investigative doctrine and terms of reference for police forces' child abuse investigation units.

2.100 Safeguarding children is not solely the role of CAIU officers – it is a fundamental part of the duties of all police officers. Patrol officers attending domestic violence incidents, for example, should be aware of the effect of such violence on any children normally resident within the household. The Children Act 2004 places a wider duty on the police to 'safeguard and promote the welfare of children'. The police also maintain relevant UK-wide databases such VISOR – the Violent and Sexual Offenders Register. This has been developed jointly between the police and the probation service to assist management of offenders in the community. Through the Safeguarding Vulnerable Groups Bill, introduced in early 2006, the Government plans to establish a new integrated Vetting and Barring Scheme, regulating all those who work with children (and vulnerable adults), which will rely on regularly updated police information. It is not the intention that the police will deploy resources into areas that are not in their normal range of duties. Separate guidance is available to help the police carry out this responsibility, but officers engaged in, for example, crime and disorder reduction partnerships, Drug Action Teams etc. must keep in mind the needs of children in their area.

2.101 The police hold important information about children who may be at risk of harm as well as those who cause such harm. They are committed to sharing information and intelligence with other organisations where this is necessary to protect children. This includes a responsibility to ensure that those officers representing the police at a child protection conference are fully informed about the case, as well as being experienced in risk assessment and the decision-making process. Similarly, they can expect other organisations to share with them information and intelligence they hold to enable the police to carry out their duties.

2.102 The police are responsible for the gathering of evidence in criminal investigations. This task can be carried out in conjunction with other agencies, but the police are ultimately accountable for the product of criminal enquiries. Any evidence gathered may be of use to LA solicitors who are preparing for civil proceedings to protect the victim. The Crown Prosecution Service (CPS) should be consulted, but evidence is normally shared if it is in the best interests of the child.

2.103 The police should be notified as soon as possible by LA children's social care whenever a case referred to them involves a criminal offence committed, or suspected of having been committed, against a child. Other agencies should consider sharing such information. (See paragraphs 5.17 onwards for detailed guidance on this point.) This does not mean that in all such cases a full investigation is required, or that there will necessarily be any further police involvement. It is important, however, that the police retain the opportunity to be informed and consulted, to ensure all relevant information can be taken into account before a final decision is made.

2.104 LSCBs should have in place a protocol, agreed between the LA and the police, to guide both organisations in deciding how child protection enquiries should be conducted and, in particular, the circumstances in which joint enquiries are appropriate.

2.105 In addition to their duty to investigate criminal offences, the police have emergency powers to enter premises and ensure the immediate protection of children believed to be suffering from, or at risk of, significant harm. Such powers should be used only when necessary, the principle being that, wherever possible, the decision to remove a child from a parent or carer should be made by a court. Home Office Circular 44/2003 (found at www.crimereduction.gov.uk/victims29.htm) gives detailed guidance on this.

National Offender Management Service

Probation services

2.106 The Probation Service supervises offenders, with the aim of reducing re-offending and protecting the public. As part of their main responsibility to supervise offenders in the community, Offender Managers are in contact with, or supervising, a number of offenders who have been identified as presenting a risk, or potential risk, to children. They also supervise offenders who are parents/carers of children. By working with these people to improve their lifestyles and enabling them to change their behaviour, Offender Managers safeguard and promote the welfare of the children for whom the offenders have a responsibility. In addition, Probation Areas provide a direct service to children by:

- offering a service to child victims of serious sexual or violent offences
- supervising 16- and 17-year-olds on Community Punishment
- seconding staff to join Youth Offending Teams

- supporting victims, and indirectly children in the family, of convicted perpetrators of domestic abuse participating in accredited domestic abuse programmes.

2.107 Offender Managers should also ensure that there is clarity and communication between Multi Agency Public Protection Arrangements (MAPPA) and other risk management processes – e.g. in the case of safeguarding children, procedures covering registered sex offenders, domestic abuse management meetings, child protection procedures and procedures for the assessment of people identified as presenting a risk or potential risk to children. These arrangements and procedures are described in Chapter 12.

Prisons

2.108 Governors of prisons (or, in the case of contracted prisons, their Directors) also have a duty to make arrangements to ensure that their functions are discharged with regard to the need to safeguard and promote the welfare of children, not least those who have been committed to their custody by the courts.

2.109 In particular, Governors/Directors of women's establishments that have Mother and Baby Units must ensure that staff working on the units are prioritised for child protection training, and that there is always a member of staff on duty in the unit who is proficient in child protection, health and safety and first aid/child resuscitation. Each baby must have a childcare plan, setting out how the best interests of the child will be maintained and promoted during the child's residence on the unit.

2.110 Governors/Directors of all prison establishments must have in place arrangements that protect the public from prisoners in their care. This includes having effective processes in place to ensure prisoners are not able to cause harm to the public, particularly children. Restrictions are placed on prisoner communications (visits, telephone and correspondence) that are proportionate to the risk they present. As a response to incidents where prisoners have attempted to 'condition and groom' future victims, all prisoners who have been identified as presenting a risk to children are not allowed contact with children, unless a favourable risk assessment has been undertaken. This assessment takes into consideration information held by the police, probation, prison and social services.

2.111 The views of the child or young person are an important element of the assessment. When seeking the views of the parent or carer (person with parental responsibility) regarding contact, it is important that the child's views are sought. In the letter to the child's parent or carer, it should be emphasised that the child's views should be taken into account. If a child is able to make an informed choice, these views must be considered. Social Care will ascertain the views of the child during the home visit.

The Secure Estate for children and young people

2.112 The Youth Justice Board for England and Wales (YJB) has statutory responsibility for the commissioning and purchasing of all secure accommodation for children and for setting standards for the delivery of those services. The Secure Estate comprises Prison

Service accommodation for juveniles – juvenile Young Offenders' Institutions (see paragraph 2.113), Secure Training Centres (see paragraph 2.114), and Secure Children's Homes provided by LAs (see paragraph 2.18).

Juvenile Young Offenders' Institutions

2.113 Governors/Directors of these establishments are required to have regard to the policies, agreed by the Prison Service and the YJB, for safeguarding and promoting the welfare of children held in custody. These are published in Prison Order 4950 *Juvenile Regimes*, and the arrangements prescribed for juvenile establishments include:

- a senior member of staff, known as the Child Protection Co-ordinator, or the Safeguards Manager, who is responsible to the Governor/Director for child protection and safeguarding matters
- a child protection committee, whose membership includes a senior manager as the Chair, multi-disciplinary staff and a representative of the LSCB, who could be a member of the LSCB (i.e. someone from another organisation) or an LSCB staff member
- a local, establishment-specific child protection and safeguarding policy, agreed with the LSCB, that has regard to the Prison Service's/YJB's overarching policy and that includes procedures for dealing with incidents or disclosures of child abuse or neglect before or during custody
- suicide and self-harm prevention and anti-bullying strategies
- procedures for dealing proactively, rigorously, fairly and promptly with complaints and formal requests, complemented by an advocacy service
- specialised training for all staff working with children, together with selection, recruitment and vetting procedures to ensure that new staff may work safely and competently with children
- action to manage and develop effective working partnerships with other organisations, including voluntary and community organisations, that can strengthen the support provided to young people and their families during custody and on release
- an initial assessment, on reception into custody, to identify the needs, abilities and aptitudes of the young person, and the formulation of a sentence plan (including an individual learning plan) designed to address those needs, followed by regular sentence plan reviews
- provision of education, training and personal development in line with the YJB's *National Specification for Learning and Skills* and the young person's identified needs
- action to encourage the young person and their family to take an active role in the preparation and subsequent reviews of their sentence plan, so that they are able to contribute to, and influence, what happens to them in custody and following release.

The same measures should apply to children in other custodial settings, such as children in adult prison settings or immigration detention centres.

Secure Training Centres

2.114 Secure Training Centres (STCs) are purpose-built secure accommodation units for vulnerable, sentenced and remanded juveniles, both male and female, between the ages of 12 and 17. The regime is focussed on childcare, and considerable time and effort is spent on individual needs so that on release young people are able to make better life choices. Each STC has a duty to protect and promote the welfare of those children in its custody. Directors must ensure that effective safeguarding policies and procedures that explain staff responsibilities in relation to safeguarding and welfare promotion are in place. These arrangements must be established in consultation with the LSCB.

Youth Offending Teams

2.115 The principal aim of the youth justice system is to prevent offending by children and young people, and this aim is achieved mainly through Youth Offending Teams (Yots). These are multi-agency teams that must include a probation officer, a police officer, a representative of the PCT, someone with experience in education, and someone with experience of social work relating to children. Yots are responsible for the supervision of children and young people subject to pre-court interventions and statutory court disposals.

2.116 Given their inter-agency membership, Yots are well placed to identify those children and young people known to relevant organisations as being most at risk of offending, and to undertake work to prevent them offending. A number of the children who are supervised by the Yots will also be children in need, and some of their needs will require safeguarding. It is necessary, therefore, for there to be clear links between youth justice and LA children's social care, both at a strategic level and at a child-specific operational level.

2.117 Yots have a duty to ensure that their functions are discharged with regard to the need to safeguard and promote the welfare of children.

Services provided under s114 of the Learning and Skills Act 2000 (the Connexions service)

2.118 There are currently 47 Connexions partnerships covering England. Each Connexions partnership has a substantial workforce working directly with young people. The workforce includes not only professionally qualified personal advisers, but also other delivery staff working under their supervision. The Connexions service is centred on young people and, as such, safeguarding and promoting the welfare of young people is a primary concern.

2.119 The Connexions partnership (including its subcontractors) is responsible for:

- identifying, keeping in touch with and giving the necessary support to young people in their geographical area. Each young person's needs are assessed and the support and continuing contact they receive is tailored to their assessed needs. A young person may receive any combination of the following according to their needs: information, advice, guidance, counselling, personal development opportunities, referral to specialist services, and advocacy to enable them to access opportunities for funding or other services. The needs of young people from vulnerable groups such as teenage mothers, care leavers, young people supervised by Yots, and young people with learning difficulties and/or disabilities are a particular priority for Connexions partnerships

- identifying young people who may be at risk from child protection issues and, in these cases, for alerting the appropriate authority. Connexions staff should be aware of the agencies and contacts to use to refer young people at risk, and should be aware of the way in which these concerns will be followed up
- minimising risk to the safety of young people on premises for which the Connexions partnership or their subcontractors are responsible. The partnership should maintain the necessary capacity to carry out relevant risk assessments
- minimising the risk that organisations to which they signpost young people, such as those providing employment and training opportunities, pose a threat to the moral development and physical and psychological wellbeing of young people
- ensuring that the recruitment of all staff (including volunteers, both to the partnership and their subcontractors) complies with current vetting regulations
- ensuring that staff (including subcontractors) are aware of risks to the welfare of young people and can exercise their legal, ethical, operational and professional obligations to safeguard them from these risks. Information sharing protocols with other agencies should give the highest priority to safeguarding and promoting the welfare of young people, and staff should comply fully with these agreements.

2.120 The Connexions partnership should work closely with other agencies concerned with child safety and welfare to analyse rigorously the nature and distribution of risk within the cohort of young people, and to use this information to design services, allocate resources and otherwise take action that addresses both causes and effects.

Schools and further education institutions

2.121 Schools (including independent schools and non-maintained special schools) and further education (FE) institutions should give effect to their duty to safeguard and promote the welfare of their pupils (students under 18 years of age in the case of FE institutions) under the Education Act 2002 and, where appropriate, under the Children Act 1989 (see paragraph 2.5) by:

- creating and maintaining a safe learning environment for children and young people
- identifying where there are child welfare concerns and taking action to address them, in partnership with other organisations where appropriate.

Schools also contribute through the curriculum by developing children's understanding, awareness and resilience.

2.122 Creating a safe learning environment means having effective arrangements in place to address a range of issues. Some arrangements are subject to statutory requirements, including child protection arrangements, pupil health and safety, and bullying. Others include arrangements for meeting the health needs of children with medical conditions, providing first aid, school security, tackling drugs and substance misuse, and having arrangements in place to safeguard and promote the welfare of children on extended vocational placements.

2.123 Education staff have a crucial role to play in helping identify welfare concerns, and indicators of possible abuse or neglect, at an early stage. They should refer to those concerns to the appropriate organisation, normally LA children's social care, contributing to the assessment of a child's needs and, where appropriate, to ongoing action to meet those needs. When a child has special educational needs or is disabled, the school will have important information about the child's level of understanding and the most effective means of communicating with the child. The school will also be well placed to give a view on the impact of treatment or intervention on the child's care or behaviour.

2.124 In addition to the features common to organisations working with children listed in paragraph 2.8, schools and FE institutions should have a senior member of staff who is designated to take lead responsibility for dealing with child protection issues, providing advice and support to other staff, liaising with the authority, and working with other organisations as necessary. A school or FE institution should remedy without delay any deficiencies or weaknesses in its arrangements for safeguarding and promoting welfare that are brought to its attention.

2.125 Staff in schools and FE institutions should not themselves investigate possible abuse or neglect. They have a key role to play by referring concerns about those issues to children's social care, providing information for police investigations and/or enquiries under s47 of the Children Act 1989, and by contributing to assessments.

2.126 Where a child of school age is the subject of an inter-agency child protection plan, the school should be involved in the preparation of the plan. The school's role and responsibilities in contributing to actions to safeguard the child, and promote his or her welfare, should be clearly identified.

2.127 Special schools, including non-maintained special schools and independent schools, that provide medical and/or nursing care should ensure that their medical and nursing staff have appropriate training and access to advice on child protection and on safeguarding and promoting the welfare of children.

2.128 Schools play an important role in making children and young people aware of behaviour towards them that is not acceptable, and of how they can help keep themselves safe. The non-statutory framework for personal, social and health education (PSHE) provides opportunities for children and young people to learn about keeping safe. For example, pupils should be taught to:

- recognise and manage risks in different situations and then decide how to behave responsibly
- judge what kind of physical contact is acceptable and unacceptable
- recognise when pressure from others (including people they know) threatens their personal safety and wellbeing and develop effective ways of resisting pressure.

2.129 PSHE curriculum materials provide resources that enable schools to tackle issues regarding healthy relationships, including domestic violence, bullying and abuse. Discussions about personal safety and keeping safe can reinforce the message that any kind of violence is unacceptable, let children and young people know that it is acceptable to talk about their own problems, and signpost sources of help.

2.130 Corporal punishment is outlawed for all pupils in all schools, including independent schools, and FE institutions. The law forbids a teacher or other member of staff from using any degree of physical contact that is deliberately intended to punish a pupil, or that is primarily intended to cause pain or injury or humiliation.

2.131 Teachers at a school are allowed to use reasonable force to control or restrain pupils under certain circumstances. Other staff may also do so, in the same way as teachers, provided they have been authorised by the head teacher to have control or charge of pupils. All schools should have a policy about the use of force to control or restrain pupils. Further guidance about this is at:
www.dfes.gov.uk/publications/guidanceonthelaw/10_98/summary.htm

Childcare services

2.132 Childcare services – family and children's centres, day nurseries, childminders, pre-schools, playgroups, and holiday and out-of-school schemes – play an important part in the lives of large numbers of children. Many childcare providers have considerable experience of working with families where a child needs to be safeguarded from harm, and many LAs provide, commission or sponsor specific services, including childminders, to work with children in need and their families.

2.133 Childminders and everyone working in day care services should know how to recognise and respond to the possible abuse or neglect of a child. Private, voluntary and LA day care providers caring for children under the age of eight must be registered by Ofsted under the Children Act 1989, and should have a written statement, based on the procedures laid out in the booklet *What To Do If You're Worried A Child Is Being Abused – Summary*. This statement should clearly set out staff responsibilities for reporting suspected child abuse or neglect in accordance with LSCB procedures, and should include contact and telephone numbers for the local police and children's social care. The statement should also include procedures to be followed in the event of an allegation being made against a member of staff or volunteer. All organisations providing group day care must have a designated person who is responsible for liaison with local child protection agencies and Ofsted on child protection issues, and other staff should be able to implement child protection procedures in the absence of that person.

Children and Family Court Advisory and Support Service (CAFCASS)

2.134 CAFCASS's functions are to:

- safeguard and promote the welfare of children who are the subject of family proceedings
- give advice to any court about any application made to it in such proceedings
- make provision for children to be represented in such proceedings
- provide information, advice and other support for children and their families.

2.135 CAFCASS appoints the individual officer, who might be a CAFCASS employee or a self-employed contractor. The CAFCASS Officer is appointed by the court to undertake one or more of their functions, and can be referred to by this general title. These CAFCASS Officers have different roles in private and public law proceedings. These roles are denoted by different titles:

- Children's Guardians, who are appointed to safeguard the interests of a child who is the subject of specified proceedings under the Children Act 1989, or who is the subject of adoption proceedings
- Parental Order Reporters, who are appointed to investigate and report to the court on circumstances relevant under the Human Fertilisation and Embryology Act 1990
- Children and Family Reporters, who prepare welfare reports for the court in relation to applications under s8 of the Children Act 1989 (private law proceedings, including applications for residence and contact). Increasingly they also work with families at the stage of their initial application to the court
- CAFCASS Officers can also be appointed to provide support under a Family Assistance Order under the Children Act 1989. (LA officers can also be appointed for this purpose.)

2.136 The CAFCASS Officer has a statutory right in public law cases to access and take copies of LA records relating to the child concerned and any application under the Children Act 1989. That power also extends to other records that relate to the child and the wider functions of the LA, or records held by an authorised body (e.g. the NSPCC) that relate to that child.

2.137 Where a CAFCASS Officer has been appointed by the court as Children's Guardian and the matter before the court relates to specified proceedings (specified proceedings include public law proceedings; applications for contact; residence, specific issue and prohibited steps orders that have become particularly difficult can also be specified proceedings) they should be invited to all formal planning meetings convened by the LA in respect of the child. This includes statutory reviews of children who are accommodated or looked after, child protection conferences, and relevant Adoption Panel meetings. The conference chair should ensure that all those attending such meetings, including the child and any family members, understand the role of the CAFCASS Officer.

The Armed Services

2.138 Young people under 18 may be in the armed forces as recruits or trainees, or may be dependants of a service family. The life of a service family differs in many respects from that of a family in civilian life, particularly for those stationed overseas, or on bases and garrisons in the UK. The services support the movement of the family in response to service commitments. The frequency and location of such moves make it essential that the service authorities are aware of any concerns regarding safeguarding and promoting the welfare of a child from a military family. The armed forces are fully committed to co-operating with statutory and other agencies in supporting families in this situation, and have procedures to help safeguard and promote the welfare of children. In areas of high concentration of service families, the armed forces seek particularly to work alongside LA children's social care, including through representation on LSCBs and at child protection conferences and reviews.

2.139 Looking after under-18s in the armed forces comes under the MoD's comprehensive welfare arrangements, which apply to all members of the armed forces. Commanding Officers are well aware of the particular welfare needs of younger recruits and trainees and, as stated above, are fully committed to co-operating with statutory and other agencies in safeguarding and promoting the welfare of under-18s. LA children's social care already has a responsibility to monitor the wellbeing of care leavers, and those joining the armed forces have unrestricted access to LA social care workers.

2.140 LAs have the statutory responsibility for safeguarding and promoting the welfare of the children of service families in the UK. All three services provide professional welfare support, including 'special to type' social work services to augment those provided by LAs. In the Royal Navy (RN) this is provided by the Naval Personal and Family Service (NPFS) and the Royal Marines Welfare Service; within the army this is provided by the Army Welfare Service (AWS); and in the Royal Air Force by the Soldiers' Sailors' and Airmen's Families Association-Forces Help (SSAFA-FH). Further details of these services and contact numbers are given in Appendix 4.

2.141 When service families or civilians working with the armed forces are based overseas, the responsibility for safeguarding and promoting the welfare of their children is vested with the MoD, who fund the British Forces Social Work Service (Overseas). This service is contracted to SSAFA-FH, who provide a fully qualified Social Work and Community Health service in major overseas locations (e.g. in Germany and Cyprus). Instructions for the protection of children overseas, which reflect the principles of the Children Act 2004 and the philosophy of inter-agency co-operation, are issued by the MoD as a 'Defence Council Instruction (Joint Service)' (DCI(JS)). Larger overseas commands issue local child protection procedures, hold a Command Child Protection Register and have a Command Safeguarding Children Board, which operates in a similar way to those set up under this guidance, in upholding standards and making sure that best practice is reflected in procedures and observed in practice.

Movement of children between the United Kingdom and overseas

2.142 LAs should ensure that SSAFA-FH, the British Forces Social Work Service (Overseas), or the NPFS for RN families is made aware of any service child who is the subject of a child protection plan and whose family is about to move overseas. In the interests of the child, SSAFA-FH, the British Forces Social Work Service (Overseas) or NPFS can confirm that appropriate resources exist in the proposed location to meet identified needs. Full documentation should be provided and forwarded to the relevant overseas command. All referrals should be made to the Director of Social Work, HQ SSAFA-FH or Area Officer, NPFS (East) as appropriate, at the addresses given in Appendix 4. Comprehensive reciprocal arrangements exist for the referral of child protection cases to appropriate UK authorities, relating to the temporary or permanent relocation of such children to the UK from overseas.

United States forces stationed in the United Kingdom

2.143 Each LA with a United States (US) base in its area should establish liaison arrangements with the base commander and relevant staff. The requirements of English child welfare legislation should be explained clearly to the US authorities, so that LAs can fulfil their statutory duties.

Enquiries about children of ex-service families

2.144 Where a LA believes that a child who is the subject of current child protection processes is from an ex-service family, NPFS, AWS or SSAFA-FH can be contacted to establish whether there is existing information that might help with enquiries. Such enquiries should be addressed to NPFS, AWS or the Director of Social Work, SSAFA-FH, at the address given in Appendix 4.

The voluntary and private sectors

2.145 Voluntary organisations and private sector providers play an important role in delivering services for children and young people, including in early-years and day care provision, family support services, youth work and children's social care and healthcare.

Many voluntary organisations are skilled in preventative work, and may be well placed to reach the most vulnerable children, young people and families.

2.146 Voluntary organisations also deliver advocacy for looked after children and young people, and for parents and children who are the subject of s47 enquiries and child protection conferences. They offer, for example:

- therapeutic work with children, young people and families, particularly in relation to child sexual abuse
- specialist support and services for children and young people with disabilities or health problems
- services for children abused through prostitution and for children who abuse other children.

2.147 Some voluntary organisations operate free 24-hour national helplines. ChildLine is a national service for all children and young people who need advice about abuse, bullying and other concerns. The NSPCC is a specialist child protection agency that operates helplines and other services throughout England, Wales and Northern Ireland. Its national child protection helpline provides advice to adults and children about child protection concerns. Parentline Plus offers support to anyone parenting a child. These services, along with many other smaller helplines, provide important routes into statutory and voluntary services.

2.148 Voluntary organisations also play a key role in providing information and resources to the wider public about the needs of children and young people, and resources to help families. Many campaign on behalf of groups on specific issues.

2.149 The NSPCC is the only voluntary organisation authorised to initiate proceedings to protect children under the terms of the Children Act 1989, but other voluntary organisations often play a key role in implementing child protection plans.

2.150 The voluntary sector is active in working to safeguard the children and young people with whom it works. A range of umbrella and specialist organisations, including the national governing bodies for sports, offer standards, guidance, training and advice for voluntary organisations on keeping children and young people safe from harm. For example, the Child Protection in Sport Unit (CPSU), established in partnership with the NSPCC and Sport England, provides advice and assistance on developing codes of practice and child protection procedures to sporting organisations.

2.151 Organisations in the voluntary and private sectors that work with children need to have the arrangements described in paragraph 2.8 in place in the same way as organisations in the public sector, and need to work effectively with LSCBs. Paid and volunteer staff need to be aware of their responsibilities for safeguarding and promoting the welfare of children, and of how they should respond to child protection concerns in line with this guidance (summarised in *What To Do If You're Worried A Child Is Being Abused.*)

Faith communities

2.152 Churches, other places of worship and faith-based organisations provide a wide range of activities for children and young people. They are some of the largest providers of children and youth work, and have an important role in safeguarding children and supporting families. Religious leaders, staff and volunteers who provide services in places of worship and in faith-based organisations will have various degrees of contact with children.

2.153 Like other organisations that work with children, churches, other places of worship and faith-based organisations need to have appropriate arrangements in place for safeguarding and promoting the welfare of children, as described in paragraph 2.8. In particular, these arrangements should include:

- procedures for staff and others to report concerns that they may have about the children they meet that are in line with *What To Do If You're Worried A Child Is Being Abused* and LSCB procedures, as well as arrangements such as those described above
- appropriate codes of practice for staff, particularly those working directly with children, such as those issued by the Churches' Child Protection Advisory Service (CCPAS) or their denomination or faith group
- recruitment procedures in accordance with *Safe from Harm* (Home Office, 1993) principles and LSCB procedures, alongside training and supervision of staff (paid or voluntary).

2.154 Churches and faith organisations can seek advice on child protection issues from the Churches' Child Protection Advisory Service (CCPAS). CCPAS can help with policies and procedures; its *Guidance to Churches* manual can assist churches, and its *Safeguarding Children and Young People* can assist other places of worship and faith-based groups

2.155 CCPAS operates a national (24-hour) telephone helpline for churches, other places of worship and faith-based groups and individuals, providing advice and support on safeguarding issues.

Chapter 3 – Local Safeguarding Children Boards

3.1 Safeguarding and promoting the welfare of children requires effective co-ordination in every local area. For this reason, the Children Act 2004 requires each local authority (LA) to establish a Local Safeguarding Children Board (LSCB).

3.2 The LSCB is the key statutory mechanism for agreeing how the relevant organisations in each local area will co-operate to safeguard and promote the welfare of children in that locality, and for ensuring the effectiveness of what they do.

LSCB role

The LSCB's relationship with wider arrangements to improve outcomes for children

3.3 The work of LSCBs is part of the wider context of children's trust arrangements that aim to improve the overall wellbeing (i.e. the five *Every Child Matters* outcomes) of all children in the local area.

3.4 While the work of LSCBs contributes to the wider goals of improving the wellbeing of all children, it has a particular focus on aspects of the 'staying safe' outcome.

3.5 Whereas the children's trust has a wider role in planning and delivery of services, LSCB objectives are about co-ordinating and ensuring the effectiveness of what their member organisations do individually and together. They will contribute to delivery and commissioning through the Children and Young People's Plan and the children's trust arrangements.

3.6 There is flexibility for a local area to decide that an LSCB should have an extended role or further functions in addition to those set out in this chapter. Those must of course still be related to its objectives. The decision should be taken as part of the scope of the wider children's trust. However, the LA and its partners should make sure that any extended role does not lessen the LSCB's ability to perform its core role effectively.

Objectives

3.7 The core objectives of the LSCB are set out in s14(1) of the Children Act 2004 as follows:

- to co-ordinate what is done by each person or body represented on the Board for the purposes of safeguarding and promoting the welfare of children in the area of the authority
- to ensure the effectiveness of what is done by each such person or body for that purpose.

3.8 As explained in Chapter 1, safeguarding and promoting the welfare of children is defined for the purposes of this guidance as:

- protecting children from maltreatment
- preventing impairment of children's health or development

Figure 1: LSCB objectives and functions

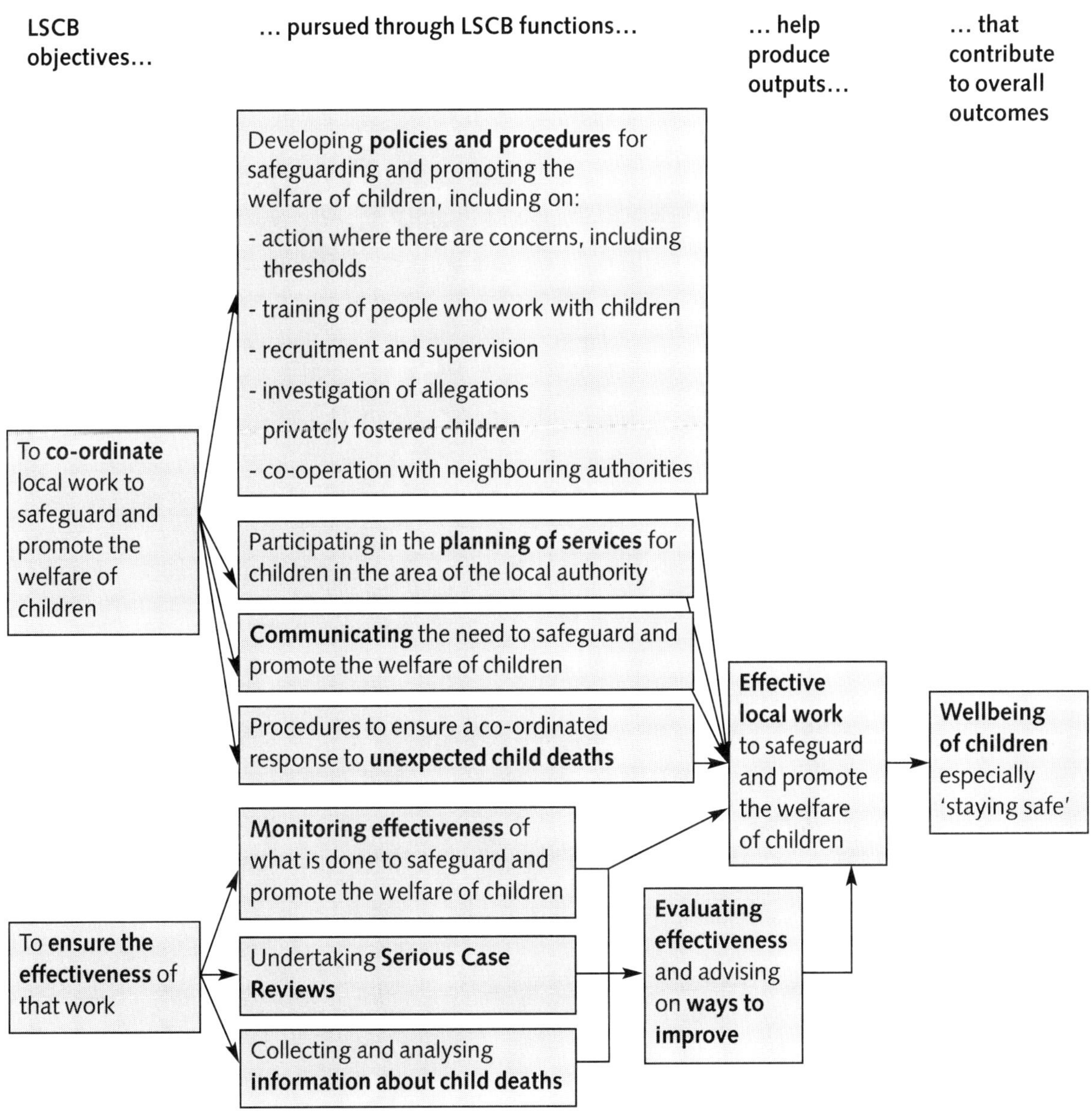

- ensuring that children are growing up in circumstances consistent with the provision of safe and effective care
- undertaking that role so as to enable those children to have optimum life chances and enter adulthood successfully.

3.9 The LSCB therefore ensures that the duty to safeguard and promote the welfare of children is carried out in such a way as to improve all five outcomes that are of importance to children.

3.10 Safeguarding and promoting the welfare of children includes protecting children from harm. Ensuring that work to protect children is properly co-ordinated and effective remains a key goal of LSCBs, and they should not focus on their wider role if the standard of this core business is inadequate. However, when this core business is secure, LSCBs should go beyond it to work to their wider remit, which includes preventative work to avoid harm being suffered in the first place.

Scope of the role

3.11 The scope of LSCBs' role includes safeguarding and promoting the welfare of children in three broad areas of activity.

3.12 First, activity that affects all children and aims to identify and prevent maltreatment, or impairment of health or development, and ensure children are growing up in circumstances consistent with safe and effective care. For example:

- mechanisms to identify abuse and neglect wherever they may occur
- work to increase understanding of safeguarding children issues in the professional and wider community, promoting the message that safeguarding is everybody's responsibility
- work to ensure that organisations working or in contact with children operate recruitment and human resources practices that take account of the need to safeguard and promote the welfare of children
- monitoring the effectiveness of organisations' implementation of their duties under s11 of the Children Act 2004
- ensuring that children know who they can contact when they have concerns about their own or others' safety and welfare
- ensuring that adults (including those who are harming children) know who they can contact if they have a concern about a child or young person.

3.13 The second area of activity is proactive work that aims to target particular groups. For example:

- developing/evaluating thresholds and procedures for work with children and families where a child has been identified as 'in need' under the Children Act 1989, but where the child is not suffering, or at risk of suffering, significant harm
- work to safeguard and promote the welfare of groups of children who are potentially more vulnerable than the general population – e.g. children living away from home, children who have run away from home, children in custody, or disabled children.

3.14 The third area is responsive work to protect children who are suffering, or at risk of suffering, harm, including:

- children abused and neglected within families, including those harmed:
  - in the context of domestic violence
  - as a consequence of the impact of substance misuse
- children abused outside families by adults known to them
- children abused and neglected by professional carers, within institutional settings, or anywhere else where children are cared for away from home
- children abused by strangers
- children abused by other young people
- young perpetrators of abuse
- children abused through prostitution.

3.15 Where particular children are the subject of interventions, then that safeguarding work should aim to help them to achieve all five outcomes, to have optimum life chances. It is within the remit of LSCBs to check the extent to which this has been achieved as part of their monitoring and evaluation work.

Accountability for operational work

3.16 While the LSCB has a role in co-ordinating and ensuring the effectiveness of local individuals' and organisations' work to safeguard and promote the welfare of children, it is not accountable for their operational work. All Board partners retain their own existing lines of accountability for safeguarding and promoting the welfare of children by their services. The LSCB does not have a power to direct other organisations.

LSCB functions

3.17 The core functions of an LSCB are set out in Regulations.[20] This guidance gives further details on what is required, as well as examples of how the functions can be carried

20 The Local Safeguarding Children Boards Regulations 2006, Statutory Instrument no. 2006/90.

out. In all their activities, LSCBs should take account of the need to promote equality of opportunity and to meet the diverse needs of children.

Policies and procedures function

3.18 This general function has a number of specific applications set out in Regulations.

a) Developing policies and procedures for safeguarding and promoting the welfare of children in the area of the authority, including policies and procedures in relation to the following:

(i) The action to be taken where there are concerns about a child's safety or welfare, including thresholds for intervention

3.19 This includes concerns under both s17 and s47 of the Children Act 1989. It may mean, for example:

- setting out thresholds for referrals to children's social care of children who may be in need, and processes for robust multi-agency assessment of children in need
- agreeing inter-agency procedures for s47 enquiries, and developing local protocols on key issues of concern such as:
    - children abused through prostitution
    - children living with domestic violence, substance abuse, or parental mental illness
    - female genital mutilation
    - forced marriage
    - children missing from school
    - children who may have been trafficked
    - safeguarding looked after children who are away from home
- setting out how s47 enquiries and associated police investigations should be conducted and, in particular, in what circumstances joint enquiries are necessary and/or appropriate.

3.20 Chapter 5 includes some further key points on which LSCBs should ensure that they have policies and procedures in place.

3.21 Clear thresholds and processes, and a common understanding of them across local partners, may help to reduce the number of inappropriate referrals and to improve the effectiveness of joint work, leading to a more efficient use of resources.

(ii) Training of people who work with children or in services affecting the safety and welfare of children

3.22 It is the responsibility of the LSCB to ensure that single-agency and inter-agency training on safeguarding and promoting welfare is provided in order to meet local needs. This covers both the training provided by single agencies to their own staff, and inter-agency training where staff from more than one agency train together.

3.23 LSCBs may wish to carry out their function by taking a view as to the priorities for inter-agency and single-agency child protection training in the local area, and feeding those priorities into the local workforce strategy. LSCBs will also wish to evaluate the quality of this training, ensuring that relevant training is provided by individual organisations and checking that the training is reaching the relevant staff within organisations.

3.24 In some areas it may be decided that the LSCB should also organise or deliver inter-agency training. As explained in Chapter 4, this is not part of the core requirement for LSCBs.

(iii) Recruitment and supervision of people who work with children

3.25 For example, by establishing effective policies and procedures, based on national guidance, for checking the suitability of people applying for work with children, and ensuring that the children's workforce is properly supervised, with any concerns acted on appropriately.

(iv) Investigation of allegations concerning people working with children

3.26 For example, policies and procedures, based on national guidance (see paragraphs 6.20 to 6.30 and Appendix 5), to ensure that allegations are dealt with properly and quickly.

(v) Safety and welfare of children who are privately fostered

3.27 For example, ensuring the co-ordination and effective implementation of measures designed to strengthen private fostering notification arrangements. These measures were amendments to the Children Act 1989 made by s44 of the Children Act 2004, the Children (Private Arrangements for Fostering) Regulations 2005, and National Minimum Standards (NMS) for private fostering, which came into effect in July 2005. LSCBs may also want to consider how they raise awareness in the community of the requirements and issues around private fostering.

(vi) Co-operation with neighbouring children's services authorities (i.e. LAs) and their Board partners

3.28 For example, by establishing procedures to safeguard and promote the welfare of children who move between LA areas, in line with the requirements in Chapter 5. This might include harmonising procedures, where appropriate, to bring coherence to liaison with an organisation (such as a police force) that spans more than one LSCB area. This could be relevant to geographically mobile families such as asylum seekers, travellers, migrant families and families in temporary accommodation.

Other policies and procedures

3.29 LSCBs should consider the need for other local protocols under this function, beyond those specifically set out in Regulations, including:

- quick and straightforward means of resolving professional differences of view in a specific case – e.g. on whether a child protection conference should be convened
- attendance at child protection conferences, including quora
- attendance at family group conferences
- involving children and family members in child protection conferences, the role of advocates, and criteria for excluding parents in exceptional circumstances
- a decision-making process for the need for a child protection plan, based on the views of the agencies present at the child protection conference
- handling complaints from families about the functioning of child protection conferences.

Communicating and raising awareness

b) Communicating to people and bodies in the area of the authority the need to safeguard and promote the welfare of children, raising their awareness of how this can best be done, and encouraging them to do so

3.30 For example, by contributing to a public campaign to raise awareness in the wider community – including faith and minority communities – and among statutory and independent agencies – including employers – about how everybody can contribute to safeguarding and promoting the welfare of children. This also involves listening to and consulting children and young people, and ensuring that their views and opinions are taken into account in planning and delivering safeguarding and promoting welfare services.

Monitoring and evaluation

c) Monitoring and evaluating the effectiveness of what is done by the LA and Board partners, individually and collectively, to safeguard and promote the welfare of children and advise them on ways to improve

3.31 The LSCB has a key role in achieving high standards in safeguarding and promoting welfare, not just through co-ordinating, but also by evaluation and continuous improvement.

3.32 For example, by asking individual organisations to self-evaluate under an agreed framework of benchmarks or indicators, and then sharing results with the Board. It might also involve leading multi-agency arrangements to contribute to self-evaluation reports.

3.33 To evaluate multi-agency working, the LSCB could perform joint audits of case files, looking at the involvement of the different agencies and identifying the quality of practice and lessons to be learned, in terms of both multi-agency and multi-disciplinary practice.

3.34 The LSCB should have a particular focus on ensuring that those key people and organisations that have a duty under s11 of the Children Act 2004, or s175 or s157 of the Education Act 2002, are fulfilling their statutory obligations about safeguarding and promoting the welfare of children.

3.35 The function also includes advising the LA and Board partners on ways to improve. The LSCB might do this by making recommendations (such as the need for further resources), by helping organisations to develop new procedures, by spreading best practice, by bringing together expertise in different bodies, or by supporting capacity building and training. Where there are concerns about the work of partners and these cannot be addressed locally, the LSCB should raise these concerns with others, as explained further in paragraph 3.86.

Function of participating in planning and commissioning

d) Participating in the local planning and commissioning of children's services to ensure that they take safeguarding and promoting the welfare of children into account

3.36 For example, by contributing to the Children and Young People's Plan and ensuring, in discussion with the children's trust partnership, that all planning and commissioning of services for children within the LA area takes account of the need to safeguard and promote children's welfare.

3.37 Where it is agreed locally that the LSCB is the 'Responsible Authority' for 'matters relating to the protection of children from harm' under the Licensing Act 2003, it must be notified of all licence variations and new applications for the sale and supply of alcohol and public entertainment.

Functions relating to child deaths

3.38 From 1 April 2008, each LSCB will have the functions set out in Regulations relating to child deaths. They become compulsory on LSCBs by that date, but can be carried out by any LSCB from 1 April 2006.

e) Collecting and analysing information about the deaths of all children in their area with a view to identifying:

i) any matters of concern affecting the safety and welfare of children in the area of the authority, including any case giving rise to the need for a serious case review

ii) any general public health or safety concerns arising from deaths of children.

f) Putting in place procedures for ensuring that there is a co-ordinated response by the authority, their Board partners and other relevant people to an unexpected death of a child.

3.39 Chapter 7 explains how these functions should be implemented.

Serious case review function

g) Undertaking reviews of cases where abuse or neglect of a child is known or suspected, a child has died or been seriously harmed, and there is cause for concern as to the way in which the authority, their Board partners or other relevant people have worked together to safeguard the child

3.40 By developing procedures and the detail of organisations' and individuals' roles, in accordance with Chapter 8, and ensuring that organisations undertake those roles. All relevant staff should be aware of the circumstances when Serious Case Reviews are required or should be considered.

3.41 By defining terms of reference, commissioning organisational and management reviews and an independent person to compile the overview report; receiving and endorsing the report, agreeing recommendations and an action plan; ensuring the action plan is carried out and that learning is disseminated, lessons acted on and local policy and practice improved.

Other activities

3.42 The Regulations make clear that, in addition to the functions set out above, an LSCB may also engage in any other activity that facilitates, or is conducive to, the achievement of its objective.

3.43 These further activities should be discussed and agreed as part of wider children's trust planning.

3.44 For example, the LSCB could agree to take the lead within a children's trust on work to tackle bullying, or could lead an initiative on domestic violence.

3.45 The LSCB is not, in general, an operational body, or one that delivers services to children, young people and their families. Its role is co-ordinating and ensuring the effectiveness of what its member organisations do, and contributing to broader planning, commissioning and delivery. It may, however, take on operational and delivery roles under this part of the Regulations.

LSCB governance and operational arrangements

3.46 County-level and unitary LAs are responsible for establishing an LSCB in their area and ensuring that it is run effectively.

3.47 An LSCB can cover more than one LA area. LAs and their partners will wish to consider whether this is desirable, perhaps to ensure a better fit with the areas covered by other bodies, or because issues are common to different areas.

Independence

3.48 It is important that, while operating in the context of the children's trust and developing a strong working relationship with the wider strategic partnerships within a LA area, LSCBs exercise their unique statutory role effectively. They must be able to form a view of the quality of local activity, to challenge organisations as necessary, and to speak with an independent voice. To ensure that this is possible, LSCBs must have a clear and distinct identity within local children's trust governance arrangements. They should not be an operational sub-committee of the children's trust board.

Chair

3.49 It is the responsibility of the LA, after consultation with the Board partners, to appoint the Chair. The Chair may be a LA employee, such as the Director of Children's Services (DCS) or the LA Chief Executive, a senior employee of one of the Board partners, or another person contracted with, or employed specifically, to fulfil this role. Where the Chair is not a senior person from the LA, such as the DCS or Chief Executive, they are accountable to the LA, via the DCS, for the effectiveness of their work as LSCB Chair. The Chair should not be an Elected Member – for more detail on the role of Elected Members, see paragraphs 3.56–3.57.

3.50 The Chair has a crucial role in making certain that the Board operates effectively and secures an independent voice for the LSCB. He or she should be of sufficient standing and expertise to command the respect and support of all partners. The Chair should act objectively and distinguish their role as LSCB Chair from any day-to-day role – e.g. as an employee of the LA.

Relationship between the LSCB and the children's trust

3.51 The LSCB and its activities are part of the wider context of children's trust arrangements. The work of LSCBs contributes to the wider goals of improving the wellbeing of all children. Within the wider governance arrangements, its role is to ensure the effectiveness of the arrangements made by individual agencies and the wider partnership to safeguard and promote the welfare of children.

3.52 The LSCB should not be subordinate to, or subsumed within, the children's trust arrangements in a way that might compromise its separate identity and independent voice. The LSCB should expect to be consulted by the partnership on issues that affect how children are safeguarded and how their welfare is promoted. The LSCB is a formal consultee during the development of the Children and Young People's Plan.

3.53 The LSCB and the wider children's trust arrangements need to establish and maintain an ongoing and direct relationship, communicating regularly. They need to ensure that action taken by one body does not duplicate that taken by another, and should work together to ensure that there are no unhelpful strategic or operational gaps in policies, protocols, services or practice.

Membership

The nature of members

3.54 As far as possible, organisations should designate particular, named people as their LSCB member, so that there is consistency and continuity in the membership of the LSCB.

3.55 Members need to be people with a strategic role in relation to safeguarding and promoting the welfare of children within their organisation. They should be able to:

- speak for their organisation with authority
- commit their organisation on policy and practice matters
- hold their organisation to account.

Role of Elected Members

3.56 LA Elected Members and non-executive directors of other Board partners should not be members of an LSCB. Their role, through their membership of governance bodies such as the cabinet of the LA or a scrutiny committee or a governance board, is to hold their organisation and its officers to account for their contribution to the effective functioning of the LSCB.

3.57 The Lead Member for children's services within the LA focuses in particular on how the LA is fulfilling its responsibilities to safeguard and promote the welfare of children, and will hold the DCS to account for the work of the LSCB.

Statutory members

3.58 The LSCB should include representatives of the LA and its Board partners, the statutory organisations that are required to co-operate with the LA in the establishment and operation of the Board and have shared responsibility for the effective discharge of its functions. These are the Board partners set out in s13(3) of the Children Act (2004):

- district councils in local government areas that have them
- the chief police officer for a police area of which any part falls within the area of the LA
- the local probation board for an area of which any part falls within the area of the LA
- the Youth Offending Team for an area of which any part falls within the area of the LA
- Strategic Health Authorities and Primary Care Trusts for an area of which any part falls within the area of the LA
- NHS Trusts and NHS Foundation Trusts, all or most of whose hospitals or establishments and facilities are situated in the LA area
- the Connexions service operating in any part of the area of the LA
- CAFCASS (Children and Family Courts Advisory and Support Service)

- the Governor or Director of any Secure Training Centre in the area of the LA
- the Governor or Director of any prison in the LA area that ordinarily detains children.

3.59 The LA should ensure that those responsible for adult social services functions are represented on the LSCB, because of the importance of adult social care in safeguarding and promoting the welfare of children. Similarly, health organisations should ensure that adult health services – in particular, mental health and disability services – are represented on the LSCB.

3.60 It is also important to ensure that the LSCB has access to appropriate expertise and advice from all the relevant sectors, including a designated doctor and nurse.

3.61 The Children Act 2004 says that the LA and its partners must co-operate in the establishment and operation of an LSCB. This places an obligation on LAs and statutory LSCB partners to support the operation of the LSCB.

Other members

3.62 The LA should also secure the involvement of other relevant local organisations and of the NSPCC where a representative is made available. The knowledge and experience of the NSPCC is an important national resource on which LSCBs should draw. At a minimum, local organisations represented should include faith groups, state and independent schools, further education colleges (including sixth-form colleges), children's centres, GPs, independent healthcare organisations, and voluntary and community sector organisations, including bodies providing specialist care to children with severe disabilities and complex health needs. In areas where they have significant local activity, the armed forces (in relation both to the families of service men and women and those personnel who are under the age of 18), the Immigration Service, and National Asylum Support Service should also be included. Where the number or size of similar organisations precludes individual representation on the LSCB – e.g. in the case of schools or voluntary youth bodies – the LA should seek to involve them via existing networks or forums, or by encouraging and developing suitable networks or forums to facilitate communication between organisations and with the LSCB.

Involvement of other agencies and groups

3.63 The LSCB should make appropriate arrangements at a strategic management level to involve others in its work as needed. For example, there may be some organisations or individuals that are, in theory, represented by the statutory Board partners, but that need to be engaged because of their particular role in service provision to children and families, or their role in public protection. The LSCB needs to link to other organisations, either through inviting them to join the LSCB or through some other mechanism. These include:

- the coronial service
- dental health services

- Domestic Violence Forums
- drug and alcohol misuse services
- Drug Action Teams
- housing, culture and leisure services
- housing providers
- LA legal services
- local MAPPA
- local sports bodies and services
- local Family Justice Council
- local Criminal Justice Board
- other health providers, such as pharmacists
- representatives of service users
- sexual health services
- the Crown Prosecution Service
- witness support services.

3.64 LSCBs also need to draw on the work of key national organisations and liaise with them when necessary – e.g. the new Child Exploitation and On-Line Protection Centre.

The role of members

3.65 The individual members of LSCBs have a duty as members to contribute to the effective work of the LSCB – e.g. in making the LSCB's assessment of performance as objective as possible, and in recommending or deciding on the necessary steps to resolve any problems. This should take precedence, if necessary, over their role as a representative of their organisation. Members of each LSCB should have a clear written statement of their roles and responsibilities.

Ways of working

3.66 The working practices of LSCB members need to be considered locally, with a view to securing effective operation of LSCB functions and ensuring that all member organisations are effectively engaged.

3.67 Where there are multiple organisations of a particular kind in the LA area – e.g. NHS Trusts or district councils – they may decide to share attendance at meetings. Organisations pooling representation in this way need to agree how they will be consulted and how their views will be fed into Board discussions.

3.68 It may be appropriate for the LSCB to set up working groups or sub-groups, on a short-term or a standing basis, to:

- carry out specific tasks – e.g. maintaining and updating procedures and protocols, reviewing serious cases and identifying inter-agency training needs
- provide specialist advice – e.g. in respect of working with specific ethnic and cultural groups, or with disabled children and/or parents
- bring together representatives of a sector to discuss relevant issues and to provide a contribution from that sector to LSCB work – e.g. schools, the voluntary and community sector, faith groups
- focus on defined geographical areas within the LSCB's boundaries.

3.69 It is possible to form a 'core group' or 'executive group' of LSCB members to carry out some of the day-to-day business by local agreement.

3.70 When LSCBs begin to operate the new child death review processes set out in Chapter 7, they will need to set up a Child Death Overview Panel that has a standing membership and whose chair is a member of the LSCB. This panel can be set up by two or more LSCBs to cover their combined area.

3.71 All groups working under the LSCB should be established by the LSCB, and should work to agreed terms of reference, with explicit lines of reporting, communication and accountability to the LSCB. This may take the form of a written constitution, detailing a job description for all members and service level agreements between the LSCB, agencies and other partnerships. Chairs of sub-groups should be LSCB members.

3.72 Where boundaries between LSCBs and their partner organisations – such as the health service and the police – are not co-terminous, there can be problems for some member organisations in having to work to different procedures and protocols according to the area involved, or having to participate in several LSCBs. It may be helpful, in these circumstances, for adjoining LSCBs to collaborate, as far as possible, in establishing common policies and procedures, and joint ways of working, under the function of 'Co-operation with neighbouring children's services authorities and their Board partners'.

3.73 LSCBs should consider how to put in place arrangements to ascertain the views of parents and carers and the wishes and feelings of children (including children who might not ordinarily be heard) about the priorities and effectiveness of local safeguarding work, including issues of access to services and contact points for children to safeguard and promote welfare. LSCBs should also consider how children, parents and carers can be given a measure of choice and control in the development of services.

Financing and staffing

3.74 To function effectively, LSCBs need to be supported by their member organisations with adequate and reliable resources.

3.75 Section 15 of the Children Act 2004 sets out that statutory Board partners (or, in the case of prisons, either the Secretary of State or the contractor) may:

- make payments towards expenditure incurred by, or for purposes connected with, an LSCB, either directly or by contributing to a fund out of which payments may be made
- provide staff, goods, services, accommodation or other resources for purposes connected with an LSCB.

3.76 The budget for each LSCB and the contribution made by each member organisation should be agreed locally. The member organisations' shared responsibility for the discharge of the LSCB's functions includes shared responsibility for determining how the necessary resources are to be provided to support it.

3.77 The core contributions should be provided by the responsible LA, the Primary Care Trusts and the police. Other organisations' contributions will vary to reflect their resources and local circumstances. For some, taking part in LSCB work may be the appropriate extent of their contribution. Other organisations may wish to contribute by committing resources in kind, rather than funds, as provided for in the legislation.

3.78 Where an LSCB member organisation provides funding, this should be committed in advance, usually into a pooled budget.

3.79 The Board may choose to use some of its funding to support the participation of some organisations, such as local voluntary or community sector groups, if they cannot otherwise afford to take part.

3.80 The funding requirement of the LSCB will depend on its circumstances and on the work it plans to undertake (which will, in turn, depend on the division of responsibilities between the LSCB and other parts of the wider children's trust). However, each LSCB will have a core minimum of work.

3.81 The LSCB's resources need to enable it to have staff to take forward its business, whether those staff are paid for from a common fund or seconded as part of a contribution in kind. The particular staffing of each LSCB should be agreed locally by the Board partners. An effective LSCB needs to be staffed so that it has the capacity to:

- drive forward the LSCB's day-to-day business in achieving its objectives, including its co-ordination and monitoring/evaluating work
- take forward any training and staff development work carried out by the LSCB, in the context of the local workforce strategy
- provide administrative and organisational support for the Board and its sub-committees, and those involved in policy and training.

Planning

3.82 On the basis of a new statutory duty, and building on best local planning practice, the Government intends that all local areas should produce a single, strategic, overarching plan for all services affecting children and young people. The Children and Young People's Plan (CYPP) and the process of joint planning should support LAs and their partners as they work together, with the LA taking the lead, to agree clear targets and priorities for all services to children and young people. It will also identify the actions and activities needed to achieve the targets and priorities and ensure delivery. Guidance on the CYPP was published in July 2005.

3.83 On the basis of the CYPP, children's trusts will develop joint commissioning arrangements. These will be based on assessment of local needs, agreeing priorities, planning provision and identifying the resources available across the partner agencies and the contribution each will make. LSCBs should contribute to, and work within, the framework established by the CYPP.

3.84 LSCBs' work needs to be properly planned. The LSCB's own activities would ordinarily be part of the overall CYPP. If not, LSCB planning should nevertheless fit clearly within the framework of priorities and action set out in the CYPP or, if there is no CYPP, within the authority's strategic planning framework. The LSCB should have a clear work programme, including measurable objectives, and a budget. It should include, in any plan or annual report, relevant management information on activity in the course of the previous year; and a review of its work in the previous year – e.g. progress against objectives. This will enable the LSCB's work to be scrutinised by the LA (perhaps by the overview and scrutiny committees), by other local partners and by other key stakeholders as well as by the inspectorates. LAs and their partners may wish to take a joint overview of LSCB work as part of the children's trust governance arrangements. It is recommended that any LSCB plan or report is endorsed by all the Board members and made publicly available.

Monitoring and inspection

3.85 The LSCB's work to ensure the effectiveness of work to safeguard and promote the welfare of children by member organisations will be a peer review process, based on self-evaluation, performance indicators and joint audit. Its aim is to promote high standards of safeguarding work and to foster a culture of continuous improvement. It will also identify and act on identified weaknesses in services. To avoid unnecessary duplication of work, the LSCB should ensure that its monitoring role complements and contributes to the work of both the children's trust and the inspectorates.

3.86 Where it is found that a Board partner is not performing effectively in safeguarding and promoting the welfare of children, and the LSCB is not convinced that any planned action to improve performance will be adequate, the LSCB Chair, or a member or employee designated by the Chair, should explain these concerns to those individuals and organisations that need to be aware of the failing and may be able to take action. For example, concerns could be explained to the most senior individual(s) in the partner organisation, to the relevant inspectorate and, if necessary, to the relevant Government department.

3.87 The local inspection framework will play an important role in reinforcing the ongoing monitoring work of the LSCB. A Joint Area Review of children's services (JAR) will take place in each LA area between 2005 and December 2008. JARs assess how children's services, taken together, contribute to improving outcomes for children and young people.

3.88 Individual services will be assessed through their own quality regimes. Annual performance assessment (APA) of council children's services, by Ofsted and the Commission for Social Care Inspection (CSCI), looks at the contribution of LAs to outcomes for children, with an overall judgement supported by separate judgements on social care services for children and on education services. It draws on performance information, inspection evidence, other documents and self-assessment. These inspectorates in their other work, plus other inspectorates such as the Healthcare Commission, and Her Majesty's Inspectorates of Constabulary, Prisons and Probation, will have as part of their remit considering the effectiveness of their agencies' role in safeguarding and promoting the welfare of children. The LSCB should draw on their work.

3.89 The LSCB will be able to feed its views about the quality of work to safeguard and promote the welfare of children into these processes.

3.90 The effectiveness of the LSCB itself should also form part of the judgement of the inspectorates, particularly through the JAR. This may be done, for example, by examining the quality of the LSCB's planning, and determining whether key objectives have been met. The LA will lead in taking action if intervention in the LSCB's own processes is necessary.

Chapter 4 – Training and development for inter-agency work

Introduction and definitions

4.1 This chapter provides guidance on the training and development of staff and volunteers to help them safeguard and promote the welfare of children effectively. This includes being able to recognise when a child may require safeguarding, and knowing what to do in response to concerns about the welfare of a child. Practitioners and managers must also be able to work effectively with others, both within their own agency and across organisational boundaries. This is best achieved by a combination of single-agency and inter-agency training.

4.2 We use particular terms to describe different types and aspects of the training. **Training for inter- and multi-agency work** means training that equips people to work effectively with those from other agencies to safeguard and promote the welfare of children. This work typically takes place in two ways:

- **single-agency training**, which is training carried out by a particular agency for its own staff; and
- **inter-agency training**, which is for employees of different agencies who either work together formally or come together for training or development. Training delivered on an inter-agency basis is a highly effective way of promoting a common and shared understanding of the respective roles and responsibilities of different professionals, and contributes to effective working relationships.

Purpose

4.3 The purpose of training for inter-agency work is to help develop and foster the following, in order to achieve better outcomes for children and young people:

- a shared understanding of the tasks, processes, principles, and roles and responsibilities outlined in national guidance and local arrangements for safeguarding children and promoting their welfare
- more effective and integrated services at both the strategic and individual case level

- improved communication between professionals, including a common understanding of key terms, definitions and thresholds for action
- effective working relationships, including an ability to work in multi-disciplinary groups or teams; and
- sound decision-making, based on information sharing, thorough assessment, critical analysis and professional judgement.

Roles and responsibilities

Role of employers

4.4 Individual agencies are responsible for ensuring that their staff are competent and confident in carrying out their responsibilities for safeguarding and promoting children's welfare.

4.5 Employers should ensure that their employees are aware of how to recognise and respond to safeguarding concerns, including signs of possible maltreatment. This knowledge and expertise should be put in place before employees attend inter-agency training.

4.6 Employers also have a responsibility to identify adequate resources and support for inter-agency training by:

- providing staff who have the relevant expertise to support the LSCB (e.g. by sitting on an LSCB training sub-group, and/or contributing to training)
- allocating the time required to complete inter-agency training tasks effectively
- releasing staff to attend the appropriate inter-agency training courses
- ensuring that staff receive relevant single-agency training that enables them to maximise the learning derived from inter-agency training, and have opportunities to consolidate learning from inter-agency training; and
- contributing to the planning, resourcing, delivery and evaluation of training.

Role of the children's trust

4.7 Local authorities (LAs), with their partners in children's trusts, are responsible for ensuring that workforce strategies are developed in their local area. This includes making sure that training opportunities to meet needs identified by the LSCBs are available. They should establish systems for the delivery of single-agency and inter-agency training on safeguarding and promoting the welfare of children. They should consider, in discussion with the LSCB, which bodies should commission or deliver the training.

Role of the LSCB

4.8 The LSCB is responsible for developing policies for safeguarding and promoting the welfare of children, in the area of the LA, in relation to the training of people who work with children or in services affecting the safety and welfare of children (see paragraphs 3.22–3.24). This includes training in relation to the child death review processes and serious case reviews.

4.9 LSCBs should contribute to, and work within, the framework of the workforce strategy. They should manage the identification of training needs, and use this information to inform the planning and commissioning of training. LSCBs should check and evaluate single- and inter-agency training to ensure it is meeting local needs – e.g. that staff within organisations are receiving relevant training. In some areas it may be agreed that the LSCBs will deliver the training themselves.

4.10 LSCBs should ensure that they are appropriately staffed and have sufficient capacity to take forward any training and development work they carry out. This includes having the necessary administrative support, and having adequate resources both to contribute to the planning of training and development and to evaluate it. Clearly, appropriate resources are required if LSCBs have responsibility for commissioning or delivering training themselves.

4.11 Effective training on safeguarding and promoting the welfare of children is most likely to be achieved if there is a member of the Board with lead responsibility for training, a training sub-group for which this Board member is responsible, and suitably skilled staff to take forward the training and development work of the LSCB.

4.12 To be effective, a training sub-group should include people with sufficient knowledge of training needs and processes to enable them to make informed contributions to the development and evaluation of a training strategy.

4.13 Many areas maintain an inter-agency training panel of suitably skilled and experienced practitioners and managers from LSCB member agencies, who work together to design, deliver and evaluate inter-agency training. The effectiveness of this approach relies on having a skilled person to co-ordinate and develop the panel, and on the allocation of time to enable panel members to undertake this work.

Ensuring effective training

4.14 This section provides further guidance on training for inter-agency work to help local agencies to ensure that this is effective.

Content and audiences

Content for all audiences

4.15 All training in safeguarding and promoting the welfare of children should create an ethos that values working collaboratively with others, respects diversity (including culture, race and disability), promotes equality, is child-centred and promotes the participation of children and families in safeguarding processes.

4.16 *The Common Core of Skills and Knowledge for the Children's Workforce*[21] sets out six areas of expertise that everyone working with children, young people and families – including those who work as volunteers – should be able to demonstrate. These are:

- effective communication and engagement with children, young people and their families and carers
- child and young person development
- safeguarding and promoting the welfare of the child
- supporting transitions
- multi-agency working
- sharing information.

4.17 Inter- and multi-agency work is an essential feature of all training in safeguarding and promoting the welfare of children. Single-agency training, and training provided in professional settings, should always equip staff for inter-agency work. All training in this field should be consistent with *The Common Core of Skills and Knowledge.*

Target audiences

4.18 It is important to ensure that the training involves and is available to all relevant partners. Some agencies involved in safeguarding and promoting the welfare of children may not be part of a local children's trust. LSCBs should ensure that the needs of those partners are included when setting up training arrangements.

4.19 Training and development for inter- and multi-agency work should be targeted at the following practitioner groups from voluntary, statutory and independent agencies:

- those in **regular contact** with children and young people and with adults who are parents or carers. These people are in a position to identify concerns about maltreatment, including those that may arise from use of the Common Assessment Framework (CAF). These people may, as a minimum, need introductory training on how to work together to safeguard and promote the welfare of children. They include housing and hospital staff, youth workers, childminders, private foster carers, those working with children in residential and day care settings and those working in sport and leisure settings in both a paid and unpaid capacity. Given the large numbers and work patterns of those involved, creative methods should be used to provide them with the essential training. For example, open learning materials may be helpful, or the inclusion of designated people from sport, community or faith groups within the

21 *The Common Core of Skills and Knowledge for the Children's Workforce* can be accessed at www.everychildmatters.gov.uk

training, who are able to support others using open learning materials or to facilitate training within their own organisation

- those who **work regularly** with children and young people, and with adults who are carers, and who may be asked to contribute to assessments of children in need. They include GPs, hospital and community health staff, family and children's centre workers, teachers, education welfare officers, social workers, mental health and learning disability staff and probation officers. This group should have a higher minimum level of expertise: a fuller understanding of how to work together to identify and assess concerns and to plan, undertake and review interventions
- those with a **particular responsibility** for safeguarding children, such as designated or named health and education professionals, police, social workers, and other professionals undertaking s47 enquiries or working with complex cases, including fabricated and induced illness. Those in this group need to have a thorough understanding of working together to safeguard and promote the welfare of children, including in complex and/or serious cases.

You can find a table with further detail on training for the different audiences at: www.everychildmatters.gov.uk/workingtogether.

4.20 Training and development are also relevant to the managers of these practitioners, and it should be relevant to their management role:

- **operational managers** at all levels – within organisations employing staff to work with children and families, or with responsibility for commissioning or delivering services – benefit from specific training on inter- and multi-agency practice to safeguard and promote the welfare of children. Practice supervisors, professional advisers/designated child protection specialists and service managers need not only a foundation level of training, but may also need training on joint planning and commissioning; managing joint services and teams; chairing multi-disciplinary meetings; negotiating joint protocols and mediating where there is conflict and difference. Specific training on the conduct of serious case reviews will be relevant to some
- those who have a **strategic and managerial responsibility** for commissioning and delivering services for children and families may also benefit from training/development. They include those in each of the agencies listed in s11 of the Children Act 2004, any other members of LSCBs, school governors and trustees. In order to be effective, LSCBs and other local bodies such as Children and Young People Strategic Partnerships should consider their own collective development needs as a group. There are significant benefits to be derived from periodically undertaking facilitated development work in order to improve effectiveness. Provision should also be made for the induction and development of members, as necessary, so that they have the required understanding, up-to-date knowledge and skills to fulfil their roles.

4.21 Training should be available at a number of levels to address the learning needs of these staff. The published table mentioned in paragraph 4.19 provides suggested learning outcomes for these target groups. Decisions should be made locally about how the levels are most appropriately delivered, as part of the planning of training.

4.22 The detailed content of training at each level of the framework should be specified locally. The content should reflect the principles, values and processes set out in this guidance on work with children and families. Steps should be taken to ensure the relevance of the content to different groups from the statutory, voluntary and independent sectors. The content of training programmes should be regularly reviewed and updated in the light of research and practice experience.

Success factors

4.23 All training to support inter- and multi-agency work should:

- be delivered by trainers who are knowledgeable about safeguarding and promoting the welfare of children and have facilitation skills. When delivering training on complex cases, trainers should have the relevant specialist knowledge and skills
- be informed by current research evidence, lessons from serious case and child death reviews, and local and national developments
- reflect an understanding of the rights of the child, and be informed by an active respect for diversity and the experience of service users, and a commitment to ensuring equality of opportunity; and
- be regularly reviewed to ensure that it meets the agreed learning outcomes.

4.24 Training on safeguarding and promoting the welfare of children can only be fully effective if it is embedded within a wider framework of commitment to inter- and multi-agency working, underpinned by shared goals, planning processes and values. It is most likely to be effective if it is delivered within a framework that includes:

- a clear mandate from senior managers (e.g. through the LSCB) with endorsement and commitment from member agencies
- adequate resources and capacity to deliver or commission training
- standards of practice[22]
- policies, procedures and practice guidelines to inform and support these standards
- opportunities to consolidate learning made available within agencies

22 *Standards for Inter-Agency Working, Education and Training* have been developed by Salford University. See www.chscc.salford.ac.uk/scswr/projects/interagency working shtml.

- the identification and periodic review of local training needs using standards for practice, followed by decisions about priorities
- a training strategy that makes clear the difference between single-agency and inter-agency training responsibilities, and which partnerships or bodies are responsible for commissioning and delivering training
- structures and processes for organising and co-ordinating delivery
- systems for the delivery of inter-agency training; and
- quality assurance processes (e.g. as part of evaluation processes put in place by the LSCB).

4.25 The systems should foster collaboration across agencies and disciplines in relation to planning, design, delivery and administration of the training. They should be efficient, as well as being designed to promote co-operation and shared ownership of the training. Training may be delivered more effectively if there is collaboration across local areas, especially where police or health boundaries embrace more than one LA area.

4.26 The government has commissioned a number of training resources that are suitable for inter-agency training. These include materials to support the implementation of the next chapter, 'Managing individual cases'. *Safeguarding Children – a shared responsibility* (2006) is a multi-media training resource (found at: www.everychildmatters.gov.uk/workingtogether) to support learners to:

- have a clear understanding of what to do when they have concerns about a child's welfare
- know how to work as part of a multi-agency or multi-disciplinary team when following the processes set out in this guidance
- be clear about their roles and responsibilities during assessment, planning, intervention and reviewing processes for children in need, including those requiring safeguarding; and
- understand the statutory requirements governing consent, confidentiality and information sharing, and how to apply these in relation to a particular child about whom they have concerns.

Quality assurance and evaluation

4.27 The LSCB, or the training sub-group acting on its behalf, has a responsibility to ensure that both single- and inter-agency training is delivered to a consistently high standard, and that a process exists for evaluating the effectiveness of training. This should include ensuring that training meets the standards set out in this chapter. The LSCB should ensure that outcomes from the evaluation of training inform the planning of training.

Chapter 5 – Managing individual cases

Introduction

5.1 This section provides advice on what should happen if somebody has concerns about the welfare of a child (including children living away from home) and, in particular, has concerns that a child may be suffering, or may be at risk of suffering, significant harm. It incorporates the guidance on information-sharing, and sets out the principles that underpin work to safeguard and promote the welfare of children. This section is not intended as a detailed practice guide, but it sets out clear expectations about the ways in which agencies and professionals should work together to safeguard and promote the welfare of children.

Working with children about whom there are child welfare concerns

5.2 Achieving good outcomes for children requires all those with responsibility for assessment and the provision of services to work together according to an agreed plan of action. Effective collaboration requires organisations and people to be clear about:

- their roles and responsibilities for safeguarding and promoting the welfare of children (see s11 of the Children Act 2004 Guidance (2005) and Chapter 2, 'Roles and responsibilities')
- the purpose of their activity, the decisions that are required at each stage of the process and the planned outcomes for the child and family members
- the legislative basis for the work
- the protocols and procedures to be followed, including the way in which information will be shared across professional boundaries and within agencies and be recorded
- which organisation, team or professional has lead responsibility, and the precise roles of everyone else who is involved, including the way in which children and family members will be involved; and
- any timescales set down in regulations or guidance that govern the completion of assessments, making of plans and timing of reviews.

Principles underpinning work to safeguard and promote the welfare of children

5.3 The following principles, which draw on findings from research, underpin work with children and their families to safeguard and promote the welfare of children (see also paragraph 2.18 in the Guidance issued under s11 of the Children Act 2004). These principles should be followed when implementing the guidance set out in this chapter. They will be relevant to varying degrees, depending on the functions and level of involvement of the organisation and the individual practitioner concerned.

5.4 Work to safeguard and promote the welfare of children should be:

- **Child-centred**
  Some of the worst failures of the system have occurred when professionals have lost sight of the child and concentrated instead on their relationship with the adults. The child should be seen by the practitioner and kept in focus throughout work with the child and family. The child's voice should be heard and account taken of their wishes and feelings.
- **Rooted in child development**
  Those working with children should be informed by a developmental perspective that recognises that, as children grow, they continue to develop their skills and abilities. Each stage, from infancy through middle years to adolescence, lays the foundation for more complex development. Plans and interventions to safeguard and promote the child's welfare should be based on a clear assessment of the child's developmental progress and the difficulties a child may be experiencing. Planned action should also be timely and appropriate for the child's age and stage of development.
- **Focused on outcomes for children**
  When working directly with a child, any plan developed for the child and their family or caregiver should be based on an assessment of the child's developmental needs and the parents'/caregivers' capacity to respond to these needs within their community contexts. This plan should set out the planned outcomes for each child and, at review, the actual outcomes should be recorded. The purpose of all interventions should be to achieve the best possible outcomes for each child, recognising that each child is unique. These outcomes should contribute to the key outcomes set out for all children in the Children Act 2004 (see paragraph 1.1).
- **Holistic in approach**
  Having a holistic approach means having an understanding of a child within the context of the child's family (parents or caregivers and the wider family) and of the educational setting, community and culture in which he or she is growing up. The interaction between the developmental needs of children, the capacities of parents or caregivers to respond appropriately to those needs, and the impact of wider family and environmental factors on children and on parenting capacity requires careful

exploration during an assessment. The ultimate aim is to understand the child's developmental needs within the context of the family, and to provide appropriate services that respond to those needs. The analysis of the child's situation will inform planning and action in order to secure the best outcomes for the child, and will inform the subsequent review of the effectiveness of actions taken and services provided. The child's context will be even more complex when they are living away from home and looked after by adults who do not have parental responsibility for them.

- **Ensuring equality of opportunity**
  Equality of opportunity means that all children have the opportunity to achieve the best possible development, regardless of their gender, ability, race, ethnicity, circumstances or age. Some vulnerable children may have been particularly disadvantaged in their access to important opportunities, and their health and educational needs will require particular attention in order to optimise their current welfare as well as their long-term outcomes in young adulthood.

- **Involving of children and families**
  In the process of finding out what is happening to a child, it is important to listen and develop an understanding of their wishes and feelings. The importance of developing a co-operative working relationship is emphasised, so that parents or caregivers feel respected and informed, they believe agency staff are being open and honest with them and, in turn, they are confident about providing vital information about their child, themselves and their circumstances. The consent of children, young people and their parents or caregivers should be obtained when sharing information, unless to do so would place the child at risk of significant harm. Decisions should also be made with their agreement, whenever possible, unless to do so would place the child at risk of significant harm.

- **Building on strengths as well as identifying difficulties**
  Identifying both strengths and difficulties within the child, their family and the context in which they are living is important, as is considering how these factors have an impact on the child's health and development. Too often it has been found that a deficit model of working with families predominates in practice, and ignores crucial areas of success and effectiveness within the family on which to base interventions. Working with a child's or family's strengths becomes an important part of a plan to resolve difficulties.

- **Multi- and inter-agency in approach**
  From birth, there will be a variety of different agencies and programmes in the community involved with children and their development, particularly in relation to their health and education. Multi- and inter-agency work to safeguard and promote children's welfare starts as soon as there are concerns about a child's welfare, not just when there are questions about possible harm.

- **A continuing process, not an event**
  Understanding what is happening to a vulnerable child, within the context of his or her family and the local community, and taking appropriate action, are continuing and interactive processes, not single events. Assessment should continue throughout a period of intervention, and intervention may start at the beginning of an assessment.

- **Providing and reviewing services**
  Action and services should be provided according to the identified needs of the child and family, in parallel with assessment where necessary. It is not necessary to await completion of the assessment process. Immediate and practical needs should be addressed alongside more complex and longer-term ones. The impact of service provision on a child's developmental progress should be reviewed.

- **Informed by evidence**
  Effective practice with children and families requires sound professional judgements that are underpinned by a rigorous evidence base and draw on the practitioner's knowledge and experience.

The processes for safeguarding and promoting the welfare of children

5.5 Four key processes underpin work with children and families, each of which has to be carried out effectively in order to achieve improvements in the lives of children in need. They are assessment, planning, intervention and reviewing, as set out in the Integrated Children's System (Department of Health, 2002).

5.6 The flow charts at the end of this chapter illustrate the processes for safeguarding and promoting the welfare of children:

- from the point that concerns are raised about a child and are referred to a statutory organisation that can take action to safeguard and promote the welfare of children (Chart 1)
- through an initial assessment of the child's situation and what happens after that (Chart 2)
- taking urgent action, if necessary (Chart 3)
- to the strategy discussion, where there are concerns about a child's safety, and beyond that to the child protection conference (Chart 4)
- what happens after the child protection conference, and the review process (Chart 5).

Being alert to children's welfare

5.7 Everybody who works or has contact with children, parents and other adults in contact with children should be able to recognise, and know how to act on, evidence that a child's health or development is, or may be, being impaired, and especially when they are suffering, or at risk of suffering, significant harm. Practitioners, foster carers and managers should be mindful always of the welfare and safety of children – including unborn children, older children and children living away from home or looked after by the local authority (LA) – in their work:

With children

5.8 For example, children's centre staff, teachers, school nurses, health visitors, GPs, A&E and all other hospital staff should be able to recognise situations where a child requires extra support to prevent impairment to their health or development or possible indicators of abuse or neglect in children. All professionals working with children, and especially those in health and social care, should be familiar with the core standards set out in the *National Service Framework for Children, Young People and Maternity Services Core Standards* and in particular Standard 5, 'Safeguarding and Promoting the Welfare of Children and Young People'. Those working with children living away from home should also be familiar with the relevant statutory Regulations and National Minimum Standards.[23]

With parents or caregivers who may need help in promoting and safeguarding their children's welfare

5.9 For example, adult mental health or substance misuse services should always consider the implications for children of patients' or users' problems. Day nurseries, children's and family centres should keep the interests of children uppermost when working with parents, work in ways intended to bring about better outcomes for children, and be alert to possible indicators of abuse or neglect. When dealing with cases of domestic violence, the police and other involved agencies should consider the implications of the situation for any children in the family.

With family members, employees or others who have contact with children

5.10 For example, the police and probation services, mental health services and housing authorities should be alert to the possibility that an individual may pose a risk of significant harm to a particular child, or to children in a local community. Employers of staff or volunteers who have substantial unsupervised access to children should guard against the potential for abuse, through rigorous selection processes, appropriate supervision and by taking steps to maintain a safe environment for children. For further details on this matter see Chapter 12.

5.11 In some circumstances, practitioners may have undertaken a common assessment because they had concerns about a child and were trying to ascertain how best to help, or the findings from the common assessment may have caused them to be concerned about a child's welfare. All staff members who have, or become aware of concerns about the welfare or safety of a child or children should know:

23 Find at: www.dh.gov.uk/PublicationsAndStatistics/Publications/PublicationsPolicyAndGuidance/fs/en

- what services are available locally
- how to gain access to them
- what sources of further advice and expertise are available
- who to contact in what circumstances, and how; and
- when and how to make a referral to LA children's social care.

5.12 These concerns should be discussed with a manager, or a named or designated health professional or a designated member of staff, depending on the organisational setting. Concerns can also be discussed – without necessarily identifying the child in question – with senior colleagues in another agency in order to develop an understanding of the child's needs and circumstances. If, after discussion, these concerns remain, and it seems that the child and family would benefit from other services – including those from within another part of the same agency – decisions should be made about to whom to make a referral. If the child is considered to be, or may be, a child in need under the Children Act 1989 (see paragraph 1.22), the child should be referred to LA children's social care. This includes a child who is believed to be, or may be at risk of, suffering significant harm. If these concerns arise about a child who is already known to LA children's social care, the allocated worker should be informed of these concerns.

5.13 Sources of information and advice should include at least one designated senior doctor and nurse within each PCT, and a designated member of staff within each school or further education institution. There should always be the opportunity to discuss child welfare concerns with, and seek advice from, colleagues, managers, a designated or named professional, or other agencies. However:

- never delay emergency action to protect a child from harm
- always record in writing concerns about a child's welfare, including whether or not further action is taken
- always record in writing discussions about a child's welfare. At the close of a discussion, always reach a clear and explicit recorded agreement about who will be taking what action, or that no further action will be taken.

The welfare of unborn children

5.14 The procedures and timescales set out in this chapter should also be followed when there are concerns about the welfare of an unborn child.

Referrals to LA children's social care where there are child welfare concerns

5.15 Councils with LA children's social services functions have particular responsibilities towards all children whose health or development may be impaired without the provision of services, or who are disabled (defined in the Children Act 1989 as children 'in need'). LAs should let children and families know how to contact them and what they might expect by way of help, advice and services. They should agree, with LSCB partners, criteria with local services and professionals as to when it is appropriate to make a referral to LA children's social care in respect of a child in need. They should also agree the format for making a referral and sharing the information recorded. The Common Assessment Framework offers a basis for early referral and information-sharing between organisations.

5.16 If somebody believes that a child may be suffering, or be at risk of suffering, significant harm, then they should always refer their concerns to LA children's social care. In addition to social care, the police and the NSPCC have powers to intervene in these circumstances. Sometimes concerns will arise within LA children's social care itself, as new information comes to light about a child and family with whom staff are already in contact. While professionals should seek, in general, to discuss any concerns with the family and, where possible, seek their agreement to make referrals to LA children's social care, **this should only be done where such discussion and agreement-seeking will not place a child at increased risk of significant harm**.

Responding to child welfare concerns where there is, or may be, an alleged crime

5.17 Whenever LA children's social care has a case referred to it that constitutes, or may constitute, a criminal offence against a child, social workers or their managers should always discuss the case with the police at the earliest opportunity.

5.18 Whenever other agencies, or the LA in its other roles, encounter concerns about a child's welfare that constitute, or may constitute, a criminal offence against a child, they must always consider sharing that information with LA children's social care or the police in order to protect the child or other children from the risk of significant harm. If a decision is taken not to share information, the reasons must be recorded.

5.19 Sharing of information in cases of concern about children's welfare enables professionals to consider jointly how to proceed in the best interests of the child and to safeguard children more generally (see paragraph 5.2).

5.20 In dealing with alleged offences involving a child victim, the police should normally work in partnership with children's social care and/or other agencies. While the responsibility to instigate a criminal investigation rests with the police, they should consider the views expressed by other agencies. There will be less serious cases where, after discussion, it is agreed that the best interests of the child are served by a children's social care led intervention rather than a full police investigation.

5.21 In deciding whether there is a need to share information, professionals need to consider their legal obligations, including whether they have a duty of confidentiality to the child. Where there is such a duty, the professional may lawfully share information if the child consents or if there is a public interest of sufficient force. This must be judged by the professional on the facts of each case. Where there is a clear risk of significant harm to a child, or serious harm to adults, the public interest test will almost certainly be satisfied. However, there will be other cases where practitioners will be justified in sharing some confidential information in order to make decisions on sharing further information or taking action – the information shared should be proportionate.

5.22 The child's best interests must be the overriding consideration in making any such decision, including in the cases of underage sexual activity, on which detailed guidance is given below. The cross-Government guidance, *Information sharing: Practitioners' guide*, provides advice on these issues – see www.everychildmatters.gov.uk. Any decision whether or not to share information must be properly documented. Decisions in this area need to be made by, or with the advice of, people with suitable competence in child protection work, such as named or designated professionals or senior managers.

Allegations of harm arising from underage sexual activity

5.23 Cases of underage sexual activity that present cause for concern are likely to raise difficult issues and should be handled particularly sensitively.[24]

5.24 A child under 13 is not legally capable of consenting to sexual activity. Any offence under the Sexual Offences Act 2003 involving a child under 13 is very serious and should be taken to indicate a risk of significant harm to the child.

5.25 Cases involving under-13s should always be discussed with a nominated child protection lead in the organisation. Under the Sexual Offences Act, penetrative sex with a child under 13 is classed as rape. Where the allegation concerns penetrative sex, or other intimate sexual activity occurs, there would always be reasonable cause to suspect that a child, whether girl or boy, is suffering, or is likely to suffer, significant harm. There should be a presumption that the case will be reported to children's social care and that a strategy discussion will be held in accordance with the guidance set out in paragraph 5.54. This should involve children's social care, police and relevant agencies, to discuss appropriate next steps with the professional. All cases involving under-13s should be fully documented, including giving detailed reasons where a decision is taken not to share information.

5.26 Sexual activity with a child under 16 is also an offence. Where it is consensual it may be less serious than if the child were under 13, but may nevertheless have serious consequences for the welfare of the young person. Consideration should be given in every case of sexual activity involving a child aged 13–15 as to whether there should be a

24 Further guidance is provided by the Department of Health 'Best practice guidance for doctors and other health professionals on the provision of advice and treatment to young people under 16 on contraception, sexual and reproductive health'.

discussion with other agencies and whether a referral should be made to children's social care. The professional should make this assessment using the considerations below. Within this age range, the younger the child, the stronger the presumption must be that sexual activity will be a matter of concern. Cases of concern should be discussed with the nominated child protection lead and subsequently with other agencies if required. Where confidentiality needs to be preserved, a discussion can still take place as long as it does not identify the child (directly or indirectly). Where there is reasonable cause to suspect that significant harm to a child has occurred or might occur, there would be a presumption that the case is reported to children's social care and a strategy discussion should be held to discuss appropriate next steps. Again, all cases should be fully documented and include detailed reasons where a decision is taken not to share information.

5.27 The following considerations should be taken into account when assessing the extent to which a child (or other children) may be suffering or at risk of harm, and therefore the need to hold a strategy discussion in order to share information:

- the age of the child – sexual activity at a young age is a very strong indicator that there are risks to the welfare of the child (whether boy or girl) and, possibly, others
- the level of maturity and understanding of the child
- what is known about the child's living circumstances or background
- age imbalance – in particular where there is a significant age difference
- overt aggression or power imbalance
- coercion or bribery
- familial child sex offences
- behaviour of the child – i.e. withdrawn, anxious
- the misuse of substances as a disinhibitor
- whether the child's own behaviour, because of the misuse of substances, places him or her at risk of harm so that he or she is unable to make an informed choice about any activity
- whether any attempts to secure secrecy have been made by the sexual partner, beyond what would be considered usual in a teenage relationship
- whether the child denies, minimises or accepts concerns
- whether the methods used are consistent with grooming; and
- whether the sexual partner/s is known by one of the agencies.

5.28 In cases of concern, when sufficient information is known about the sexual partner/s, the agency concerned should check with other agencies, including the police, to establish what information is known about that person/s. The police should normally share the required information without beginning a full investigation if the agency making the check requests this.

5.29 Sexual activity involving a 16- or 17-year-old, though unlikely to involve an offence, may still involve harm or the risk of harm. Professionals should still bear in mind the considerations and processes outlined in this guidance in assessing that risk, and should share information as appropriate. It is an offence for a person to have a sexual relationship with a 16- or 17-year-old if that person holds a position of trust or authority in relation to them.

5.30 Implementation of this guidance should be through the development of local protocols, supported by inter-agency training. Examples will be available at: www.everychildmatters.gov.uk/workingtogether.

Response of LA children's social care to a referral

5.31 When a parent, professional, or another person contacts LA children's social care with concerns about a child's welfare, it is the responsibility of LA children's social care to clarify with the referrer (including self-referrals from children and families):

- the nature of concerns
- how and why they have arisen; and
- what appear to be the needs of the child and family.

This process should always identify clearly whether there are concerns about maltreatment, what is their foundation, and whether it may be necessary to consider taking urgent action to ensure the child(ren) are safe from harm.

5.32 Professionals who phone LA children's social care should confirm referrals in writing within 48 hours. The Common Assessment Framework provides a structure for the written referral. At the end of any discussion or dialogue about a child, the referrer (whether a professional or a member of the public or family) and LA children's social care should be clear about proposed action, timescales and who will be taking it, or that no further action will be taken. The decision should be recorded by LA children's social care and by the referrer (if a professional in another service). LA children's social care should acknowledge a written referral within one working day of receiving it. If the referrer has not received an acknowledgement within three working days, they should contact LA children's social care again.

5.33 LA children's social care should decide and record next steps of action within one working day. This information should be consistent with the information set out in the Referral and Information Record (Department of Health, 2002). This decision should normally follow discussion with any referring professional/service and consideration of information held in any existing records, and involve discussion with other professionals and services as necessary (including the police, where a criminal offence may have been committed against a child). This initial consideration of the case should address – on the basis of the available evidence – whether there are concerns about either the child's health and development or actual and/or potential harm that justifies an initial assessment to establish whether this child is possibly a child in need. Further action may also include referral to other agencies, the provision of advice or information, or no further action.

5.34 Parents' permission, or the child's permission where appropriate, should be sought before discussing a referral about them with other agencies, unless permission-seeking may itself place a child at increased risk of significant harm. When responding to referrals from a member of the public rather than another professional, LA children's social care should bear in mind that personal information about referrers, including identifying details, should only be disclosed to third parties (including subject families and other agencies) with the consent of the referrer. In all cases where the police are involved, the decision about when to inform the parents (about referrals from third parties) will have a bearing on the conduct of police investigations.

5.35 Where LA children's social care decides to take no further action at this stage, feedback should be provided to the referrer, who should be told of this decision and the reasons for making it. In the case of public referrals, this should be done in a manner consistent with respecting the confidentiality of the child. Sometimes it may be apparent at this stage that emergency action should be taken to safeguard and promote the welfare of a child (see paragraph 5.49). Such action should normally be preceded by an immediate strategy discussion between the police, LA children's social care and other agencies as appropriate.

5.36 New information may be received about a child or family where the child or family member is already known to LA children's social care. If the child's case is open, and there are concerns that the child is or may be suffering harm, then a decision should be made about whether a strategy discussion should be initiated (see paragraph 5.54). In these circumstances, it may not be necessary to undertake an initial assessment before deciding what to do next. It may, however, be appropriate to undertake a core assessment or to update a previous one, in order to understand the child's current needs and circumstances and inform future decision-making.

Initial assessment

5.37 The initial assessment is a brief assessment of each child referred to LA children's social care, in which it is necessary to determine whether the child is in need, the nature of any services required, and whether a further, more detailed core assessment should be undertaken (paragraph 3.9 of the *Framework for the Assessment of Children in Need and their Families* (2000)). It should be completed by LA children's social care, working with colleagues, within a maximum of seven working days of the date of referral. The initial assessment period may be very brief if the criteria for initiating s47 enquiries are met. The initial assessment should be undertaken in accordance with the *Framework for the Assessment of Children in Need and their Families* (Department of Health et al., 2000) (the 'Assessment Framework' – summarised in Appendix 2). Where a common assessment has been completed, this information should be used to inform the initial assessment. Information should be gathered and analysed within the three domains of the Assessment Framework (see Figure 2), namely:

- the child's developmental needs
- the parents' or caregivers' capacity to respond appropriately to those needs; and
- the wider family and environmental factors.

Figure 2: The Assessment Framework

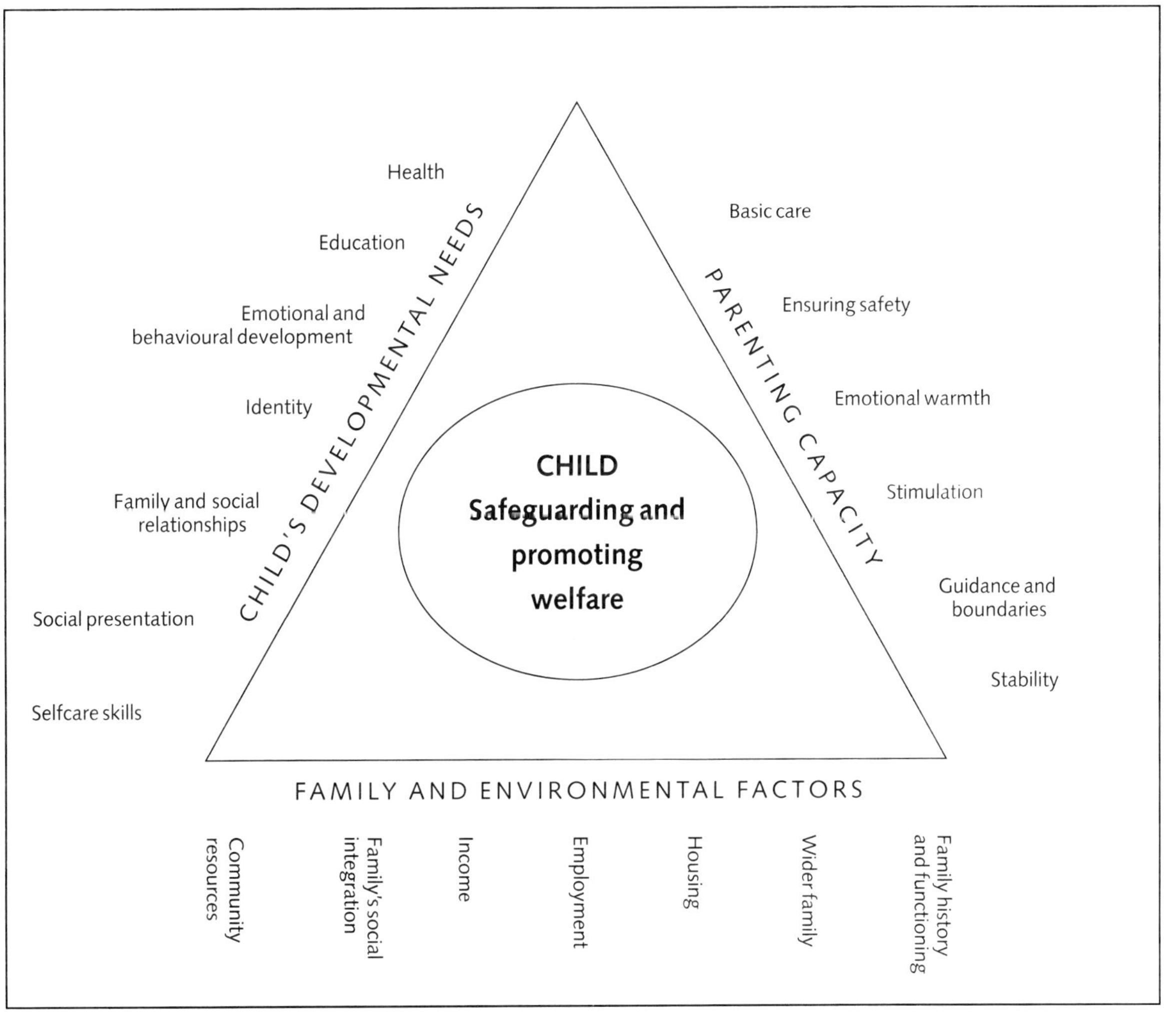

5.38 The initial assessment should address the following questions.

- What are the developmental needs of the child?
- Are the parents able to respond appropriately to the child's identified needs? Is the child being adequately safeguarded from significant harm, and are the parents able to promote the child's health and development?
- What impact are family functioning and history, the wider family and environmental factors having on the parents' capacity to respond to their child's needs and the child's developmental progress?
- Is action required to safeguard and promote the welfare of the child?

5.39 The initial assessment should be led by a qualified and experienced social worker. It should be carefully planned, with clarity about who is doing what, as well as when and what information is to be shared with the parents. The planning process and decisions about the timing of the different assessment activities should be undertaken in collaboration with all those involved with the child and family. The process of initial assessment should involve:

- seeing and speaking to the child (according to age and understanding) and family members as appropriate
- drawing together and analysing available information from a range of sources (including existing records); and
- involving and obtaining relevant information from professionals and others in contact with the child and family.

All relevant information (including historical information) should be taken into account. This includes seeking information from relevant services if the child and family have spent time abroad. Professionals from agencies such as health, LA children's social care or the police should request this information from their equivalent agencies in the country or countries in which the child has lived. Information about who to contact can be obtained via the Foreign and Commonwealth Office on 0207 008 1500 or the appropriate Embassy or Consulate based in London (see the London Diplomatic List (The Stationery Office), ISBN 0 11 591772 1 or the FCO website www.fco.gov.uk).

5.40 The child should be seen within a timescale that is appropriate to the nature of concerns expressed at the time of the referral, according to the agreed plan (which may include seeing the child without his or her caregivers present). This includes observing and communicating with the child in a manner appropriate to his or her age and understanding. LA children's social care is required by the Children Act 1989 (as amended by s53 of the Children Act 2004) to ascertain the child's wishes and feelings about the provision of services and give them due consideration before determining what (if any) services to provide. Interviews with the child should be undertaken in the preferred language of the child. For some disabled children, interviews may require the use of non-verbal communication methods.

5.41 **It will not necessarily be clear whether a criminal offence has been committed**, which means that even initial discussions with the child should be undertaken in a way that minimises distress to them and maximises the likelihood that she or he will provide accurate and complete information, avoiding leading or suggestive questions.

5.42 Interviews with family members (which may include the child) should also be undertaken in their preferred language and, where appropriate for some people, using non-verbal communication methods.

5.43 In the course of an initial assessment, LA children's social care should ascertain:

- is this a child in need? (s17 of the Children Act 1989); and
- is there reasonable cause to suspect that this child is suffering, or is likely to suffer, significant harm? (s47 of the Children Act 1989).

5.44 The focus of the initial assessment should be the welfare of the child. It is important to remember that even if the reason for a referral was a concern about abuse or neglect that is not subsequently substantiated, a family may still benefit from support and practical help to promote a child's health and development. When services are to be provided, a child's plan should be developed, based on the findings from the initial assessment and on any previous plans – e.g. those made following the completion of a common assessment. If the child's needs and circumstances are complex, a more in-depth core assessment under s17 of the Children Act 1989 is required in order to decide what other types of services are necessary to assist the child and family (see the *Framework for the Assessment of Children in Need and their Families*). Appendix 1 sets out the Statutory Framework, including relevant sections of the Children Act 1989. Appendix 3, 'Use of questionnaires and scales to evidence assessment and decision-making', is intended for use by practitioners to support evidence-based assessment and decision-making.

5.45 Following an initial assessment, LA children's social care should decide on the next course of action, following discussion with the child and family, unless such a discussion may place a child at increased risk of significant harm. If there are concerns about a parent's ability to protect a child from harm, careful consideration should be given to what the parents should be told, when and by whom, taking account of the child's welfare. Where it is clear that there should be a police investigation in parallel with a s47 enquiry, the considerations at paragraph 5.64 should apply. Whatever decisions are taken, they should be endorsed at a managerial level, agreed within LA children's social care and recorded in writing. This information should be consistent with that contained in the Initial Assessment Record (Department of Health, 2002). The record should also include the reasons for these decisions and future action to be taken. The family, the original referrer and other professionals and services involved in the assessment should, as far as possible, be told what action has been and will be taken, consistent with respecting the confidentiality of the child and family concerned, and not jeopardising further action in respect of concerns about harm (which may include police investigations). This information should be confirmed in writing to the agencies and the family.

Next steps – child in need but no suspected actual or likely significant harm

5.46 An initial assessment may indicate that a child is a 'child in need', as defined by s17 of the Children Act 1989, but that there are no substantiated concerns that the child may be suffering, or at risk of suffering, significant harm. There may be sufficient information available on which to decide what services (if any) should be provided by whom according to an agreed plan. On the other hand, a more in-depth assessment may be necessary in order to understand the child's needs and circumstances. In these circumstances, the *Framework for the Assessment of Children in Need and their Families* provides guidance on undertaking a core assessment that builds on the findings from the initial assessment and addresses the central or most important aspects of the needs of a child and the capacity of his or her parents or caregivers to respond appropriately to these needs within the wider family and community context. This core assessment can provide a sound evidence base for professional judgements on what types of services are most likely to bring about good outcomes for the child. Family Group Conferences (see paragraphs 10.2–10.4) may be an effective vehicle for taking forward work in such cases.

5.47 The definition of a 'child in need' is wide and embraces children in a diverse range of circumstances. The types of services that may help such children and their families vary greatly according to their needs and circumstances.

The rest of the guidance in this chapter is concerned with the processes that should be followed where a child is suspected to be suffering, or is likely to suffer, significant harm.

Initial assessment and enquiries: ten pitfalls and how to avoid them

1. Not enough weight is given to information from family, friends and neighbours.

Ask yourself: Would I react differently if these reports had come from a different source? How can I check whether or not they have substance? Even if they are not accurate, could they be a sign that the family is in need of some help or support?

2. Not enough attention is paid to what children say, how they look and how they behave.

Ask yourself: Have I been given appropriate access to all the children in the family? If I have not been able to see any child, is there a very good reason, and have I made arrangements to see him/her as soon as possible? How should I follow up any uneasiness about the child(ren)'s health or development? If the child is old enough and has the communication skills, what is the child's account of events? If the child uses a language other than English, or alternative non-verbal communication, have I made every effort to enlist help in understanding him/her? What is the evidence to support or refute the child or young person's account?

3. Attention is focused on the most visible or pressing problems and other warning signs are not appreciated.

Ask yourself: What is the most striking thing about this situation? If this feature were to be removed or changed, would I still have concerns?

4. Pressures from high status referrers or the press, with fears that a child may die, lead to over precipitate action.

Ask yourself: Would I see this referral as a safeguarding matter if it came from another source?

5. Professionals think that when they have explained something as clearly as they can, the other person will have understood it.

Ask yourself: Have I double-checked with the family and the child(ren) that they understand what will happen next?

6. Assumptions and pre-judgements about families lead to observations being ignored or misinterpreted.

Ask yourself: What were my assumptions about this family? What, if any, is the hard evidence which supports them? What, if any, is the hard evidence which refutes them?

Continued

7. Parents' behaviour, whether co-operative or unco-operative, is often misinterpreted.

Ask yourself: What were the reasons for the parents' behaviour? Are there other possibilities besides the most obvious? Could their behaviour have been a reaction to something I did or said rather than to do with the child?

8. When the initial enquiry shows that the child is not at risk of significant harm, families are seldom referred to other services that they need to prevent longer-term problems.

Ask yourself: Is this family's situation satisfactory for meeting the child(ren)'s needs? Whether or not there is a concern about harm, does the family need support or practical help? How can I make sure they know about services they are entitled to, and can access them if they wish?

9. When faced with an aggressive or frightening family, professionals are reluctant to discuss fears for their own safety and ask for help.

Ask yourself: Did I feel safe in this household? If not, why not? If I or another professional should go back there to ensure the child(ren)'s safety, what support should I ask for? If necessary, put your concerns and requests in writing to your manager.

10. Information taken at the point of referral is not adequately recorded, facts are not checked and reasons for decisions are not noted.

Ask yourself: Am I sure the information I have noted is 100% accurate? If I didn't check my notes with the family during the interview, what steps should I take to verify them? Do my notes show clearly the difference between the information the family gave me, my own direct observations, and my interpretation or assessment of the situation? Do my notes record what action I have taken/will take? What action all other relevant people have taken/will take?

From: Cleaver, H., Wattam, C. and Cawson, P. (1998). *Assessing Risk in Child Protection.* London: NSPCC

Next steps – child in need and suspected actual or likely significant harm

5.48 Where a child is suspected to be suffering, or likely to suffer, significant harm, the LA is required by s47 of the Children Act 1989 to make enquiries, to enable it to decide whether it should take any action to safeguard and promote the welfare of the child. The *Framework for the Assessment of Children in Need and their Families* provides a structured framework for collecting, drawing together and analysing available information about a child and family within the following three domains:

- the child's developmental needs
- parenting capacity; and
- family and environmental factors.

It helps provide sound evidence on which to base often difficult professional judgements about whether to intervene to safeguard and promote the welfare of a child and, if so, how best to do so and with what intended outcomes.

Immediate protection

5.49 Where there is a risk to the life of a child or a likelihood of serious immediate harm, an agency with statutory child protection powers[25] **should act quickly to secure the immediate safety of the child**. Emergency action might be necessary as soon as a referral is received, or at any point in involvement with children and families. (See Appendix 1, paragraph 17 for the range of emergency protection powers available.) The need for emergency action may become apparent only over time as more is learned about the circumstances of a child or children. Neglect, as well as abuse, can pose such a risk of significant harm to a child that urgent protective action is necessary. When considering whether emergency action is required, an agency should always consider whether action is also required to safeguard and promote the welfare of other children in the same household (e.g. siblings), the household of an alleged perpetrator, or elsewhere.

5.50 Planned emergency action normally takes place following an immediate strategy discussion between police, LA children's social care and other agencies as appropriate (including the NSPCC where involved). Where a single agency has to act immediately to protect a child, a strategy discussion should take place as soon as possible after such action to plan next steps. Legal advice should normally be obtained before initiating legal action, in particular when an Emergency Protection Order is to be sought.

5.51 In some cases, it may be sufficient to secure a child's safety by a parent taking action to remove an alleged perpetrator, or by the alleged perpetrator agreeing to leave the home. In other cases, it may be necessary to ensure either that the child remains in a safe place or is removed to a safe place, either on a voluntary basis or by obtaining an emergency protection order. The police also have powers to remove a child to suitable accommodation in cases of emergency. If it is necessary to remove a child, a LA should, wherever possible, and unless a child's safety is otherwise at immediate risk, apply for an emergency protection order. **Police powers should only be used in exceptional circumstances where there is insufficient time to seek an Emergency Protection Order, or for reasons relating to the immediate safety of the child.**

5.52 The LA in whose area a child is found, in circumstances that require emergency action, is responsible for taking that action. If the child is looked after by or is the subject of

25 Agencies with statutory child protection powers are the local authority, the police and the NSPCC.

a child protection plan in another authority, the first authority should consult the authority responsible for the child. Only when the second LA explicitly accepts responsibility is the first authority relieved of the responsibility to take emergency action. Such acceptance should subsequently be confirmed in writing.

5.53 Emergency action addresses only the immediate circumstances of the child(ren). It should be followed quickly by s47 enquiries as necessary. The agencies primarily involved with the child and family should then assess the needs and circumstances of the child and family, and agree action to safeguard and promote the welfare of the child in the longer term. Where an emergency protection order applies, LA children's social care must consider quickly whether to initiate care or other proceedings, or to let the order lapse and the child return home.

Strategy discussion

5.54 Whenever there is reasonable cause to suspect that a child is suffering, or is likely to suffer, significant harm, there should be a strategy discussion involving LA children's social care and the police, and other bodies as appropriate (e.g. children's centre/school and health), in particular any referring agency. The strategy discussion should be convened by LA children's social care, and those participating should be sufficiently senior and able, therefore, to contribute to the discussion of available information and to make decisions on behalf of their agencies. If the child is a hospital patient (inpatient or outpatient) or receiving services from a child development team, the medical consultant responsible for the child's healthcare should be involved, as should the senior ward nurse if the child is an inpatient. Where a medical examination may be necessary or has taken place, a senior doctor from those providing services should also be involved.

5.55 A strategy discussion may take place following a referral, or at any other time (e.g. if concerns about significant harm emerge in respect of a child receiving support under s17). The discussion should be used to:

- share available information
- agree the conduct and timing of any criminal investigation
- decide whether a core assessment under s47 of the Children Act 1989 (s47 enquiries) should be initiated, or continued if it has already begun
- plan how the s47 enquiry should be undertaken (if one is to be initiated), including the need for medical treatment, and who will carry out what actions, by when and for what purpose
- agree what action is required immediately to safeguard and promote the welfare of the child, and/or provide interim services and support. If the child is in hospital, decisions should also be made about how to secure the safe discharge of the child

- determine what information from the strategy discussion will be shared with the family, unless such information sharing may place a child at increased risk of significant harm or jeopardise police investigations into any alleged offence(s); and
- determine if legal action is required.

5.56 Relevant matters include:

- agreeing a plan for how the core assessment under s47 of the Children Act 1989 will be carried out – what further information is required about the child(ren) and family and how it should be obtained and recorded
- agreeing who should be interviewed, by whom, for what purpose and when. The way in which interviews are conducted can play a significant part in minimising any distress caused to children, and in increasing the likelihood of maintaining constructive working relationships with families. When a criminal offence may have been committed against a child, the timing and handling of interviews with victims, their families and witnesses can have important implications for the collection and preservation of evidence
- agreeing, in particular, how the child's wishes and feelings will be ascertained so that they can be taken into account when making decisions under s47 of the Children Act 1989
- in the light of the race and ethnicity of the child and family, considering how this should be taken into account, and establishing whether an interpreter is required
- considering the needs of other children who may be affected – e.g. siblings and other children, such as those living in the same establishment, in contact with alleged abusers.

5.57 A strategy discussion may take place at a meeting or by other means (e.g. by telephone). In complex types of maltreatment, a meeting is likely to be the most effective way of discussing the child's welfare and planning future action. More than one strategy discussion may be necessary. This is likely to be where the child's circumstances are very complex and a number of discussions are required to consider whether – and, if so, when – to initiate s47 enquiries, as well as how best to undertake them. Such a meeting should be held at a convenient location for the key attendees, such as a hospital, school, police station or children's social care office. Any information shared, all decisions reached, and the basis for those decisions should be clearly recorded by the chair of the strategy discussion and circulated within one working day to all parties to the discussion. LA children's social care should record information that is consistent with the information set out in the Record of Strategy Discussion (Department of Health, 2002). Any decisions about taking immediate action should be kept under constant review.

5.58 Significant harm to children gives rise to both child welfare concerns and law enforcement concerns, and s47 enquiries may run concurrently with police investigations concerning possible associated crime(s). The police have a duty to carry out thorough and professional investigations into allegations of crime, and the obtaining of clear, strong evidence is in the best interests of a child, since it makes it less likely that a child victim will have to give evidence in a criminal court. Enquiries may, therefore, give rise to information that is relevant to decisions that will be taken by both LA children's social care and the police. The findings from the assessment and/or police investigation should be used to inform plans about future support and help to the child and family. They may also contribute to legal proceedings, whether criminal, civil or both.

5.59 Each LSCB should have in place a protocol for LA children's social care and the police, to guide both agencies in deciding how s47 enquiries and associated police investigations should be conducted jointly and, in particular, in what circumstances s47 enquiries and linked criminal investigations are necessary and/or appropriate. When joint enquiries take place, the police have the lead for the criminal investigation and LA children's social care has the lead for the s47 enquiries and the child's welfare.

Section 47 enquiries and core assessment

5.60 The core assessment is the means by which a s47 enquiry is carried out. It should be led by a qualified and experienced social worker. LA children's social care has lead responsibility for the core assessment under s47 of the Children Act 1989. In these circumstances, the objective of the LA's involvement is to determine whether action is required to safeguard and promote the welfare of the child or children who are the subjects of the enquiries. The *Framework for the Assessment of Children in Need and their Families* provides the structure for helping to collect and analyse information obtained in the course of s47 enquiries. The core assessment should begin by focusing primarily on the information identified during the initial assessment as being of most importance when considering whether the child is suffering, or is likely to suffer, significant harm. It should, however, cover all relevant dimensions in the Assessment Framework before its completion. Those making enquiries about a child should always be alert to the potential needs and safety of any siblings or other children in the household of the child in question. In addition, enquiries may also need to cover children in other households with whom the alleged offender may have had contact. At the same time, the police have to (where relevant) establish the facts about any offence that may have been committed against a child and collect evidence.

5.61 The Children Act 1989 places a statutory duty on health, education and other services to help the LA in carrying out its social services functions under Part III of the Children Act 1989 and s47 enquiries. The professionals conducting s47 enquiries should do their utmost to secure willing co-operation and participation from all professionals and services, by being prepared to explain and justify their actions, and to demonstrate that the process is being managed in a way that can help to bring about better outcomes for children. The LSCB has an important role to play in cultivating and promoting a climate of trust and understanding between different professionals and services.

5.62 Assessing the needs of a child and the capacity of their parents or wider family network adequately to ensure their safety, health and development very often depends on building a picture of the child's situation on the basis of information from many sources. Enquiries should always involve separate interviews with the child who is the subject of concern and – in the great majority of cases – interviews with parents and/or caregivers and observation of the interactions between parents and child(ren). Enquiries may also include:

- interviews with those who are personally and professionally connected with the child
- specific examinations or assessments of the child by other professionals (e.g. medical or developmental checks, assessment of emotional or psychological state); and
- interviews with those who are personally and professionally connected with the child's parents and/or caregivers.

5.63 Individuals should always be enabled to participate fully in the enquiry process. Where a child or parent is disabled, it may be necessary to provide help with communication to enable the child or parent to express him/herself to the best of his or her ability. Where a child or parent speaks a language other than that spoken by the interviewer, an interpreter should be provided. If the child is unable to take part in an interview because of age or understanding, alternative means of understanding the child's wishes or feelings should be used, including observation where children are very young or where they have communication impairments.

5.64 Children are a key, and sometimes the only, source of information about what has happened to them – especially in child sexual abuse cases, but also in physical and other forms of abuse. Accurate and complete information is essential for taking action to promote the welfare of the child, as well as for any criminal proceedings that may be instigated concerning an alleged perpetrator of abuse. When children are first approached, the nature and extent of any harm suffered by them may not be clear, nor may it be clear whether a criminal offence has been committed. It is important that even initial discussions with children are conducted in a way that minimises any distress caused to them and maximises the likelihood that they will provide accurate and complete information. It is important, wherever possible, to have separate communication with a child. Leading or suggestive communication should always be avoided. Children may need time, and more than one opportunity, to develop sufficient trust to communicate any concerns they may have, especially if they have a communication impairment, learning disabilities, are very young or are experiencing mental health problems.

5.65 Exceptionally, a joint enquiry/investigation team may need to speak to a suspected child victim without the knowledge of the parent or caregiver. Relevant circumstances would include the possibility that a child would be threatened or otherwise coerced into silence; a strong likelihood that important evidence would be destroyed; or that the child in question did not wish the parent to be involved at that stage and is competent to take that decision. As at paragraph 5.41, in all cases where the police are involved, the decision about when to inform the parent or caregiver will have a bearing on the conduct of police investigations, and the strategy discussion should decide on the most appropriate timing of parental participation.

5.66 In accordance with the *Achieving Best Evidence* guidance (2002), all such joint interviews with children should be conducted by those with specialist training and experience in interviewing children. Additional specialist help may be required if:

- the child does not speak English at a level that enables him or her to participate in the interview
- the child appears to have a degree of psychiatric disturbance but is deemed competent
- the child has an impairment
- the interviewers do not have adequate knowledge and understanding of the child's racial, religious or cultural background.

Consideration should also be given to the gender of interviewers, particularly in cases of alleged sexual abuse.

5.67 Criminal justice legislation, in particular the Youth Justice and Criminal Evidence Act 1999, creates particular obligations for courts that are dealing with witnesses under 17 years of age. These include the presumption of evidence-giving through pre-recorded videos, as well as the use of live video links for further evidence-giving and cross-examination. Cross-examination in pre-trial video hearings may also occur in relevant cases.

Child assessment orders

5.68 LA children's social care should make all reasonable efforts to persuade parents to co-operate with s47 enquiries. If, despite these efforts, the parents continue to refuse access to a child for the purpose of establishing basic facts about the child's condition – but concerns about the child's safety are not so urgent as to require an emergency protection order – a LA may apply to the court for a child assessment order. In these circumstances, the court may direct the parents/caregivers to co-operate with an assessment of the child, the details of which should be specified. The order does not take away the child's own right to refuse to participate in an assessment – e.g. a medical examination – so long as he or she is of sufficient age and understanding.

The impact of s47 enquiries on the family and child

5.69 Section 47 enquiries should always be carried out in such a way as to minimise distress to the child, and to ensure that families are treated sensitively and with respect. LA children's social care should explain the purpose and outcome of s47 enquiries to the parents and child (having regard to age and understanding) and be prepared to answer questions openly, unless to do so would affect the safety and welfare of the child. It is particularly helpful for families if LA children's social care provides written information about the purpose, process and potential outcomes of s47 enquiries. The information should be both general and specific to the particular circumstances under enquiry. It should include information about how advice, advocacy and support may be obtained from independent sources.

5.70 In the great majority of cases, children remain with their families following s47 enquiries, even where concerns about abuse or neglect are substantiated. As far as possible, s47 enquiries should be conducted in a way that allows for future constructive working relationships with families. The way in which a case is handled initially can affect the entire subsequent process. Where handled well and sensitively, there can be a positive effect on the eventual outcome for the child.

5.71 Where a child is living in a residential establishment, consideration should be given to the possible impact on other children living in the same establishment.

The outcome of s47 enquiries

5.72 LA children's social care should decide how to proceed following s47 enquiries, after discussion between all those who have conducted, or been significantly involved in those enquiries – including relevant professionals and agencies, as well as foster carers where involved and the child and parents themselves. The information recorded on the outcome of the s47 enquiries should be consistent with the information set out in the Outcome of the s47 Enquiries Record (Department of Health, 2002). Parents and children of sufficient age and appropriate level of understanding (together with professionals and agencies who have been significantly involved) should receive a copy of this record, in particular in advance of any initial child conference that is convened. This information should be conveyed in an appropriate format for younger children and for those people whose preferred language is not English. Consideration should be given to whether the core assessment has been completed or what further work is required before it is completed. It may be valuable, following an evaluation of the outcome of enquiries, to make recommendations for action in an inter-disciplinary forum, if the case is not going forward to a child protection conference. Enquiries may result in a number of outcomes. Where the child concerned is living in a residential establishment that is subject to inspection, the relevant inspectorate should be informed.

Concerns are not substantiated

5.73 Section 47 enquiries may not substantiate the original concerns about the child being at risk of, or suffering, significant harm, but it is important that the core assessment is completed. In some circumstances it may be decided that the core assessment has been completed and no further action is necessary. However, LA children's social care and other relevant agencies as necessary should always consider, with the family, what support and/or services may be helpful, how the child and family might be provided with these services if they wish it, and by whom. The focus of s47 enquiries is the welfare of the child, and the assessment may well reveal a range of needs. The provision of services to these children and their families should not be dependent on the presence of abuse and neglect. Help and support to children in need and their families may prevent problems escalating to a point where a child is abused or neglected.

5.74 In some cases, there may remain concerns about significant harm, despite there being no real evidence. It may be appropriate to put in place arrangements to monitor the child's welfare. Monitoring should never be used as a means of deferring or avoiding difficult decisions. The purpose of monitoring should always be clear – i.e. what is being monitored and why, in what way and by whom. It is also important to inform parents about the nature of any ongoing concern. There should be a time set for reviewing the monitoring arrangements by holding a further discussion or meeting.

Concerns are substantiated, but the child is not judged to be at continuing risk of significant harm

5.75 There may be substantiated concerns that a child has suffered significant harm, but it is agreed between the agencies most involved, and the child and family, that a plan for ensuring the child's future safety and welfare can be developed and implemented without having a child protection conference or a child protection plan. Such an approach is of particular relevance where it is clear to the agencies involved that there is no continuing risk of significant harm.

5.76 A child protection conference may not be required when there are sound reasons, based on an analysis of evidence obtained through s47 enquiries, for judging that a child is not at continuing risk of significant harm. This may be because, for example, the caregiver has taken responsibility for the harm they caused the child, the family's circumstances have changed or the person responsible for the harm is no longer in contact with the child. It may be because significant harm was incurred as the result of an isolated abusive incident (e.g. abuse by a stranger).

5.77 The agencies most involved may judge that a parent, caregiver or members of the child's wider family are willing and able to co-operate with actions to ensure the child's future safety and welfare, and that the child is therefore not at continuing risk of significant harm. This judgement can only be made in the light of all relevant information obtained during a s47 enquiry, and a soundly based assessment of the likelihood of successful intervention, based on clear evidence and mindful of the dangers of misplaced professional optimism. LA children's social care has a duty to seek children's views and take account of their wishes and feelings, according to their age and understanding. A meeting of involved professionals and family members may be useful to agree what actions should be undertaken by whom, and with what intended outcomes for the child's health and development, including the provision of therapeutic services. Whatever process is used to plan future action, the resulting plan should be informed by the core assessment findings. It should set out who will have responsibility for what actions, including what course of

action should be followed if the plan is not being successfully implemented. It should also include a timescale for review of progress against planned outcomes. Family Group Conferences (see paragraphs 10.2–10.4) may have a role to play in fulfilling these tasks.

5.78 LA children's social care should take carefully any decision not to proceed to a child protection conference where it is known that a child has suffered significant harm. A suitably experienced and qualified social work manager within LA children's social care should endorse the decision. Those professionals and agencies who are most involved with the child and family, and those who have taken part in the s47 enquiry, have the right to request that LA children's social care convene a child protection conference if they have serious concerns that a child's welfare may not otherwise be adequately safeguarded. Any such request that is supported by a senior manager, or a named or designated professional, should normally be agreed. Where there remain differences of view over the necessity for a conference in a specific case, every effort should be made to resolve them through discussion and explanation, but as a last resort LSCBs should have in place a quick and straightforward means of resolving differences of opinion.

Concerns are substantiated and the child is judged to be at continuing risk of significant harm

5.79 Where the agencies most involved judge that a child may continue to suffer, or to be at risk of suffering, significant harm, LA children's social care should convene a child protection conference. The aim of the conference is to enable those professionals most involved with the child and family, and the family themselves, to assess all relevant information and plan how best to safeguard and promote the welfare of the child.

The initial child protection conference

Purpose

5.80 The initial child protection conference brings together the child (where appropriate), family members and those professionals most involved with the child and family, following s47 enquiries. Its purpose is to:

- bring together and analyse, in an inter-agency setting, the information that has been obtained about the child's developmental needs, and the parents' or carers' capacity to respond to these needs to ensure the child's safety and promote the child's health and development within the context of their wider family and environment
- consider the evidence presented to the conference, make judgements about the likelihood of a child suffering significant harm in future, and decide whether the child is at continuing risk of significant harm; and
- decide what future action is required to safeguard and promote the welfare of the child, how that action will be taken forward, and with what intended outcomes.

Timing

5.81 The timing of an initial child protection conference depends on the urgency of the case and on the time required to obtain relevant information about the child and family. If the conference is to reach well-informed decisions based on evidence, it should take place following adequate preparation and assessment of the child's needs and circumstances. At the same time, cases where children are at risk of significant harm should not be allowed to drift. Consequently, all initial child protection conferences should take place within 15 working days of the strategy discussion, or the last strategy discussion if more than one has been held (see paragraph 5.57).

Attendance

5.82 Those attending conferences should be there because they have a significant contribution to make, arising from professional expertise, knowledge of the child or family or both. The LA social work manager should consider whether to seek advice from, or have present, a medical professional who can present the medical information in a manner which can be understood by conference attendees and enable such information to be evaluated from a sound evidence base. There should be sufficient information and expertise available – through personal representation and written reports – to enable the conference to make an informed decision about what action is necessary to safeguard and promote the welfare of the child, and to make realistic and workable proposals for taking that action forward. At the same time, a conference that is larger than it needs to be can inhibit discussion and intimidate the child and family members. Those who have a relevant contribution to make may include:

- the child, or his or her representative
- family members (including the wider family)
- LA children's social care staff who have led and been involved in an assessment of the child and family
- foster carers (current or former)
- residential care staff
- professionals involved with the child (e.g. health visitors, midwife, school nurse, children's guardian, paediatrician, school staff, early-years staff, the GP, NHS Direct)
- professionals involved with the parents or other family members (e.g. family support services, adult mental health services, probation, the GP, NHS Direct)
- professionals with expertise in the particular type of harm suffered by the child or in the child's particular condition – e.g. a disability or long-term illness
- those involved in investigations (e.g. the police)
- LA legal services (child welfare)

- NSPCC or other involved voluntary organisations; and
- a representative of the Armed Services, in cases where there is a service connection.

5.83 The relevant LSCB protocol should specify a required quorum for attendance, and list those who should be invited to attend, provided that they have a relevant contribution to make. As a minimum, at every conference there should be attendance by LA children's social care, and at least two other professional groups or agencies who have had direct contact with the child who is the subject of the conference. In addition, attendees may include those whose contribution relates to their professional expertise or responsibility for relevant services. In exceptional cases, where a child has not had relevant contact with three agencies (i.e. LA children's social care and two others), this minimum quorum may be breached. Professionals and agencies who are invited but are unable to attend should submit a written report.

Involving the child and family members

5.84 Before a conference is held, the purpose of a conference, who will attend, and the way in which it will operate should always be explained to a child of sufficient age and understanding, and to the parents and involved family members. Where the child/family members do not speak English well enough to understand the discussions and express their views, an interpreter should be used. The parents (including absent parents) should normally be invited to attend the conference and helped to participate fully. Children's social care staff should give parents information about local advice and advocacy agencies, and explain that they may bring an advocate, friend or supporter. The child, subject to consideration about age and understanding, should be invited to attend and to bring an advocate, friend or supporter if s/he wishes. Where the child's attendance is neither desired by him/her nor appropriate, the LA children's social care professional who is working most closely with the child should ascertain what his/her wishes and feelings are and make these known to the conference.

5.85 The involvement of family members should be planned carefully. It may not always be possible to involve all family members at all times in the conference – e.g. if one parent is the alleged abuser, or if there is a high level of conflict between family members. Adults and any children who wish to make representations to the conference may not wish to speak in front of one another. Exceptionally, it may be necessary to exclude one or more family members from a conference, in whole or in part. The conference is primarily about the child, and while the presence of the family is normally welcome, those professionals attending must be able to share information in a safe and non-threatening environment. Professionals may themselves have concerns about violence or intimidation, which should be communicated in advance to the conference chair.

5.86 LSCB procedures should set out criteria for excluding a parent or caregiver, including the evidence required. A strong risk of violence or intimidation by a family member at or subsequent to the conference, towards a child or anybody else, might be one reason for exclusion. The possibility that a parent or caregiver may be prosecuted for an offence against a child is not in itself a reason for exclusion, although in these circumstances the Chair should take advice from the police about any implications arising from an alleged perpetrator's attendance. If criminal proceedings have been instigated, the view of the Crown Prosecution Service should be taken into account. The decision to exclude a parent or caregiver from the child protection conference rests with the Chair of the conference, acting within LSCB procedures. If the parents are excluded, or are unable or unwilling to attend a child protection conference, they should be enabled to communicate their views to the conference by another means.

Chairing the conference

5.87 A professional who is independent of operational or line management responsibilities for the case should chair the conference. The conference Chair is accountable to the Director of Children's Services. The status of the Chair should be sufficient to ensure inter-agency commitment to the conference and the child protection plan. Wherever possible, the same person should also chair subsequent child protection reviews in respect of a specific child. The responsibilities of the Chair include:

- meeting the child and family members in advance, to ensure that they understand the purpose of the conference and what will happen
- setting out the purpose of the conference to all present, determining the agenda and emphasising the confidential nature of the occasion
- enabling all those present, and absent contributors, to make their full contribution to discussion and decision-making
- ensuring that the conference takes the decisions required of it in an informed, systematic and explicit way; and
- being accountable to the Director of Children's Services for the conduct of conferences.

5.88 A conference Chair should be trained in the role and should have:

- a good understanding and professional knowledge of children's welfare and development, and best practice in working with children and families
- the ability to look objectively at, and assess the implications of, the evidence on which judgements should be based
- skills in chairing meetings in a way that encourages constructive participation, while maintaining a clear focus on the welfare of the child and the decisions that have to be taken
- knowledge and understanding of anti-discriminatory practice

- knowledge of relevant legislation, including that relating to children's services and human rights.

Information for the conference

5.89 LA children's social care should provide the conference with a written report. This should summarise and analyse the information obtained in the course of the initial assessment and the core assessment undertaken under s47 of the Children Act 1989 (in as far as it has been completed within the available time period) and information in existing records relating to the child and family. Where decisions are being made about more than one child in a family, there should be a report prepared on each child. The report for a child protection conference should be consistent with the information set out in the Initial Child Protection Conference Report (Department of Health, 2002). The core assessment is the means by which a s47 enquiry is carried out. Although a core assessment will have been commenced, it is unlikely it will have been completed in time for the conference, given the 35 working day period that such assessments can take. The child protection conference report should include:

- a chronology of significant events and agency and professional contact with the child and family
- information on the child's current and past state of developmental needs
- information on the capacity of the parents and other family members to ensure the child is safe from harm, and to respond to the child's developmental needs, within their wider family and environmental context
- the expressed views, wishes and feelings of the child, parents and other family members; and
- an analysis of the implications of the information obtained for the child's future safety and meeting of his or her developmental needs.

5.90 Where relevant, the parents and each child should be provided with a copy of the report in advance of the conference. The contents of the report should be explained and discussed with the child and relevant family members in advance of the conference itself, in the preferred language(s) of the child and family members.

5.91 Other professionals attending the conference should bring with them details of their involvement with the child and family, as well as information concerning their knowledge of the child's developmental needs and the capacity of the parents to meet the needs of their child within their family and environmental context. Contributors should, wherever possible, provide in advance a written report to the conference that should be made available to those attending. The child and family members should be helped in advance to think about what they want to convey to the conference and about how best to get their points across on the day. Some may find it helpful to provide their own written report, which they may be assisted to prepare by their adviser/advocate.

5.92 Those providing information should take care to distinguish between fact, observation, allegation and opinion. When information is provided from another source – i.e. it is second- or third-hand – this should be made clear.

Action and decisions for the conference

5.93 The conference should consider the following question when determining whether the child should be the subject of a child protection plan:

Is the child at continuing risk of significant harm?

5.94 The test should be that either:

- the child can be shown to have suffered ill-treatment or impairment of health or development as a result of physical, emotional or sexual abuse or neglect, and professional judgement is that further ill-treatment or impairment are likely; or
- professional judgement, substantiated by the findings of enquiries in this individual case or by research evidence, is that the child is likely to suffer ill-treatment or the impairment of health or development as a result of physical, emotional or sexual abuse or neglect.

5.95 If the child is at continuing risk of significant harm, safeguarding the child will therefore require inter-agency help and intervention, delivered through a formal child protection plan. It is also the role of the initial child protection conference to formulate the outline child protection plan, in as much detail as possible.

5.96 Conference participants should base their judgements on all the available evidence obtained through existing records, the initial assessment and the in-depth core assessment undertaken following the initiation of s47 enquiries. The method of reaching a decision within the conference on whether the child should be the subject of a child protection plan should be set out in the relevant LSCB protocol. The decision-making process should be based on the views of all agencies represented at the conference, and also take into account any written contributions that have been made. The decision of the conference – and, where appropriate, details of the category of abuse or neglect, the name of the key worker who is also the lead professional and the core group membership – should be recorded in a manner that is consistent with the Initial Child Protection Conference Report (Department of Health, 2002) and circulated to all those invited to the conference within one working day.

5.97 If a decision is taken that the child is at continuing risk of significant harm and hence a child protection plan is necessary, the Chair should determine which category of abuse or neglect the child has suffered or is at risk of suffering. The category used (i.e. physical, emotional, sexual abuse or neglect) will indicate to those consulting the child's social care record the primary presenting concerns at the time the child became the subject of a child protection plan.

5.98 A child may not be the subject of a child protection plan, but he or she may nonetheless require services to promote his or her health or development. In these circumstances the conference, together with the family, should consider the child's needs and what further help would assist the family in responding to them. Subject to the family's views and consent, it may be appropriate to continue with and complete a core assessment of the child's needs to help determine what support might best help promote the child's welfare. Where the child's needs are complex, inter-agency working will continue to be important. Where appropriate, a child in need plan should be drawn up and reviewed at regular intervals – no less frequent than every six months (see paragraphs 4.33 and 4.36 of the *Framework for the Assessment of Children in Need and their Families*).

5.99 Where a child is to be the subject of a child protection plan, it is the responsibility of the conference to consider and make recommendations on how agencies, professionals and the family should work together to ensure that the child will be safeguarded from harm in the future. This should enable both professionals and the family to understand exactly what is expected of them and what they can expect of others. Specific tasks include:

- appointing the lead statutory body (either LA children's social care or the NSPCC) and a key worker (the lead professional), who should be a qualified, experienced social worker and an employee of the lead statutory body
- identifying the membership of a core group of professionals and family members who will develop and implement the child protection plan as a detailed working tool
- establishing how the child, their parents (including all those with parental responsibility) and wider family members should be involved in the ongoing assessment, planning and implementation process, and the support, advice and advocacy available to them
- establishing timescales for meetings of the core group, production of a child protection plan, and for child protection review meetings
- identifying in outline what further action is required to complete the core assessment, and what other specialist assessments of the child and family are required to make sound judgements on how best to safeguard and promote the welfare of the child
- outlining the child protection plan – in particular, identifying what needs to change in order to achieve the planned outcomes to safeguard and promote the welfare of the child
- ensuring a contingency plan is in place if agreed actions are not completed and/or circumstances change – e.g. if a caregiver fails to achieve what has been agreed, a court application is not successful or a parent removes the child from a place of safety

- clarifying the different purpose and remit of the initial conference, the core group and the child protection review conference; and
- agreeing a date for the first child protection review conference, and under what circumstances it might be necessary to convene the conference before that date.

5.100 The outline child protection plan should:

- identify factors associated with the likelihood of the child suffering significant harm and ways in which the child can be protected through an inter-agency plan, based on the current findings from the assessment and information held from any previous involvement with the child and family
- establish short-term and longer-term aims and objectives that are clearly linked to reducing the likelihood of harm to the child and promoting the child's welfare, including contact with family members
- be clear about who will have responsibility for what actions – including actions by family members – within what specified timescales
- outline ways of monitoring and evaluating progress against the planned outcomes set out in the plan; and
- be clear about which professional is responsible for checking that the required changes have taken place, and what action will be taken, by whom, when they have not.

Complaints about a child protection conference

5.101 Parents/caregivers – and, on occasion, children – may have concerns about which they may wish to make representations or complain, in respect of one or more of the following aspects of the functioning of child protection conferences:

- the process of the conference
- the outcome, in terms of the fact of and/or the category of primary concern at the time the child became the subject of a child protection plan
- a decision for the child to become, or not to become, the subject of a child protection plan or not to cease the child being the subject of a child protection plan.

5.102 Complaints about individual agencies, their performance and provision (or non-provision) of services should be responded to in accordance with the relevant agency's complaints handling process. For example, LA children's social care is required (by s26 of the Children Act 1989) to establish complaints procedures to deal with complaints arising in respect of Part III of the Act.

5.103 Complaints about aspects of the functioning of conferences described above should be addressed to the conference Chair. Such complaints should be passed on to LA children's social care and, since they relate to Part V of the Children Act 1989, should be responded to in accordance with the Complaints Directions 1990.[26] (This section will be updated when regulations on the revision of LA Complaints Procedures under the Children Act 1989 are revised.) In considering and responding to complaints, the LA should form an inter-agency panel made up of senior representatives from LSCB member agencies. The panel should consider whether the relevant inter-agency protocols and procedures have been observed correctly, and whether the decision that is being complained about follows reasonably from the proper observation of the protocol(s).

5.104 In addition, representations and complaints may be received by individual agencies in respect of services provided (or not provided) as a consequence of assessments and conferences, including those set out in child protection plans. Such concerns should be responded to by the relevant agency in accordance with its own processes for responding to such matters.

Administrative arrangements and record-keeping

5.105 Those attending should be notified of conferences as far in advance as possible, and the conference should be held at a time and place likely to be convenient to as many people as possible. All child protection conferences, both initial and review, should have a dedicated person to take notes and produce a record of the meeting. The record of the conference is a crucial working document for all relevant professionals and the family. It should include:

- the essential facts of the case
- a summary of discussion at the conference, which accurately reflects contributions made
- all decisions reached, with information outlining the reasons for decisions; and
- a translation of decisions into an outline or revised child protection plan, enabling everyone to be clear about their tasks.

5.106 A copy should be sent as soon as possible after the conference to all those who attended, or were invited to attend, including family members, except for any part of the conference from which they were excluded. This is in addition to sharing the main decisions within one working day of the conference (see paragraph 5.96). The record is confidential and should not be passed by professionals to third parties without the consent of either the conference Chair or the key worker. However, in cases of criminal proceedings, the police may reveal the existence of the notes to the CPS in accordance with the Criminal Procedure and Investigation Act 1996. The recipient agencies and professionals should retain the record of the decisions of the child protection conference in accordance with their record retention policies.

26 The directions are based on s7B of the Local Authority Social Services Act 1970, inserted by s50 of the National Health Service and Community Care Act 1990.

Action following the initial child protection conference

The role of the key worker

5.107 When a conference decides that a child should be the subject of a child protection plan, one of the child welfare agencies with statutory powers (LA children's social care or the NSPCC) should carry future child welfare responsibility for the case and designate a qualified and experienced member of its social work staff to be the key worker (the lead professional). Each child who is the subject of a child protection plan should have a named key worker.

5.108 The key worker is responsible for making sure that the outline child protection plan is developed into a more detailed inter-agency plan. S/he should complete the core assessment of the child and family, securing contributions from core group members and others as necessary. The key worker is also responsible for acting as the lead professional for the inter-agency work with the child and family. S/he should co-ordinate the contribution of family members and other agencies to planning the actions that need to be taken, putting the child protection plan into effect and reviewing progress against the planned outcomes set out in the plan. It is important that the role of the key worker is fully explained at the initial child protection conference and at the core group.

5.109 The key worker should also regularly ascertain the child's wishes and feelings, and keep the child up-to-date with the child protection plan and any developments or changes.

The core group

5.110 The core group is responsible for developing the child protection plan as a detailed working tool, and implementing it, within the outline plan agreed at the initial child protection conference. Membership should include the key worker, who leads the core group, the child if appropriate, family members, and professionals or foster carers who will have direct contact with the family. Although the key worker has the lead role, all members of the core group are jointly responsible for the formulation and implementation of the child protection plan, refining the plan as needed, and monitoring progress against the planned outcomes set out in the plan.

5.111 Core groups are an important forum for working with parents, wider family members, and children of sufficient age and understanding. It can often be difficult for parents to agree to a child protection plan within the confines of a formal conference. Their agreement may be gained later when details of the plan are worked out in the core group. Sometimes there may be conflicts of interest between family members who have a relevant interest in the work of the core group. The child's best interests should always take precedence over the interests of other family members.

5.112 The first meeting of the core group should take place within 10 working days of the initial child protection conference. The purpose of this first meeting is to flesh out the child protection plan and decide what steps need to be taken by whom to complete the core assessment on time. Thereafter, core groups should meet sufficiently regularly to facilitate working together, monitor actions and outcomes against the child protection plan, and make any necessary alterations as circumstances change.

5.113 There should be a written note recording the decisions taken and actions agreed at core group meetings. The child protection plan should be updated as necessary.

Completion of the core assessment

5.114 Completion of the core assessment, within 35 working days, should include an analysis of the child's developmental needs and the parents' capacity to respond to those needs, including parents' capacity to ensure that the child is safe from harm. It may be necessary to commission specialist assessments (e.g. from child and adolescent mental health services) that it may not be possible to complete within this time period. This should not delay the drawing together of the core assessment findings at this point.

5.115 The analysis of the child's needs should provide evidence on which to base judgements and decisions on how best to safeguard and promote the welfare of a child and support parents in achieving this aim. Decisions based on analysis of the child's developmental needs should be used to develop the child protection plan.

The child protection plan

5.116 The initial child protection conference is responsible for agreeing an outline child protection plan. Professionals and parents/caregivers should develop the details of the plan in the core group. The overall aim of the plan is to:

- ensure the child is safe and prevent him or her from suffering further harm
- promote the child's health and development – i.e. his or her welfare; and
- provided it is in the best interests of the child, support the family and wider family members to safeguard and promote the welfare of their child.

5.117 The child protection plan should be based on the findings from the assessment and follow the dimensions relating to the child's developmental needs, parenting capacity and family and environmental factors, drawing on knowledge about effective interventions. The content of the child protection plans should be consistent with the information set out in the exemplar for the Child Protection Plan (Department of Health, 2002). It should set out what work needs to be done, why, when and by whom. The plan should:

- describe the identified developmental needs of the child, and what therapeutic services are required
- include specific, achievable, child-focused outcomes intended to safeguard and promote the welfare of the child
- include realistic strategies and specific actions to achieve the planned outcomes

- include a contingency plan to be followed if circumstances change significantly and require prompt action
- clearly identify roles and responsibilities of professionals and family members, including the nature and frequency of contact by professionals with children and family members
- lay down points at which progress will be reviewed, and the means by which progress will be judged; and
- set out clearly the roles and responsibilities of those professionals with routine contact with the child – e.g. health visitors, GPs and teachers – as well as those professionals providing specialist or targeted support to the child and family.

5.118 The child protection plan should take into consideration the wishes and feelings of the child, and the views of the parents, insofar as they are consistent with the child's welfare. The key worker should make every effort to ensure that the children and parents have a clear understanding of the planned outcomes, that they accept the plan and are willing to work to it. The plan should be constructed with the family in their preferred language and they should receive a written copy in this language. If family members' preferences are not accepted about how best to safeguard and promote the welfare of the child, the reasons for this should be explained. Families should be told about their right to complain and make representations, and how to do so.

Agreeing the plan with the child

5.119 The child protection plan should be explained to and agreed with the child in a manner appropriate to their age and understanding. An interpreter should be used if the child's level of English means that s/he is not able to participate fully in these discussions unless they are conducted in her/his own language. The child should be given a copy of the plan written at a level appropriate to his or her age and understanding, and in his or her preferred language.

Agreeing the plan with parents

5.120 Parents should be clear about the evidence of significant harm that resulted in the child becoming the subject of a child protection plan, about what needs to change, and what is expected of them as part of the plan for safeguarding and promoting the child's welfare. All parties should be clear about the respective roles and responsibilities of family members and different agencies in implementing the plan. The parents should receive a written copy of the plan so that they are clear about who is doing what when and the planned outcomes for the child.

Intervention

5.121 Decisions about how to intervene, including what services to offer, should be based on evidence about what is likely to work best to bring about good outcomes for the child. A number of aspects of intervention should be considered in the context of the child protection plan, in the light of evidence from assessment of the child's developmental needs, the parents' capacity to respond appropriately to the child's needs, and the wider family circumstances.

5.122 It is important that services are provided to give the child and family the best chance of achieving the required changes. If a child cannot be cared for safely by his or her caregiver(s) he or she will have to be placed elsewhere while work is being undertaken with the child and family. Irrespective of where the child is living, interventions should specifically address:

- the developmental needs of the child
- the child's understanding of what has happened to him or her
- the abusing caregiver/child relationship and parental capacity to respond to the child's needs
- the relationship between the adult caregivers both as adults and parents
- family relationships; and
- possible changes to the family's social and environmental circumstances.

5.123 Intervention may have a number of inter-related components:

- action to make a child safe
- action to help promote a child's health and development – i.e. welfare
- action to help a parent(s)/caregiver(s) in safeguarding a child and promoting his or her welfare
- therapy for an abused child; and
- support or therapy for a perpetrator of abuse.

5.124 The development by the child of a secure attachment to the parent is critical to his or her healthy development. The quality and nature of the attachment will be a key issue to be considered in decision-making, especially if decisions are being made about moving a child from one setting to another, reuniting a child with his or her birth family, or considering a permanent placement away from the child's family. If the plan is to assess whether the child can be reunited with the caregiver(s) responsible for the maltreatment, very detailed work is required to help the caregiver(s) develop the necessary parenting skills.

5.125 A key issue in deciding on suitable interventions is whether the child's developmental needs can be responded to within his or her family context and **within timescales that are appropriate for the child**. These timescales may not be compatible with those for the caregiver(s) who are receiving therapeutic help. The process of decision-making and planning should be as open as possible, from an ethical as well as a practical point of view. Where the family situation is not improving or changing fast enough to respond to the child's needs, decisions are necessary about the long-term future of the child. In the longer term it may be in the best interests of the child to be placed in an alternative family context. Key to these considerations is what is in the child's best interests, informed by the child's wishes and feelings.

5.126 Children who have suffered significant harm may continue to experience the consequences of this abuse irrespective of where they are living: whether remaining with or being reunited with their families, or alternatively being placed in new families. This relates particularly to their behavioural and emotional development. Therapeutic work with the child should continue, therefore, irrespective of where the child is placed, in order to ensure the needs of the child are responded to appropriately.

5.127 More information to assist with making decisions about interventions is available in Chapter 4 of the *Assessment Framework* and the accompanying practice guidance (Department of Health, 2000).

The child protection review conference

Timescale

5.128 The first child protection review conference should be held within three months of the initial child protection conference, and further reviews should be held at intervals of not more than six months for as long as the child remains the subject of a child protection plan. This is to ensure that momentum is maintained in the process of safeguarding and promoting the welfare of the child. Where necessary, reviews should be brought forward to address changes in the child's circumstances. Attendees should include those most involved with the child and family in the same way as at an initial child protection conference, and the LSCB protocols for establishing a quorum should apply.

Purpose

5.129 The purposes of the child protection review are to:

- review the safety, health and development of the child against planned outcomes set out in the child protection plan
- ensure that the child continues to be safeguarded from harm; and
- consider whether the child protection plan should continue in place or should be changed.

5.130 The reviewing of the child's progress and the effectiveness of interventions are critical to achieving the best possible outcomes for the child. The child's wishes and feelings should be sought and taken into account during the reviewing process.

5.131 The review requires as much preparation, commitment and management as the initial child protection conference. Every review should consider explicitly whether the child continues to be at risk of significant harm, and hence continues to require safeguarding from harm through adherence to a formal child protection plan. If not, then the child should no longer be the subject of a child protection plan. The same LSCB decision-making procedure should be used to reach a judgement on a child protection plan as is used at the initial child protection conference. As with initial child protection conferences, the relevant LSCB protocol should specify a required quorum for attendance at review conferences.

5.132 The core group has a collective responsibility to produce reports for the child protection review. Together, these reports provide an overview of work undertaken by family members and professionals, and evaluate the impact on the child's welfare against the planned outcomes set out in the child protection plan. The content of the report to the review child protection conference should be consistent with the information set out in the Child Protection Review (Department of Health, 2002).

Discontinuing the child protection plan

5.133 A child should no longer be the subject of a child protection plan in the following circumstances:

- it is judged that the child is no longer at continuing risk of significant harm requiring safeguarding by means of a child protection plan (e.g. the likelihood of harm has been reduced by action taken through the child protection plan; the child and family's circumstances have changed; or re-assessment of the child and family indicates that a child protection plan is not necessary). Under these circumstances, only a child protection review conference can decide that a child protection plan is no longer necessary
- the child and family have moved permanently to another LA area. In such cases, the receiving LA should convene a child protection conference within 15 working days of being notified of the move. Only after this event may discontinuing the child protection plan take place in respect of the original LA's child protection plan.
- the child has reached 18 years of age, has died or has permanently left the UK.

5.134 When a child is no longer the subject of a child protection plan, notification should be sent, as minimum, to all those agency representatives who were invited to attend the initial child protection conference that led to the plan.

5.135 A child who is no longer the subject of a child protection plan may still require additional support and services, and discontinuing the child protection plan should never lead to the automatic withdrawal of help. The key worker should discuss with the parents and the child what services might be wanted and required, based on the re-assessment of the needs of the child and family.

Children looked after by the local authority

5.136 The Review of Children's Cases Regulations 1991, as amended by The Review of Children's Cases (Amendment) (England) Regulations 2004, set out the requirements for:

- LAs as Responsible Authorities for looked after children
- voluntary organisations that accommodate children under s59 of the Children Act 1989; and
- registered children's homes that accommodate children

to review each child's care plan. The Regulations make provision for the minimum frequency of the review and the matters that must be discussed.

5.137 The Review of Children's Cases (Amendment) Regulations 2004 require each Responsible Authority to appoint an independent reviewing officer (IRO). The IROs are responsible for monitoring the LA's review of the care plan, with the aim of ensuring that actions required to implement the care plan are carried out and outcomes monitored. The Regulations give IROs power to refer a case to the Children and Family Court Advisory and Support Service (CAFCASS) to take legal action as a last resort where a child's human rights are considered to be in breach through failure to implement the care plan.

5.138 Where children looked after are also subject to a child protection review conference, the overriding principle must be that the systems are integrated and carefully monitored in a way that promotes a child-centred and not a bureaucratic approach. It is important to link the timing of a child protection review conference with the review under the Review Regulations, to ensure that information from the former is brought to the review meeting and informs the overall care planning process. It should be remembered that significant changes to the care plan can only be made at the looked after children review meeting.

5.139 IROs may be employed to chair child protection conferences as well as looked after children reviews. The appropriateness of the IRO undertaking this role should be considered on a case-by-case basis. This must be managed in a way that ensures that the independence of the IRO is not compromised.

Pre-birth child protection conferences and reviews

5.140 Where a core assessment under s47 of the Children Act 1989 gives rise to concerns that an unborn child may be at future risk of significant harm, LA children's social care may decide to convene an initial child protection conference prior to the child's birth. Such a conference should have the same status, and proceed in the same way, as other initial child protection conferences, including decisions about a child protection plan. Child protection review conferences should also proceed in the same way. The involvement of midwifery services is vital in such cases.

Recording that a child is the subject of a child protection plan

5.141 LA children's social care IT systems should be capable of recording, in the child's case record, when the child is the subject of a child protection plan. Each LA's IT system that supports the Integrated Children's System (ICS) (required to be fully operational by 1 January 2007) should be capable of producing a list of all the children resident in the area (including those who have been placed there by another LA or agency) who are considered to be at continuing risk of significant harm and for whom there is a child protection plan.

5.142 The principal purpose of having the IT capacity to record that a child is the subject of a child protection plan is to enable agencies and professionals to be aware of those children who are judged to be at continuing risk of significant harm and who are the subject of a child protection plan. It is equally important that agencies and professionals can obtain relevant information about other children who are known, or have been known, to the LA. Consequently, agencies and professionals who have concerns about a child should be able to obtain information about a child that is recorded on the LAs ICS IT system (www.everychildmatters.gov.uk/ics). It is essential that legitimate enquirers such as police and health professionals are able to obtain this information both in and outside office hours.

5.143 Children should be recorded as having been abused or neglected under one or more of the categories of physical, emotional, or sexual abuse or neglect, according to a decision by the Chair of the child protection conference. These categories help indicate the nature of the current concerns. Recording information in this way also allows for the collation and analysis of information locally and nationally and for its use in planning the provision of services. The categories selected should reflect all the information obtained in the course of the initial assessment and core assessment under s47 or the Children Act 1989 and subsequent analysis, and should not just relate to one or more abusive incidents.

Managing and providing information about a child

5.144 Each LA should designate a manager, normally an experienced social worker, who has responsibility for:

- ensuring that records on children who have a child protection plan are kept up-to-date
- ensuring enquiries about children about whom there are concerns, or who have child protection plans, are recorded and considered in accordance with paragraph 5.152
- managing other notifications of movements of children into or out of the LA area, such as children who have a child protection plan and looked after children
- managing notifications of people who may pose a risk of significant harm to children who are either identified with the LA area or have moved into the LA area
- managing requests for checks to be made to ensure unsuitable people are prevented from working with children.

5.145 This manager should be accountable to the Director of Children's Services.

5.146 Information on each child known to LA children's social care should be kept up-to-date on the LA's ICS IT system, and the content of the child's record should be confidential, available only to legitimate enquirers. This information should be accessible at all times to such enquirers. The details of enquirers should always be checked and recorded on the system before information is provided.

5.147 If an enquiry is made about a child and the child's case is open to LA children's social care, the enquirer should be given the name of the child's key worker, and the key worker should be informed of this enquiry so that they can follow it up. If an enquiry is made about a child living at the same address as a child who is the subject of a child protection plan, this information should be sent to the key worker of the child who is the subject of the child protection plan. If an enquiry is made but the child is not known to LA children's social care, this enquiry should be recorded on a contact sheet, together with the advice given to the enquirer. In the event of a second enquiry about a child who is not known to children's social care, not only should the fact of the earlier enquiry be notified to the later enquirer, but the designated manager in LA children's social care should ensure that LA children's social care considers whether this is, or may be, a child in need.

5.148 The Department for Education and Skills holds lists of the names of designated managers, and should be notified of any changes in designated managers.

Recording

5.149 Good record-keeping is an important part of the accountability of professionals to those who use their services. It helps to focus work, and it is essential to working effectively across agency and professional boundaries. Clear and accurate records ensure that there is a documented account of an agency's or professional's involvement with a child and/or family. They help with continuity when individual workers are unavailable or change, and they provide an essential tool for managers to monitor work or for peer review. Records are an essential source of evidence for investigations and enquiries, and may also be required to be disclosed in court proceedings. Cases where s47 enquiries do not result in the substantiation of referral concerns should be retained in accordance with agency retention policies. These policies should ensure that records are stored safely and can be retrieved promptly and efficiently.

5.150 To serve these purposes, records should use clear, straightforward language, be concise, and be accurate not only in fact, but also in differentiating between opinion, judgement and hypothesis.

5.151 Well-kept records provide an essential underpinning to good professional practice. Safeguarding and promoting the welfare of children requires information to be brought together from a number of sources, and careful professional judgements to be made on the basis of this information. Records should be clear, accessible and comprehensive, with judgements made and decisions and interventions carefully recorded. Where decisions have been taken jointly across agencies, or endorsed by a manager, this should be made clear.

5.152 The exemplars (Department of Health, 2002) produced to support the implementation of the Integrated Children's System contain the information requirements for LA children's social care, together with others, when recording information about children in need and their families. The appropriate record to use at different stages of working with children and families is referenced throughout this chapter.

Request for a change of worker

5.153 Occasions may arise where relationships between parents, or other family members, and professionals are not productive in terms of working to safeguard and promote the welfare of their children. In such instances, agencies should respond sympathetically to a request for a change of worker, provided that such a change can be identified as being in the interests of the child who is the focus of concern.

Effective support and supervision

5.154 Working to ensure children are protected from harm requires sound professional judgements to be made. It is demanding work that can be distressing and stressful. All of those involved should have access to advice and support from, for example, peers, managers, or named and designated professionals.

5.155 For many practitioners involved in day-to-day work with children and families, effective supervision is important to promote good standards of practice and to support individual staff members. Supervision should help to ensure that practice is soundly based and consistent with LSCB and organisational procedures. It should ensure that practitioners fully understand their roles, responsibilities and the scope of their professional discretion and authority. It should also help to identify the training and development needs of practitioners, so that each has the skills to provide an effective service.

5.156 Supervision should include reflecting on, scrutinising and evaluating the work carried out, assessing the strengths and weaknesses of the practitioner and providing coaching, development and pastoral support. Supervisors should be available to practitioners as an important source of advice and expertise, and may be required to endorse judgements at certain key points in time. Supervisors should also record key decisions within the child's case records.

Flow chart 1: Referral

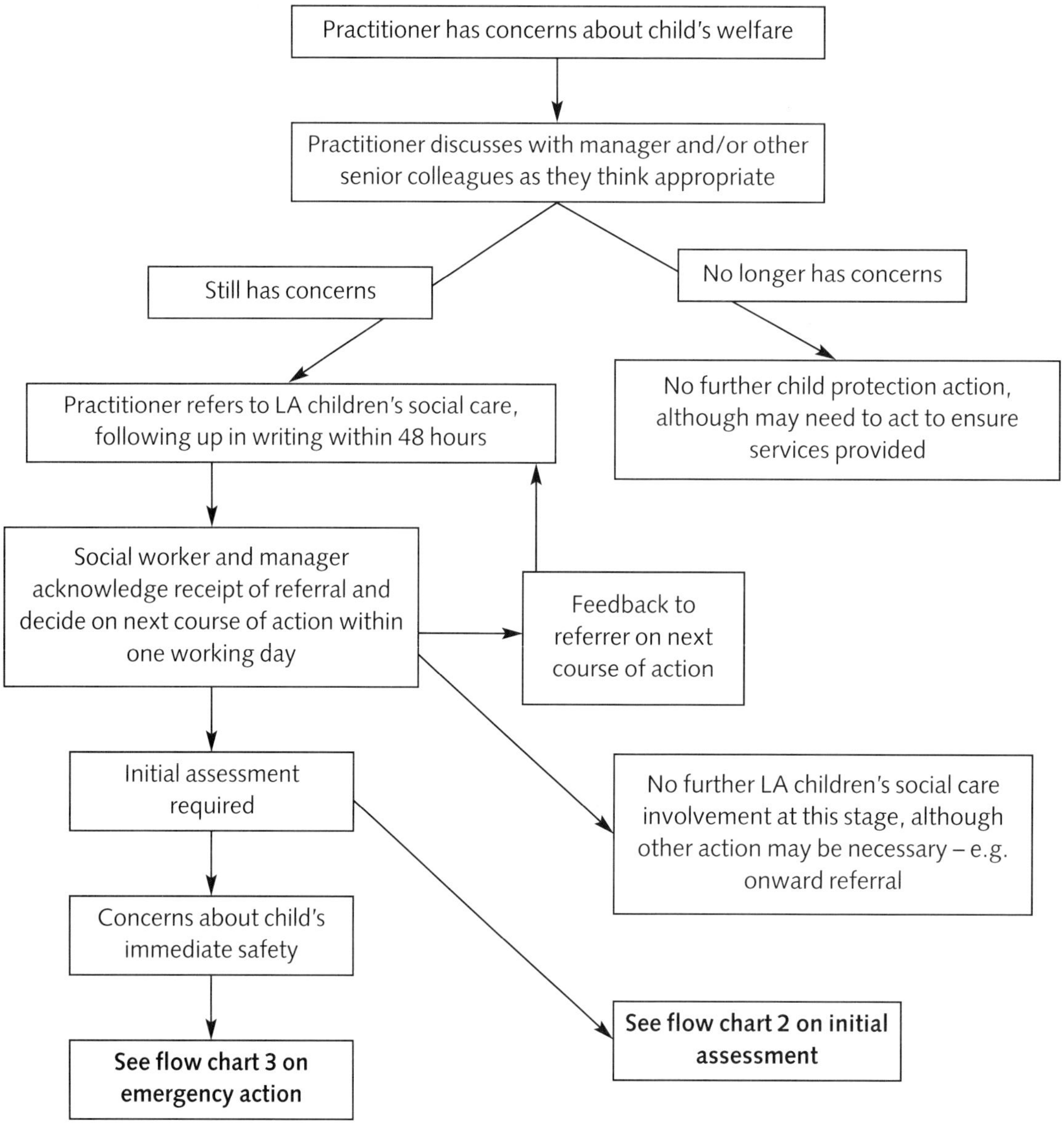

Flow chart 2: What happens following initial assessment?

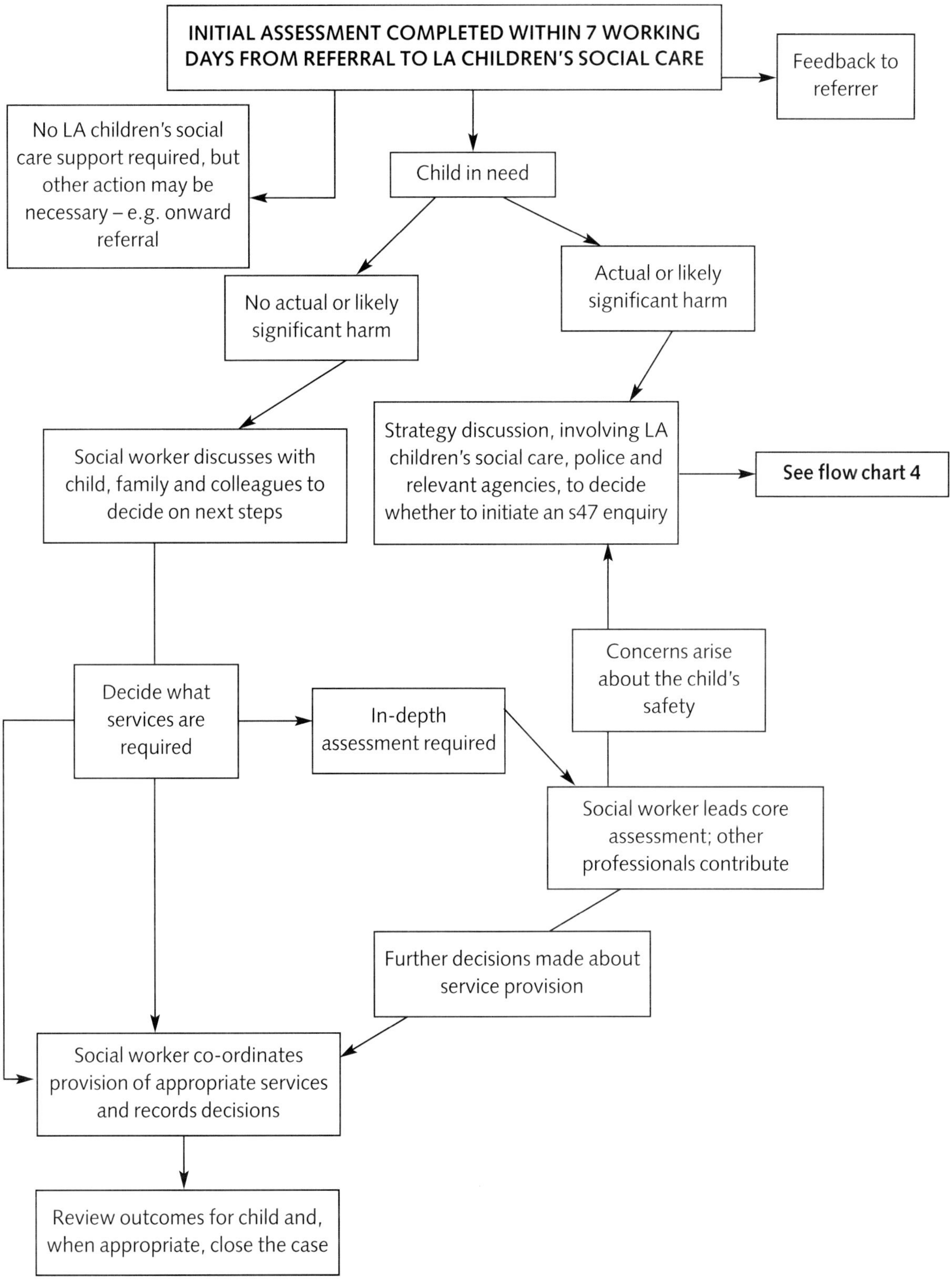

Flow chart 3: Urgent action to safeguard children

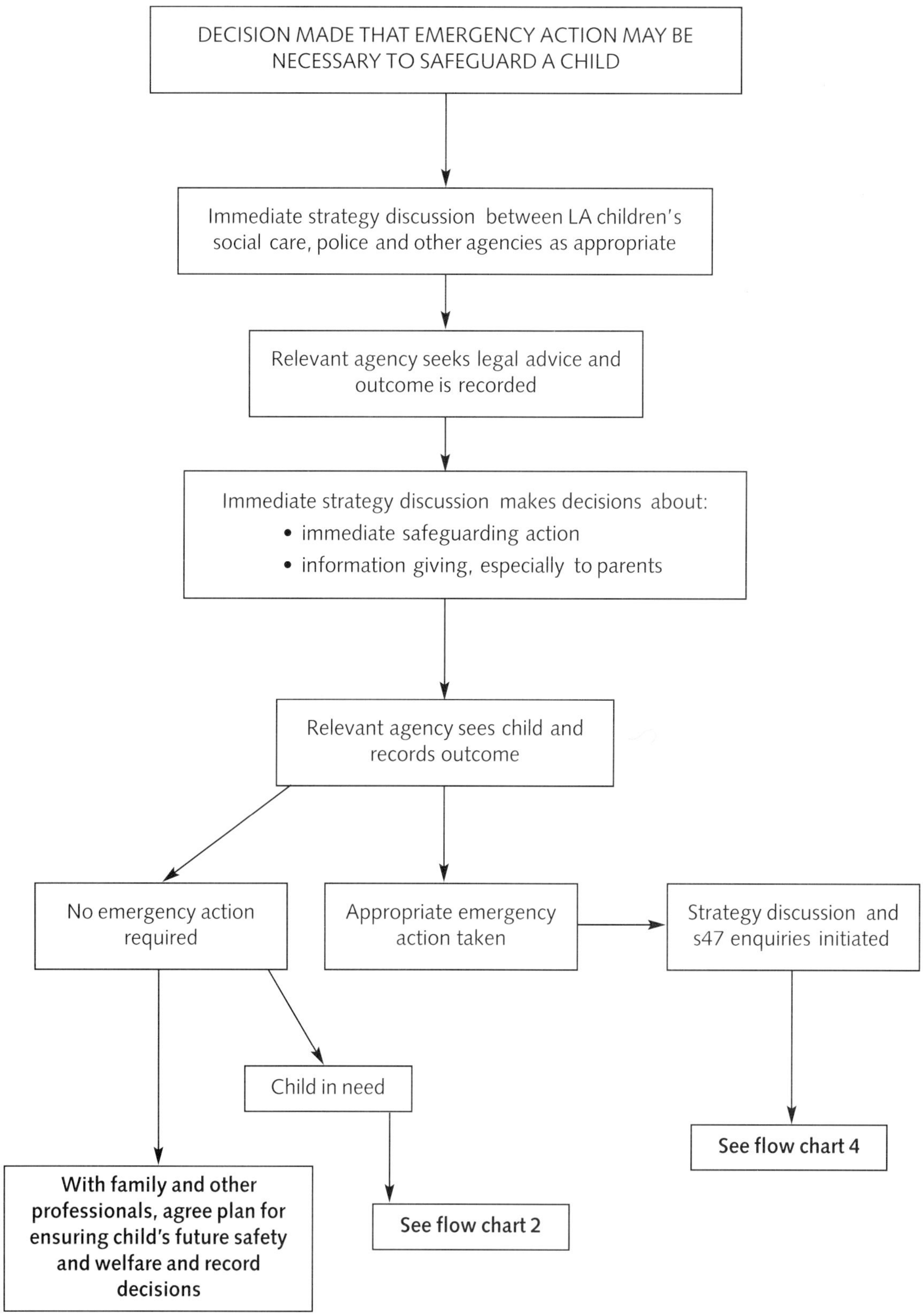

Flow chart 4: What happens after the strategy discussion?

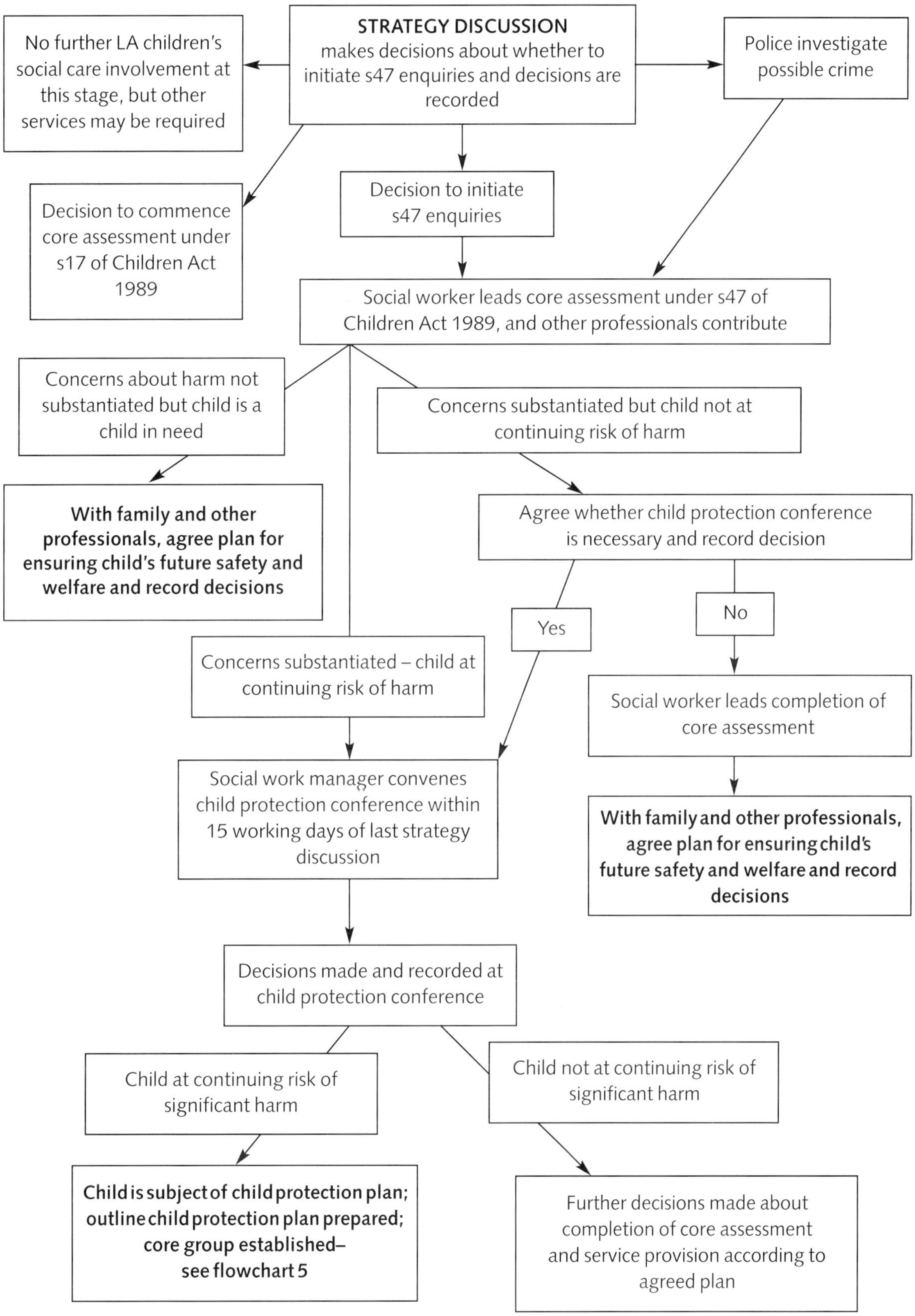

Flow chart 5: What happens after the child protection conference, including the review process?

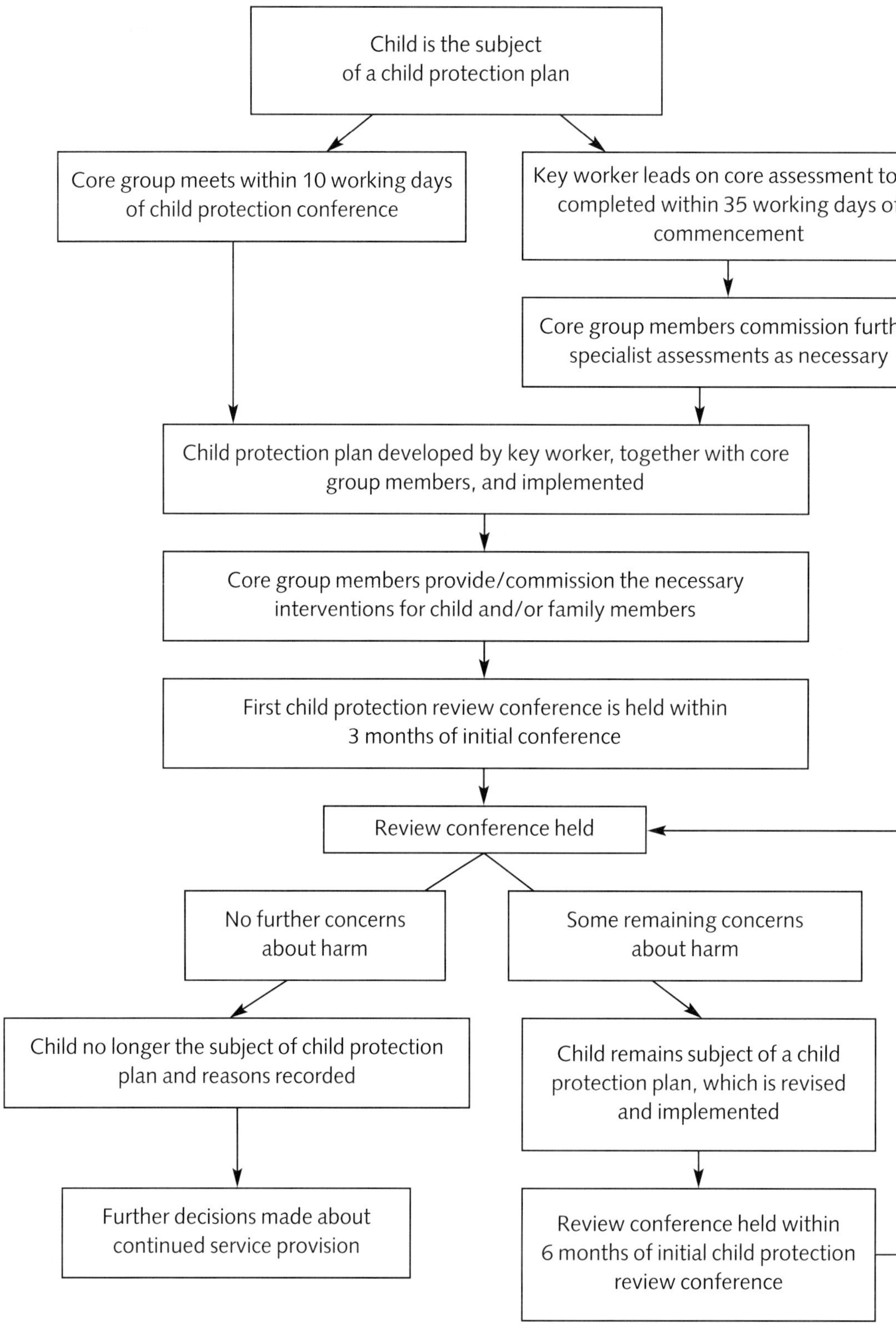

Chapter 6 – Supplementary guidance on safeguarding and promoting the welfare of children

Introduction

6.1 This chapter summarises supplementary guidance to *Working Together to Safeguard Children* and other guidance relevant to safeguarding and promoting children's welfare. The supplementary guidance follows the processes set out in Chapter 5 on how to respond to concerns about the welfare of a child or children, but is developed in more detail to reflect the specialist nature of the particular issues covered.

Children abused through prostitution

6.2 Children involved in prostitution and other forms of commercial sexual exploitation should be treated primarily as the victims of abuse, and their needs require careful assessment. They are likely to be in need of welfare services and, in many cases, protection under the Children Act 1989 (see www.crimereduction.gov.uk/toolkits for further guidance). This group may include children who have been victims of human trafficking. The LSCB should actively enquire into the extent to which children are involved in prostitution in the local area. They should assume that this is a local issue unless there is clear evidence to the contrary. The Home Office and Department of Health jointly published guidance in May 2000 on *Safeguarding Children Involved in Prostitution*. The guidance promotes an approach whereby agencies should work together to:

- recognise the problem
- treat the child primarily as a victim of abuse
- safeguard the children involved and promote their welfare
- work together to prevent abuse and provide children with opportunities and strategies to exit from prostitution; and
- investigate and prosecute those who coerce, exploit and abuse children.

6.3 The guidance states that local agencies should develop inter-agency protocols to guide action when there are concerns that a child is involved in prostitution, including guidance on sharing concerns about a child's safety. The protocols should be consistent with LSCB procedures for safeguarding and promoting the welfare of children, with procedures for working with children in need, and with relevant aspects of youth offending protocols. The identification of a child involved in prostitution, or at risk of being drawn into prostitution, should always trigger the agreed local procedures to ensure the child's safety and welfare, and to enable the police to gather evidence about abusers and coercers. The strong links that have been identified between prostitution, running away from home, human trafficking and substance misuse should be borne in mind in the development of protocols.

Fabricated or induced illness (FII)

6.4 Concerns may be raised when it is considered that the health or development of a child is likely to be significantly or further impaired by a parent or caregiver who has fabricated or induced illness. These concerns may arise when:

- reported symptoms and signs found on examination are not explained by any medical condition from which the child may be suffering; or
- physical examination and results of medical investigations do not explain reported symptoms and signs; or
- there is an inexplicably poor response to prescribed medication and other treatment; or
- new symptoms are reported on resolution of previous ones; or
- reported symptoms and found signs are not seen to begin in the absence of the caregiver; or
- over time, the child is repeatedly presented by the parent or caregiver with a range of symptoms; or
- the child's normal activities are being curtailed beyond what might be expected for any medical disorder from which the child is known to suffer.

There may be a number of explanations for these circumstances, and each requires careful consideration and review. Concerns about a child's health or suspicion of FII should be discussed with the GP or paediatrician responsible for the child's health.

6.5 There are three main ways of fabricating or inducing illness in a child:

- fabrication of signs and symptoms – this may include fabrication of past medical history
- fabrication of signs and symptoms and falsification of hospital charts and records, and specimens of bodily fluids – this may also include falsification of letters and documents
- induction of illness by a variety of means.

These are not mutually exclusive.

6.6 In 2002 the Government published *Safeguarding Children in Whom Illness is Fabricated or Induced* (found at: www.dh.gov.uk/PublicationsAndStatistics/Publications/PublicationsPolicyAndGuidance/fs/en). This Guidance provides a national framework within which agencies and professionals at a local level – individually and jointly – draw up and agree their own more detailed ways of working together where illness may be being fabricated or induced in a child by a caregiver who has parenting responsibilities for him or her. LSCBs should incorporate this Guidance, and its references to covert video surveillance, into their local procedures for safeguarding and promoting the welfare of children, rather than having separate procedures on fabricated or induced illness in children. Within the local procedures, the section on the use of covert video surveillance should make reference to the good practice advice for police officers, which is available to them from the National Crime Faculty.

Investigating complex (organised or multiple) abuse

6.7 Complex (organised or multiple) abuse may be defined as abuse involving one or more abusers and a number of children. The abusers concerned may be acting in concert to abuse children, sometimes acting in isolation, or may be using an institutional framework or position of authority to recruit children for abuse.

6.8 Complex abuse occurs both as part of a network of abuse across a family or community, and within institutions such as residential homes or schools. Such abuse is profoundly traumatic for the children who become involved. Its investigation is time-consuming and demanding work, requiring specialist skills from both police and social work staff. Some investigations become extremely complex, because of the number of places and people involved and the timescale over which abuse is alleged to have occurred. The complexity is heightened where, as in historical cases, the alleged victims are no longer living in the setting where the incidents occurred, or where the alleged perpetrators are no longer linked to the setting or employment role.

6.9 Each investigation of organised or multiple abuse is different, according to the characteristics of each situation and the scale and complexity of the investigation. Although there has been much reporting in recent years about complex abuse in residential settings, complex abuse can occur in day care, in families, and in other provisions such as youth services, sports clubs and voluntary groups. Children being abused via the use of the internet is a new form of abuse that agencies have to address.

6.10 Each complex abuse case requires thorough planning, good inter-agency working, and attention to the welfare needs of the child victims or adult survivors involved. The guidance, *Complex Child Abuse Investigations: Inter-agency issues* (Home Office and Department of Health, 2002) (found at: www.dh.gov.uk/PublicationsAndStatistics/Publications/PublicationsPolicyAndGuidance/fs/en) seeks to help agencies confronted with difficult investigations by sharing the accumulated learning from serious case reviews. It sets out the overarching policy and practice framework to inform and shape the detailed strategic plans that agencies will need to develop when confronted with a complex child abuse case. It does not, however, provide detailed operational guidance on all aspects of such investigations. This guidance is equally relevant to investigating organised or multiple abuse within an institution. In addition, Appendix A in the *Complex Child Abuse Investigations* guidance identifies the issues that should be addressed in all major investigations, and that should be reflected in local procedures.

Female genital mutilation

6.11 Female genital mutilation (FGM) is a collective term for procedures that include the removal of part or all of the external female genitalia, for cultural or other non-therapeutic reasons. The practice is medically unnecessary, extremely painful and has serious health consequences, both at the time when the mutilation is carried out and in later life. The procedure is typically performed on girls aged between four and 13, but in some cases FGM is performed on newborn infants or on young women before marriage or pregnancy. A number of girls die as a direct result of the procedure, from blood loss or infection.

6.12 FGM has been a criminal offence in the UK since the Prohibition of Female Circumcision Act 1985 was passed. The Female Genital Mutilation Act 2003 replaced the 1985 Act and makes it an offence, for the first time, for UK nationals or permanent UK residents to carry out FGM abroad, or to aid, abet, counsel or procure the carrying out of FGM abroad, even in countries where the practice is legal. Further information about the Act can be found in *Home Office Circular 10/2004*, which is available at www.homeoffice.gov.uk.

6.13 FGM is much more common than most people realise, both worldwide and in the UK. It is reportedly practised in 28 African countries and in parts of the Middle and Far East, but is increasingly found in Western Europe and other developed countries, primarily among immigrant and refugee communities. There are substantial populations from countries where FGM is endemic in London, Liverpool, Birmingham, Sheffield and Cardiff, but it is likely that communities in which FGM is practised reside throughout the UK.

6.14 Suspicions may arise in a number of ways that a child is being prepared for FGM to take place abroad. These include knowing that the family belongs to a community in which FGM is practised and is making preparations for the child to take a holiday, arranging vaccinations or planning absence from school. The child may also talk about a 'special procedure' taking place. Indicators that FGM may already have occurred include prolonged absence from school, with noticeable behaviour change on return and long periods away from classes or other normal activities, possibly with bladder or menstrual problems. Midwives and doctors may become aware that FGM has been practised on an older woman, and this may prompt concern for female children in the same family.

6.15 A local authority (LA) may exercise its powers under s47 of the Children Act 1989 if it has reason to believe that a child has suffered, or is likely to suffer, FGM. However, despite the very severe health consequences, parents and others who have this done to their daughters do not intend it as an act of abuse. They genuinely believe that it is in the girl's best interests to conform to their prevailing custom. So, where a child has been identified as at risk of significant harm, it may not be appropriate to consider removing the child from an otherwise loving family environment. Where a child appears to be in immediate danger of mutilation, consideration should be given to getting a prohibited steps order. If a child has already undergone FGM, particular attention should be paid to the potential risk of harm to other female children in the same family.

6.16 In local areas where there are communities who traditionally practise FGM, consideration should be given to incorporating more detailed guidance on responding to concerns about FGM into existing procedures to safeguard and promote the welfare of children. LSCB policy should focus on a preventive strategy involving community education. Further information in support of these guidelines can be found in *Local Authority Social Services Letter LASSL (2004)4*, which is available at www.dfes.gov.uk.

Forced marriage

6.17 A forced marriage is a marriage conducted without the full consent of both parties and where duress is a factor.

6.18 In 2004 the Government's definition of domestic violence was extended to include acts perpetrated by extended family members as well as intimate partners. Consequently, acts such as forced marriage and other so-called 'honour crimes', which can include abduction and homicide, can now come under the definition of domestic violence. Many of these acts are committed against children. The Government's Forced Marriage Unit produced guidelines, in conjunction with children's social care and the Department for Education and Skills, on how to identify and support young people threatened by forced marriage. The guidelines are available at www.adss.org.uk/publications/guidance/marriage.pdf and www.homeoffice.gov.uk/comrace/race/forcedmarriage/index.html.

6.19 If there are concerns that a child (male or female) is in danger of a forced marriage, local agencies and professionals should contact the Forced Marriage Unit, where experienced caseworkers are able to offer support and guidance (www.fco.gov.uk or 020 7008 0230). The police and children's social care should also be contacted. All those involved should bear in mind that **mediation as a response to forced marriage can be extremely dangerous**. Refusal to go through with a forced marriage has, in the past, been linked to so-called 'honour crimes'.

Allegations of abuse made against a person who works with children

6.20 Children can be subjected to abuse by those who work with them in any and every setting. All allegations of abuse or maltreatment of children by a professional, staff member, foster carer or volunteer must therefore be taken seriously and treated in accordance with consistent procedures. LSCBs have responsibility for ensuring that there are effective inter-agency procedures in place for dealing with allegations against people who work with children, and for monitoring and evaluating the effectiveness of those procedures – see Chapter 3.

6.21 In evaluating the effectiveness of local procedures, LSCBs should have regard to the need to complete cases expeditiously. Data about allegations made against education staff show that it is reasonable to expect that 80 per cent of cases should be resolved within one month, 90 per cent within three months, and all but the most exceptional cases should be completed within 12 months. However, it is unlikely that cases which require a criminal prosecution or a complex police investigation can be completed in less than three months.

6.22 All organisations that provide services for children, or provide staff or volunteers to work with or care for children, should operate a procedure for handling such allegations that is consistent with the guidance in Appendix 5.[27]

6.23 LSCB member organisations should have a named senior officer who has overall responsibility for:

- ensuring that the organisation operates procedures for dealing with allegations in accordance with the guidance in Appendix 5
- resolving any inter-agency issues; and
- liaising with the LSCB on the subject.

County-level and unitary LAs should also designate officers to be involved in the management and oversight of individual cases – providing advice and guidance to employers and voluntary organisations, liaising with the police and other agencies, and monitoring the progress of cases to ensure that they are dealt with as quickly as possible, consistent with a thorough and fair process.

6.24 Police forces should also identify officers to fill similar roles. There should be a senior officer to have strategic oversight of the arrangements, liaise with the LSCBs in the force area and ensure compliance. There should be others, perhaps unit managers, who are responsible for liaising with the designated LA officer(s), taking part in the strategy discussion (see paragraphs 5.54–5.59), subsequently reviewing the progress of those cases in which there is a police investigation, and sharing information on completion of the investigation or any prosecution.

[27] Specific advice for the education sector was published in November 2005, *Safeguarding Children in Education: Dealing with Allegations of Abuse Against Teachers and Other Staff*

6.25 The scope of inter-agency procedures in this area is not limited to allegations involving significant harm, or risk of significant harm, to a child. The guidance in Appendix 5 should be followed in respect of any allegation that a person who works with children has:

- behaved in a way that has harmed, or may have harmed, a child
- possibly committed a criminal offence against, or related to, a child; or
- behaved towards a child or children in a way that indicates s/he is unsuitable to work with children

in connection with the person's employment or voluntary activity. If concerns arise about the person's behaviour in regard to his/her own children, the police and/or social care need to consider informing the person's employer in order to assess whether there may be implications for children with whom the person has contact at work.

6.26 The child or children concerned should receive appropriate support. They and their parents or carers should be helped to understand the process, told the result of any enquiry or disciplinary process and, where necessary, helped to understand the outcomes reached.[28] The provision of information and advice must take place in a manner that does not impede the proper exercise of enquiry, disciplinary and investigative processes.

6.27 Staff, foster carers, volunteers and other individuals about whom there are concerns should be treated fairly and honestly, and should be provided with support throughout the investigation process, as should others who are involved. They should be helped to understand the concerns expressed and the processes being operated, and be clearly informed of the outcome of any investigation and the implications for disciplinary or related processes. However, the police and other relevant agencies should always be consulted before informing a person who is the subject of allegations that may possibly require a criminal investigation.

6.28 There have been a number of widely reported cases of historical abuse, usually of an organised or multiple nature (see paragraph 6.9). Such cases have generally come to light after adults have reported abuse that they experienced as children, while living away from home in settings provided by LAs, the voluntary sector or independent providers. When such allegations are made, they should be responded to in the same way as contemporary concerns. In those cases it is also important to find out whether the person accused is still working with children and, if so, to inform the person's current employer or voluntary organisation.

6.29 Those undertaking investigations should be alert to any sign or pattern that suggests that the abuse is more widespread or organised than it appears at first sight, or that it involves other perpetrators or institutions. It is important not to assume that initial

28 In deciding what information to disclose, careful consideration should be given to duties under the Data Protection Act 1998, the law of confidence and, where relevant, the Humans Right Act 1998.

signs are necessarily related directly to abuse, and to consider occasions where boundaries have been blurred, inappropriate behaviour has taken place, and matters such as fraud, deception or pornography have been involved.

6.30 If an allegation is substantiated, the managers or commissioners of the relevant service should think widely about the lessons of the case and how they should be acted on. This should include whether there are features of the organisation that may have contributed to, or failed to prevent, the abuse occurring. In some circumstances, a serious case review may be appropriate (see Chapter 8).

Chapter 7 – Child death review processes

Introduction

7.1 This chapter sets out the procedures to be followed when a child dies in the LSCB area(s) covered by the Child Death Overview Panel. There are two interrelated processes for reviewing child deaths (either of which can trigger a Serious Case Review – see paragraph 8.2):

a. a rapid response by a group of key professionals who come together for the purpose of enquiring into and evaluating each unexpected death of a child (see paragraphs 7.18–7.49)

b. an overview of all child deaths (under 18 years) in the LSCB area(s), undertaken by a panel (see paragraphs 7.50–7.56).

Overall principles

7.2 Each unexpected death of a child is a tragedy for his or her family, and subsequent enquiries/investigations should keep an appropriate balance between forensic and medical requirements and the family's need for support. Children with a known disability or a medical condition should be responded to in the same manner as other children. A minority of unexpected deaths are the consequence of abuse or neglect, or are found to have abuse or neglect as an associated factor. In all cases, enquiries should seek to understand the reasons for the child's death, address the possible needs of other children in the household, the needs of all family members, and also consider any lessons to be learnt about how best to safeguard and promote children's welfare in the future.

7.3 Families should be treated with sensitivity, discretion and respect at all times, and professionals should approach their enquiries with an open mind.

The Regulations relating to child deaths

7.4 One of the LSCB functions, set out in Regulation 6, in relation to the deaths of any children normally resident in their area is as follows:

(a) collecting and analysing information about each death with a view to identifying –

(i) any case giving rise to the need for a review mentioned in Regulation 5(1)(e);

(ii) any matters of concern affecting the safety and welfare of children in the area of the authority; and

(iii) any wider public health or safety concerns arising from a particular death or from a pattern of deaths in that area;

(b) putting in place procedures for ensuring that there is a coordinated response by the authority, their Board partners and other relevant persons to an unexpected death.

7.5 As explained in Chapter 3, the LSCB regulations mean that the child death review functions will become compulsory on 1 April 2008, but can be carried out by any LSCB from 1 April 2006. This chapter should not be regarded as statutory guidance in every local authority area until 1 April 2008, but when an LSCB takes on this function before that date, it should follow the guidance in this chapter.

Definition of an unexpected death of a child

7.6 In this guidance an unexpected death is defined as the death of a child that was not anticipated as a significant possibility 24 hours before the death, or where there was a similarly unexpected collapse leading to or precipitating the events that led to the death (Fleming et al., 2000; The Royal College of Pathologists and the Royal College of Paediatrics and Child Health, 2004).[29, 30] The designated paediatrician responsible for unexpected deaths in childhood (see paragraph 7.18) should be consulted where professionals are uncertain about whether the death is unexpected. If in doubt, these procedures should be followed until the available evidence enables a different decision to be made.

LSCB responsibilities for the child death review processes

7.7 A sub-committee of the LSCB(s) should be responsible for reviewing information on all child deaths, and should be accountable to the LSCB Chair. The disclosure of information about a deceased child is to enable the LSCB to carry out its statutory functions relating to child deaths. The LSCB should use the aggregated findings from all child deaths, collected according to a nationally agreed minimum data set[31], to inform local strategic planning on how best to safeguard and promote the welfare of the children in their area.

7.8 Neighbouring LSCBs may decide to share a Child Death Overview Panel, depending on the local configuration of services and population served. (Experience shows that the

29 Fleming, P. J., Blair, P. S., Bacon, C. and Berry, P. J. (2000). *Sudden Unexpected Death in Infancy. The CESDI SUDI Studies 1993-1996*. London: The Stationery Office. ISBN 0 11 3222 9988.

30 Royal College of Pathologists and the Royal College of Paediatrics and Child Health (2004). *Sudden unexpected death in infancy. A multi-agency protocol for care and investigation. The Report of a working group convened by the Royal College of Pathologists and the Royal College of Paediatrics and Child Health.* London: Royal College of Pathologists and the Royal College of Paediatrics and Child Health. www.rcpath.org

31 This data set is being developed by The Confidential Enquiry into Maternal and Child Health (CEMACH) www.cemach.org.uk/child_health_enquiry1.htm

population to be covered should be greater than 500,000.) In this situation the LSCBs should agree lines of accountability with the Child Death Overview Panel in accordance with this guidance.

7.9 Guidance in this chapter relates to the deaths of all children and young people from birth (excluding those babies who are stillborn) up to the age of 18 years. In 2004 there were 3,026 infant deaths and 1,680 child deaths in England. Implementation of some parts of the guidance may therefore need to take into account the needs of different age groups.

7.10 In each partner agency of the LSCB(s), a senior person with relevant expertise should be identified as having responsibility for advising on the implementation of the local procedures on responding to child deaths within their agency. Each agency should expect to be involved in a child's death at some time.

7.11 Each PCT should have access to a consultant paediatrician who has a designated role to provide advice on:

- the commissioning of paediatric services from paediatricians with expertise in undertaking enquiries into unexpected deaths in childhood and the medical investigative services such as radiology, laboratory and histopathology services; and
- the organisation of such services.

The designated paediatrician for unexpected deaths in childhood may provide advice to more than one PCT, and is likely to be a member of the local child death overview panel. This is a separate role to the designated doctor for child protection, but is not necessarily be filled by a different person. These responsibilities should be recognised in the job plan agreed between the consultant and his/her employer.

7.12 The LSCB should ensure that appropriate single and inter-agency training (see Chapter 4) is made available to ensure successful implementation of these procedures. LSCB partner agencies should ensure that relevant staff have access to this training.

7.13 The paragraphs below set out the roles of the various professionals for enquiring into and evaluating all unexpected child deaths, reaching conclusions about whether and how they could have been prevented, and undertaking an overview of the deaths of all children normally resident in the LSCB area(s). When a child dies unexpectedly, several investigative processes may be instigated, particularly when abuse or neglect is a factor. This guidance intends that the relevant professionals and organisations work together in a co-ordinated way, in order to minimize duplication and ensure that the lessons learnt contribute to safeguarding and promoting the welfare of children in the future.

Other related processes

7.14 Where there is an ongoing criminal investigation, the Crown Prosecution Service must be consulted as to what it is appropriate for the professionals to be doing, and what actions to take in order not to prejudice any criminal proceeding.

7.15 Where a child dies unexpectedly, all Trusts, including PCTs, should follow their locally agreed procedures for reporting and handling serious patient safety incidents (see the National Patient Safety Agency's website www.npsa.nhs.uk and the core standard on patient safety in the *Standards for Better Health* www.dh.gov.uk/publications).

7.16 If it is thought, at any time, that the criteria for a serious case review might apply, the Chair of the LSCB should be contacted and the serious case review procedures set out in the next chapter should be followed.

7.17 If, during the enquiries, concerns are expressed in relation to the needs of surviving children in the family, discussions should take place with LA children's social care. It may be decided that it is appropriate to initiate an initial assessment using the *Framework for the Assessment of Children in Need and their Families* (2000). If concerns are raised at any stage about the possibility of surviving children in the household being abused or neglected, the inter-agency procedures set out in Chapter 5 in this guidance should be followed. LA children's social care has lead responsibility for safeguarding and promoting the welfare of children. The police will be the lead agency for any criminal investigation. The police must be informed immediately that there is a suspicion of a crime, to ensure that the evidence is properly secured and that any further interviews with family members and other relevant people accord with the requirements of the Police and Criminal Evidence Act 1984.

Roles and responsibilities when responding rapidly to an unexpected death of a child

7.18 It is intended that those professionals involved (before or after the death) with a child who dies unexpectedly should come together to enquire into and evaluate the child's death. This means that some roles may require an on-call rota for responding to unexpected child deaths in their area. The work of the team convened in response to each child's death should be co-ordinated, usually, by a local designated paediatrician responsible for unexpected deaths in childhood. LSCBs may choose to designate particular professionals to be standing members of a team because of their roles and particular expertise. The professionals who come together as a team will carry out their normal functions – i.e. as a paediatrician, GP, nurse, health visitor, midwife, mental health professional, social worker, probation or police officer – in response to the unexpected death of a child in accordance with this guidance. They should also work according to a protocol agreed with the local coronial service. The joint responsibilities of these professionals include:

- responding quickly to the unexpected death of a child

- making immediate enquiries into and evaluating the reasons for and circumstances of the death, in agreement with the Coroner
- undertaking the types of enquiries/investigations that relate to the current responsibilities of their respective organisations when a child dies unexpectedly. This includes liaising with those who have ongoing responsibilities for other family members
- collecting information in a standard, nationally agreed manner
- following the death through and maintaining contact at regular intervals with family members and other professionals who have ongoing responsibilities for other family members, to ensure they are informed and kept up-to-date with information about the child's death.

Procedures for a rapid response from professionals to all unexpected deaths of children (0–18 years)

Care of parents/family members

7.19 Where a child has died in, or been taken to, a hospital their parents/carers should be allocated a member of the hospital staff to remain with and support them throughout the process. The parents should normally be given the opportunity to hold and spend time with their baby or child. During this time the allocated member of staff should maintain a discreet presence.

7.20 Within the local procedures there should be provision for an identified professional to provide similar support to families where the child has died and not been taken to a hospital.

7.21 Where a child is living in England but their parents live abroad, careful consideration should be given to how best to contact and support the bereaved family members.

7.22 Parents/carers should be kept up-to-date with information about their child's death and the involvement of each professional, unless such sharing of information would jeopardise police investigations or other criminal processes.

Responding to the unexpected death of a child

7.23 The type of response to each child's unexpected death will depend to a certain extent on the age of the child, but there are some key elements that underpin all subsequent work. Supplementary information is required for making enquiries into, for example, infant deaths, deaths that are the result of trauma, deaths in hospital and suicides.

7.24 Once the death of a child has been referred to the Coroner and s/he has accepted it, the Coroner has jurisdiction over the body and all that pertains to it. Coroners must therefore be consulted over the local implementation of national procedures and protocols, and should be asked to give general approval for the measures agreed to reduce the need to obtain specific approval on each occasion.

7.25 A multi-professional approach is required to ensure collaboration among all involved, including ambulance staff, A&E department staff, Coroners' Officers, police, GPs, health visitors, school nurses, midwives, paediatricians, mental health professionals, hospital bereavement staff, voluntary agencies, Coroners, pathologists, forensic medical examiners, LA children's social care, probation, schools, and any others who may find themselves with a contribution to make in individual cases (e.g. fire fighters or faith leaders).

Immediate response to the unexpected death of a child taken to a hospital

7.26 Babies who die suddenly and unexpectedly at home should be taken to an A&E department rather than a mortuary, and resuscitation should always be initiated unless clearly inappropriate. Resuscitation, once commenced, should be continued according to the *UK Resuscitation Guidelines* (2005) (found at: www.resus.org.uk/pages/guide.htm) until an experienced doctor (usually the consultant paediatrician on call) has made a decision that it is appropriate to stop further efforts. Older children may also be taken to A&E unless this is inappropriate (e.g. if the circumstances of the death require the body to remain at the scene for forensic examination).

7.27 As soon as practicable (i.e. as a response to an emergency) after arrival at a hospital, the baby or child should be examined by the consultant paediatrician on call (in some cases this might be together with a consultant in emergency medicine or, for some young people over 16 years of age, the consultant in emergency medicine may be more appropriate than a paediatrician). A detailed and careful history of events leading up to and following the discovery of the child's collapse should be taken from the parents/carers. This should begin the process of collecting a nationally agreed data set. The purpose of obtaining high-quality information at this stage is to understand the cause of the death when appropriate and to identify anything suspicious about it.

7.28 Where the cause of death or factors contributing to it are uncertain, investigative samples should be taken immediately on arrival and after the death is confirmed. These need to be agreed in advance with the Coroner (see paragraph 7.25) and should include the standard set for SUDI (Royal College of Pathologists and Royal College of Paediatrics and Child Health, 2004) and standard sets for other types of death presentation as they are developed. Consideration should always be given to undertaking a full skeletal survey and, when appropriate, it should be made before the autopsy starts as this may significantly alter the required investigations.

7.29 When the baby or child is pronounced dead, the consultant clinician should inform the parents, having first reviewed all the available information. S/he should explain future police and Coroner involvement, including the Coroner's authority to order a postmortem examination. This may involve taking particular tissue blocks and slides to ascertain the cause of death. Consent from those with parental responsibility for the child is required for tissue to be retained beyond the period required by the Coroner (e.g. for use in research or for possible future review).

7.30 The consultant clinician who has seen the child should inform the designated paediatrician with responsibility for unexpected deaths in childhood immediately after the Coroner is informed.

7.31 The same processes apply to a child who is admitted to a hospital ward and subsequently dies unexpectedly in hospital.

Immediate response to the unexpected death of a child in the community

7.32 Where a child is not taken immediately to A&E, the professional confirming the fact of death should inform the designated paediatrician with responsibility for unexpected deaths in childhood at the same time as the Coroner is informed.

7.33 The police will be involved and may decide that it is not appropriate to move the child's body. This may typically occur if there are clear signs that lead to suspicion. In most cases, however, it is expected that the child's body will already have been held or moved by the carer and, therefore, removal to A&E will not normally jeopardize an investigation.

Whenever and wherever an unexpected death of a child has occurred

7.34 The professional confirming the fact of death should consult the designated paediatrician with responsibility for unexpected deaths in childhood, who will ensure that relevant professionals (i.e. the Coroner, the police and LA children's social care) are informed of the death. This task may be undertaken by a person on behalf of the designated paediatrician. Contact may be required with more than one LA if the child died away from home. Any relevant information identified by LA children's social care should be shared promptly with the police and on-call paediatrician. The health visitor or school nurse and GP should also be informed as a matter of routine and relevant information should be shared.

7.35 When a child dies unexpectedly, a paediatrician (on-call or designated) should initiate an immediate information-sharing and planning discussion between the lead agencies (i.e. health, police and LA children's social care) to decide what should happen next and who will do what. This will also include the Coroner's Officer and consultant paediatrician on call, and any others who are involved (e.g. the GP if called out by family or, for older children, the professional certifying the fact of death if s/he has already been involved in the child's care/death). The agreed plan should include a commitment to collaborate closely and communicate as often as necessary, often by telephone. Where the death occurred in a hospital, the plan should also address the actions required by the Trust's serious incidents protocol. Where the death occurred in a custodial setting, the plan should ensure appropriate liaison with the investigator from the Prisons and Probation Ombudsman.

7.36 For all unexpected deaths of children (including those not seen in A&E) urgent contact should be made with any other agencies who know or are involved with the child (including CAMHS, school or early years) to inform them of the child's death and to obtain information on the history of the child, the family and other members of the household. If a young person is under the supervision of a Youth Offending Team (Yot), the Yot should also be approached.

7.37 The police will begin an investigation into the sudden or unexpected death of a child on behalf of the Coroner. They will carry this out in accordance with relevant ACPO guidelines.

7.38 When a baby or older child dies unexpectedly in a non-hospital setting, the senior investigating officer and senior healthcare professional should make a decision about whether a visit to the place where the child died should be undertaken. This should almost always take place for infants who die unexpectedly (see paragraph 5.1 in the Kennedy Report).[32] As well as deciding if the visit should take place, it should be decided how soon (within 24 hours) and who should attend. It is likely to be a senior investigating police officer and a healthcare professional (experienced in responding to unexpected child deaths and who may be a paediatrician) who will visit, talk with the parents and inspect the scene. They may make this visit together, or they may visit separately and then confer (details should be included in the local child death review protocol). After this visit the senior investigating police officer, visiting health care professional, GP, health visitor or school nurse and children's social care representative should review whether there is any additional information that could raise concerns about the possibility of abuse or neglect having contributed to the child's death. If there are concerns about surviving children in the household, the procedures set out in Chapter 5 should be followed. If there are grounds for considering initiating a serious case review, the process set out in Chapter 8 should be followed.

Involvement of Coroner and pathologist

7.39 If s/he deems it necessary (and in almost all cases of an unexpected child death it will be), the Coroner will order a postmortem examination to be carried out as soon as possible by the most appropriate pathologist available (this may be a paediatric pathologist, forensic pathologist or both) who will perform the examination according to the guidelines and protocols laid down by The Royal College of Pathologists. The designated paediatrician should collate information collected by those involved in responding to the child's death and share it with the pathologist conducting the postmortem in order to inform this process. Where the death may be unnatural, or the cause of death has not yet been determined, the Coroner will in due course hold an inquest.

7.40 All information collected relating to the circumstances of the death – including a review of all relevant medical, social and educational records – must be included in a report

32 *Sudden Unexpected Death in Infancy: a multi-agency protocol for care and investigation. The report of a working party convened by the Royal Colleges of Pathologists and the Royal College of Paediatrics and Child Health* (2004). London: RCPath.

for the Coroner. This report should be delivered to the Coroner within 28 days of the death, unless some of the crucial information is not yet available.

Case discussion following the preliminary results of the postmortem examination becoming available

7.41 The preliminary results of the postmortem examination belong to the commissioning Coroner. In most cases it is possible for these to be discussed by the paediatrician and pathologist, together with the senior investigating police officer, as soon as possible, and the Coroner should be informed immediately of the initial results. At this stage the core data set should be updated and, if necessary, previous information corrected to enable this change to be audited. If the initial postmortem findings or findings from the child's history suggest evidence of abuse or neglect as a possible cause of death, the police, child protection team and LA children's social care should be informed immediately, and the serious case review processes in Chapter 8 of this Guidance should be followed. If there are concerns about surviving children living in the household, the procedures set out in Chapter 5 should be followed with respect to these children.

7.42 In all cases, the designated paediatrician for unexpected child deaths should convene a further multi-agency discussion (usually on the telephone) very shortly after the initial postmortem results are available. This discussion usually takes place five to seven days after the death, and should involve the pathologist, police, LA children's social care and the paediatrician, plus any other relevant healthcare professionals, to review any further information that has come to light and that may raise additional concerns about safeguarding issues.

Case discussion following the final results of the postmortem examination becoming available

7.43 A case discussion meeting should be held as soon as the final postmortem result is available. The timing of this discussion varies according to the circumstances of the death. This may range from immediately after the postmortem to eight to 12 weeks after the death. The type of professionals involved in this meeting depends on the age of the child. The meeting should include those who knew the child and family, and those involved in investigating the death – i.e. the GP, health visitor or school nurse, paediatrician(s), pathologist, senior investigating police officers and, where appropriate, social workers.

7.44 The designated paediatrician with responsibility for unexpected deaths in childhood should convene and chair this meeting. At this stage, the collection of the core data set should be completed and, if necessary, previous information corrected to enable this change to the information to be audited.

7.45 The main purpose of the case discussion is to share information to identify the cause of death and/or those factors that may have contributed to the death, and then to plan future care for the family. Potential lessons to be learnt may also be identified by this process. Another purpose is to inform the inquest.

7.46 There should be an explicit discussion of the possibility of abuse or neglect either causing or contributing to the death. If no evidence is identified to suggest maltreatment, this should be documented as part of the minutes of the meeting.

7.47 It should be agreed how detailed information about the cause of the child's death will be shared, and by whom, with the parents, and who will offer the parents ongoing support.

7.48 The results of the postmortem examination should be discussed with the parents at the earliest opportunity, except in those cases where abuse is suspected and/or the police are conducting a criminal investigation. In these situations, the paediatrician should discuss with LA children's social care, the police and the pathologist what information should be shared with the parents and when. This discussion with the parents is usually part of the role of the paediatrician responsible for the child's care and she or he will, therefore, have responsibility for initiating and leading the meeting. A member of the primary healthcare team should usually attend this meeting.

7.49 An agreed record of the case discussion meeting and all reports should be sent to the Coroner, to take into consideration in the conduct of the inquest and in the cause of death notified to the Registrar of Births and Deaths. The record of the case discussions and the record of the core data set should also be made available to the local Child Death Overview Panel when the child dies away from their residential area (see paragraph 7.52). This information can then be analysed and decisions can be made about what actions should be taken to prevent similar deaths in the future.

Reviewing deaths of all children

7.50 An overview of all child deaths in the LSCB area(s) covered by the Child Death Overview Panel will be undertaken. This is a paper exercise, based on information available from those who were involved in the care of the child, both before and immediately after the death, and other sources including, perhaps, the Coroner. The panel:

- has a fixed core membership to review these cases, with flexibility to co-opt other relevant professionals as and when appropriate
- holds meetings at regular intervals to enable each child's case to be discussed in a timely manner
- reviews the appropriateness of the professionals' responses to each unexpected death of a child, their involvement before the death, and relevant environmental, social, health and cultural aspects of each death, to ensure a thorough consideration of how such deaths might be prevented in the future; and
- identifies any patterns or trends in the local data and reports these to the LSCB.

Procedures to be followed by the local Child Death Overview Panel (for all child deaths)

7.51 The LSCB has responsibility for reviewing the deaths of all children. In order to fulfil its responsibilities, it should be informed of all deaths of children normally resident in its geographical area. The LSCB Chair should decide who will be the designated person to whom the death notification and other data on each death should be sent. The Chair of the Overview Panel is responsible for ensuring that this process operates effectively.

7.52 Deaths should be notified by the professional confirming the fact of the child's death. For unexpected deaths, this will be at the same time as they inform the Coroner and the person designated by the LSCB to be notified of all children's deaths in the area in which the child's death occurred. If this is not the area in which the child is normally resident, the designated person should inform their opposite number in the area where the child normally resides. In these situations, it should be decided on a case-by-case basis which Panel should take responsibility for gathering the necessary information for a Panel's consideration. In some cases this may be done jointly. The Registrar and ONS respectively send a notification of each death to the local PCT, and this provides a check to ensure that all child deaths have been notified to the LSCB Chair. Any professional (or member of the public) hearing of a local child death in circumstances that mean it may not yet be known about (e.g. a death occurring abroad) can inform the Chair of the LSCB.

7.53 The Child Death Overview Panel has a permanent core membership drawn from the key organisations represented on the LSCB (see paragraph 3.58), although not all core members are necessarily involved in discussing all cases. The Panel should include a professional from public health as well as child health. Other members may be co-opted, either as permanent members to reflect the characteristics of the local population (e.g. a representative of a large local ethnic or religious community), to provide a perspective from the independent or voluntary sector, or to contribute to the discussion of certain types of death when they occur (e.g. fire fighters for house fires). The Panel will be chaired by the LSCB Chair or his or her representative, who will be a member of the LSCB. The Panel Chair should not be involved in providing direct services to children and families in the area.

7.54 There should be a clear relationship and agreed channels of communication with the local Coronial Service.

7.55 The functions of the Child Death Overview Panel include:

- implementing, in consultation with the local Coroner, local procedures and protocols that are in line with this guidance on enquiring into unexpected deaths, and evaluating these together with information about all deaths in childhood
- collecting and collating an agreed minimum data set and, where relevant, seeking information from professionals and family members
- meeting frequently to evaluate the routinely collected data (see paragraph 7.50) on the deaths of all children, and thereby identifying lessons to be learnt or issues of concern,

with a particular focus on effective inter-agency working to safeguard and promote the welfare of children

- having a mechanism to evaluate specific cases in depth, where necessary, at subsequent meetings
- monitoring the appropriateness of the response of professionals to an unexpected death of a child, reviewing the reports produced by the rapid response team on each unexpected death of a child, making a full record of this discussion and providing the professionals with feedback on their work. Where there is an ongoing criminal investigation, the Crown Prosecution Service must be consulted as to what it is appropriate for the Panel to consider and what actions it might take in order not to prejudice any criminal proceedings
- referring to the Chair of the LSCB any deaths where, on evaluating the available information, the Panel considers there may be grounds to undertake further enquiries, investigations or a Serious Case Review and explore why this had not previously been recognised
- informing the Chair of the LSCB where specific new information should be passed to the Coroner or other appropriate authorities
- providing relevant information to those professionals involved with the child's family so that they, in turn, can convey this information in a sensitive and timely manner to the family
- monitoring the support and assessment services offered to families of children who have died
- monitoring and advising the LSCB on the resources and training required locally to ensure an effective inter-agency response to child deaths
- organising and monitoring the collection of data for the nationally agreed minimum data set, and making recommendations (to be approved by LSCBs) for any additional data to be collected locally
- identifying any public health issues and considering, with the Director(s) of Public Health, how best to address these and their implications for both the provision of services and for training; and
- co-operating with regional and national initiatives – e.g. the Confidential Enquiry into Maternal and Child Health (CEMACH) (found at: www.cemach.org.uk/) – to identify lessons on the prevention of unexpected child deaths.

7.56 The Child Death Overview Panel is responsible for developing its work plan, which should be approved by the LSCB. It will prepare an annual report for the LSCB, which is responsible for publishing relevant, anonymised information.

7.57 The LSCB takes responsibility for disseminating the lessons to be learnt to all relevant organisations, ensures that relevant findings inform the Children and Young People's Plan and acts on any recommendations to improve policy, professional practice and inter-agency working to safeguard and promote the welfare of children. The LSCB is also required to supply data regularly on every child death to bodies commissioned by the Department for Education and Skills, so that the Department can commission bodies to undertake and publish nationally comparable, anonymised analyses of these deaths.

Flow chart 6: Interface between the child death and serious case review processes

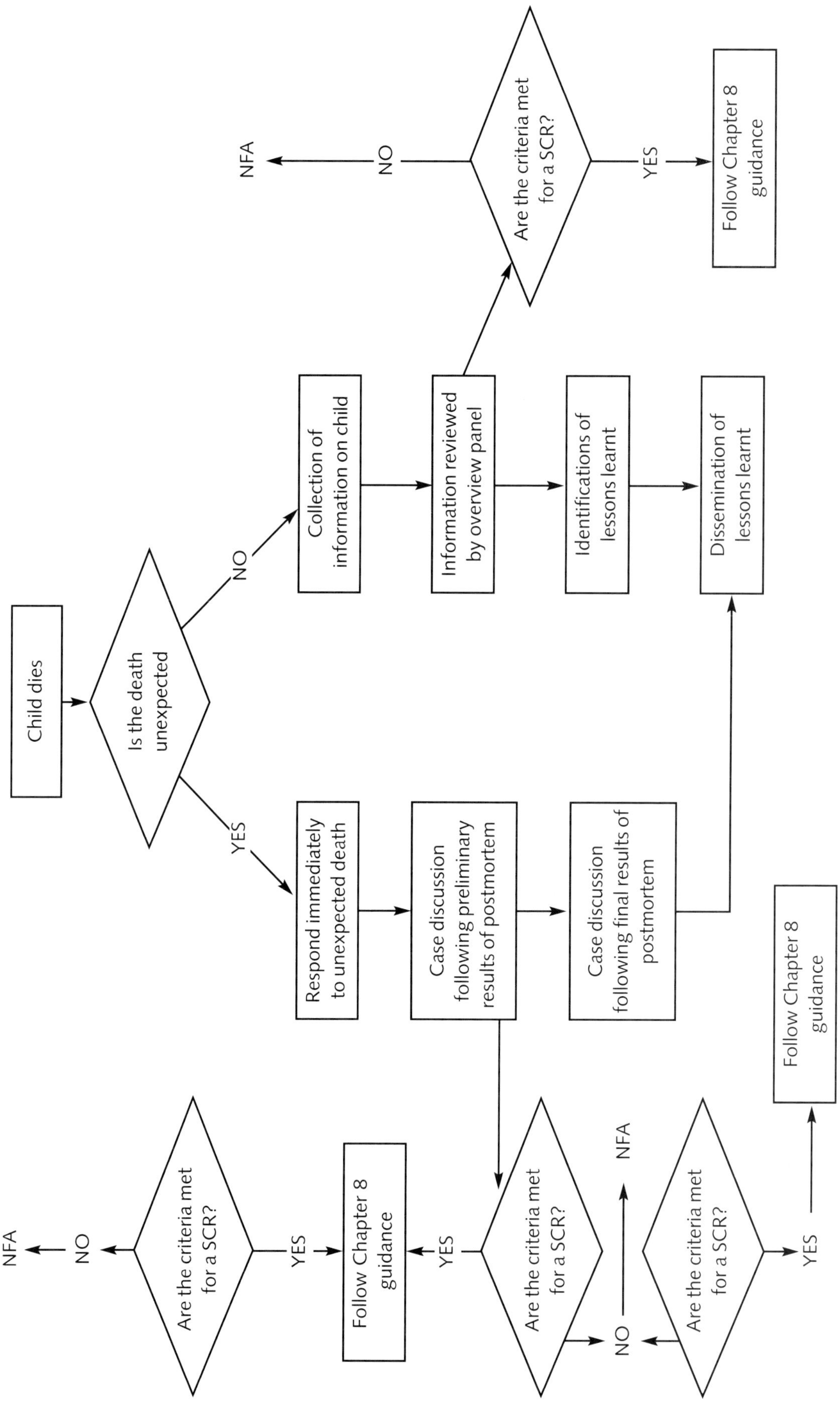

Chapter 8 – Serious case reviews

Reviewing and investigative functions of LSCBs

8.1 Regulation 5 requires LSCBs to undertake reviews of serious cases. They should be undertaken in accordance with the procedures set out in this chapter. The same criteria apply to disabled children as to non-disabled children.

Serious case reviews

8.2 When a child dies, and abuse or neglect is known or suspected to be a factor in the death, local organisations should consider immediately whether there are other children at risk of harm who require safeguarding (e.g. siblings, or other children in an institution where abuse is alleged). Thereafter, organisations should consider whether there are any lessons to be learnt about the ways in which they work together to safeguard and promote the welfare of children. Consequently, when a child dies in such circumstances, the LSCB should always conduct a serious case review into the involvement with the child and family of organisations and professionals. Additionally, LSCBs should always consider whether a serious case review should be conducted where:

- a child sustains a potentially life-threatening injury or serious and permanent impairment of health and development through abuse or neglect; or
- a child has been subjected to particularly serious sexual abuse; or
- a parent has been murdered and a homicide review is being initiated; or
- a child has been killed by a parent with a mental illness; or
- the case gives rise to concerns about inter-agency working to protect children from harm.

The purpose of serious case reviews

8.3 The purpose of serious case reviews carried out under this guidance is to:

- establish whether there are lessons to be learnt from the case about the way in which local professionals and organisations work together to safeguard and promote the welfare of children
- identify clearly what those lessons are, how they will be acted on, and what is expected to change as a result; and
- as a consequence, improve inter-agency working and better safeguard and promote the welfare of children.

8.4 Serious case reviews are not inquiries into how a child died or who is culpable. That is a matter for Coroners and criminal courts, respectively, to determine as appropriate.

When should a LSCB undertake a serious case review?

8.5 A LSCB should always undertake a serious case review when a child dies (including death by suicide) and abuse or neglect is known or suspected to be a factor in the child's death. This is irrespective of whether LA children's social care is, or has been, involved with the child or family.

8.6 A LSCB should always consider whether to undertake a serious case review where a child has sustained a potentially life-threatening injury through abuse or neglect, serious sexual abuse, or sustained serious and permanent impairment of health or development through abuse or neglect, **and** the case gives rise to concerns about the way in which local professionals and services work together to safeguard and promote the welfare of children. This includes situations where a parent has been killed in a domestic violence situation, or where a child has been killed by a parent who has a mental illness.

8.7 Where more than one LSCB has knowledge of a child, the LSCB for the area in which the child is/was normally resident should take lead responsibility for conducting any review. Any other LSCBs that have an interest or involvement in the case should be included as partners in jointly planning and undertaking the review. In the case of looked after children, the Responsible Authority should exercise lead responsibility for conducting any review, again involving other LSCBs with an interest or involvement.

8.8 Any professional may refer such a case to the LSCB if it is believed that there are important lessons for inter-agency working to be learned from the case. In addition, the Secretary of State for the Department for Education and Skills has powers to demand an inquiry be held under the Inquiries Act 2005.

8.9 The following questions may help in deciding whether or not a case should be the subject of a serious case review in circumstances other than when a child dies. The answer 'yes' to several of these questions is likely to indicate that a review could yield useful lessons.

- Was there clear evidence of a risk of significant harm to a child that was:
    - not recognised by organisations or individuals in contact with the child or perpetrator **or**
    - not shared with others **or**
    - not acted on appropriately?
- Was the child killed by a mentally ill parent?
- Was the child abused in an institutional setting (e.g. school, nursery, family centre, YOI, STC, children's home or Armed Services training establishment)?
- Did the child die in a custodial setting (prison, Young Offenders' Institution or Secure Training Centre)?
- Was the child abused while being looked after by the local authority (LA)?
- Did the child commit suicide, or die while absent having run away from home?
- Does one or more agency or professional consider that its concerns were not taken sufficiently seriously, or acted on appropriately, by another?
- Does the case indicate that there may be failings in one or more aspects of the local operation of formal safeguarding children procedures, which go beyond the handling of this case?
- Was the child the subject of a child protection plan, or had they previously been the subject of a plan or on the child protection register?
- Does the case appear to have implications for a range of agencies and/or professionals?
- Does the case suggest that the LSCB may need to change its local protocols or procedures, or that protocols and procedures are not being adequately promulgated, understood or acted on?

Instigating a serious case review

Does the case meet serious case review criteria?

8.10 The LSCB should first decide whether or not a case should be the subject of a serious case review, applying the criteria at paragraphs 8.5 and 8.6. In making this decision where a child has died, the LSCB should draw on information available from the professionals involved in reviewing the child's death (see Chapter 7). LSCBs should establish a Serious Case Review Panel, involving at least LA children's social care, health, education and the police, to consider questions such as whether a serious case review should take place. In some cases, it may be valuable to conduct individual management reviews, or a smaller-scale audit of individual cases that give rise to concern but that do not meet the criteria for a full serious case review. In such cases, arrangements should be made to share relevant findings with the Serious Case Review Panel.

8.11 The Review Panel's decision should be forwarded as a recommendation to the Chair of the LSCB, who has ultimate responsibility for deciding whether or not to conduct a serious case review. Immediately following the making of this decision, the LA should inform the local region of the Commission for Social Care Inspection of every case that becomes the subject of a serious case review.

Determining the scope of the review

8.12 The Review Panel should consider, in the light of each case, the scope of the review process, and draw up clear terms of reference. Relevant issues include the following.

- What appear to be the most important issues to address in trying to learn from this specific case? How can the relevant information best be obtained and analysed?
- Who should be appointed as the independent author for the overview report?
- Are there features of the case that indicate that any part of the review process should involve, or be conducted by, a party independent of the professionals/organisations who will be required to participate in the review? Might it help the Review Panel to bring in an outside expert at any stage, to shed light on crucial aspects of the case?
- Over what time period should events be reviewed, – i.e. how far back should enquiries cover, and what is the cut-off point? What family history/background information will help better to understand the recent past and present?
- Which organisations and professionals should contribute to the review including, where appropriate, for example, the proprietor of an independent school or playgroup leader should be asked to submit reports or otherwise contribute?
- How should family members contribute to the review, and who should be responsible for facilitating their involvement?
- Will the case give rise to other parallel investigations of practice – e.g. independent health investigations or multi-disciplinary suicide reviews, a homicide review where a parent has been murdered, a YJB Serious Incident Review and a Prisons and Probation Ombudsman investigation where the child has died in a custodial setting? And if so, how can a co-ordinated or jointly commissioned review process best address all the relevant questions that need to be asked, in the most economical way?
- Is there a need to involve organisations/professionals in other LSCB areas (see paragraph 8.7), and what should be the respective roles and responsibilities of the different LSCBs with an interest?
- How should the review process take account of a Coroner's inquiry, and (if relevant) any criminal investigations or proceedings related to the case? How best to liaise with the Coroner and/or the Crown Prosecution Service?

- How should the serious case review process fit in with the processes for other types of reviews – e.g. for homicide, mental health or prisons?
- Who will make the link with relevant interests outside the main statutory organisations – e.g. independent professionals, independent schools, voluntary organisations?
- When should the review process start, and by what date should it be completed?
- How should any public, family and media interest be managed before, during and after the review?
- Does the LSCB need to obtain independent legal advice about any aspect of the proposed review?

8.13 Some of these issues may need to be revisited as the review progresses and new information emerges. The PCT should always inform its SHA of every case that becomes the subject of a serious case review.

Timing

8.14 Reviews vary widely in their breadth and complexity but, in all cases, lessons should be learnt and acted on as quickly as possible. Within one month of a case coming to the attention of the LSCB Chair, he or she should decide, following a recommendation from the Review Panel, whether a review should take place. Individual organisations should secure case records promptly and begin work quickly to draw up a chronology of involvement with the child and family.

8.15 Reviews should be completed within a further four months, unless an alternative timescale is agreed with the Commission for Social Care Inspection Region at the outset. Sometimes the complexity of a case does not become apparent until the review is in progress. As soon as it emerges that a review cannot be completed within four months of the LSCB Chair's decision to initiate it, there should be a discussion with the Commission for Social Care Inspection Region to agree a timescale for completion.

8.16 In some cases, criminal proceedings may follow the death or serious injury of a child. Those co-ordinating the review should discuss with the relevant criminal justice agencies, at an early stage, how the review process should take account of such proceedings. For example, how does this affect timing, the way in which the review is conducted (including interviews of relevant personnel), its potential impact on criminal investigations, and who should contribute at what stage? Serious case reviews should not be delayed as a matter of course because of outstanding criminal proceedings or an outstanding decision on whether or not to prosecute. Much useful work to understand and learn from the features of the case can often proceed without risk of contamination of witnesses in criminal proceedings. In some cases, it may not be possible to complete or to publish a review until after the Coroner's or criminal proceedings have been concluded, but this should not prevent early lessons learnt from being implemented.

Who should conduct reviews?

8.17 The initial scoping of the review should identify those who should contribute, although it may emerge, as information becomes available, that the involvement of others would be useful. In particular, information of relevance to the review may become available through criminal proceedings.

8.18 Each relevant service should undertake a separate management review of its involvement with the child and family. This should begin as soon as a decision is taken to proceed with a review, and even sooner if a case gives rise to concerns within the individual organisation. Relevant independent professionals (including GPs) should contribute reports of their involvement. Designated professionals should review and evaluate the practice of all involved health professionals and providers within the PCT area. This may involve reviewing the involvement of individual practitioners and Trusts, and advising named professionals and managers who are compiling reports for the review. Designated professionals have an important role in providing guidance on how to balance confidentiality and disclosure issues. Where a children's guardian contributes to a review, the prior agreement of the courts should be sought so that the guardian's duty of confidentiality under the court rules can be waived to the degree necessary.

8.19 The LSCB should commission an overview report that brings together and analyses the findings of the various reports from organisations and others, and that makes recommendations for future action.

8.20 The overview report should be commissioned from a person who is independent of all the agencies/professionals involved. Those conducting management reviews of individual services should not have been directly concerned with the child or family, or the immediate line manager of the practitioner(s) involved.

Individual management reviews

8.21 Once it is known that a case is being considered for review, each organisation should secure records relating to the case to guard against loss or interference.

8.22 The aim of management reviews should be to look openly and critically at individual and organisational practice to see whether the case indicates that changes could and should be made and, if so, to identify how those changes will be brought about. The findings from the management review reports should be accepted by the senior officer in the organisation who has commissioned the report and who will be responsible for ensuring that recommendations are acted on.

8.23 On completion of each management review report, there should be a process for feedback and debriefing for staff involved, in advance of completion of the overview report by the LSCB. There may also be a need for a follow-up feedback session if the LSCB overview report raises new issues for the organisation and staff members.

8.24 Serious case reviews are not a part of any disciplinary enquiry or process, but information that emerges in the course of reviews may indicate that disciplinary action should be taken under established procedures. Alternatively, reviews may be conducted concurrently with disciplinary action. In some cases (e.g. alleged institutional abuse) disciplinary action may be needed urgently to safeguard and promote the welfare of other children.

8.25 Where a child dies in a custodial setting (prison, Young Offenders' Institution or Secure Training Centre) the Prisons and Probation Ombudsman investigates and reports on the circumstances surrounding the death of that child. The investigation examines the child's period in custody and assesses the clinical care they received. The report is normally made available to assist any serious case review process.

8.26 The following outline format should guide the preparation of management reviews, to help ensure that the relevant questions are addressed, and to provide information to LSCBs in a consistent format to help with preparing an overview report. The questions posed do not comprise a comprehensive checklist relevant to all situations. Each case may give rise to specific questions or issues that need to be explored, and each review should consider carefully the circumstances of individual cases and how best to structure a review in the light of those particular circumstances.

8.27 Where staff or others are interviewed by those preparing management reviews, a written record of such interviews should be made and this should be shared with the relevant interviewee.

Management reviews

What was our involvement with this child and family?

Construct a comprehensive chronology of involvement by the organisation and/or professional(s) in contact with the child and family over the period of time set out in the review's terms of reference. Briefly summarise decisions reached, the services offered and/or provided to the child(ren) and family, and other action taken.

Analysis of involvement

Consider the events that occurred, the decisions made, and the actions taken or not taken. Where judgements were made, or actions taken, which indicate that practice or management could be improved, try to get an understanding not only of what happened but why. Consider specifically the following.

- Were practitioners sensitive to the needs of the children in their work, knowledgeable about potential indicators of abuse or neglect, and about what to do if they had concerns about a child?

Continued

- Did the organisation have in place policies and procedures for safeguarding and promoting the welfare of children and acting on concerns about their welfare?
- What were the key relevant points/opportunities for assessment and decision-making in this case in relation to the child and family? Do assessments and decisions appear to have been reached in an informed and professional way?
- Did actions accord with assessments and decisions made? Were appropriate services offered/provided, or relevant enquiries made, in the light of assessments?
- Where relevant, were appropriate child protection or care plans in place, and child protection and/or looked after reviewing processes complied with?
- When, and in what way, were the child(ren)'s wishes and feelings ascertained and taken account of when making revisions about children's services. Was this information recorded?
- Was practice sensitive to the racial, cultural, linguistic and religious identity of the child and family?
- Were more senior managers or other organisations and professionals involved at points where they should have been?
- Was the work in this case consistent with each organisation's and the LSCBs policy and procedures for safeguarding and promoting the welfare of children, and with wider professional standards?

What do we learn from this case?

Are there lessons from this case for the way in which this organisation works to safeguard and promote the welfare of children? Is there good practice to highlight, as well as ways in which practice can be improved? Are there implications for ways of working; training (single- and inter-agency); management and supervision; working in partnership with other organisations; resources?

Recommendations for action

What action should be taken by whom and when? What outcomes should these actions bring, and how will the organisation evaluate whether they have been achieved?

The LSCB overview report

8.28 The LSCB overview report should bring together, and draw overall conclusions from, the information and analysis contained in the individual management reviews, information from the child death review processes, and reports commissioned from any other relevant interests. Overview reports should be produced according to the following outline format although, as with management reviews, the precise format depends on the features of the case. This outline is most relevant to abuse or neglect that has taken place in a family setting.

LSCB overview report

Introduction

- Summarise the circumstances that led to a review being undertaken in this case.
- State terms of reference of review.
- List contributors to review and the nature of their contributions (for example, management review by LA, report from adult mental health service). List Review Panel members and author of overview report.

The facts

- Prepare a genogram showing membership of family, extended family and household.
- Compile an integrated chronology of involvement with the child and family on the part of all relevant organisations, professionals and others who have contributed to the review process. Note specifically in the chronology each occasion on which the child was seen and the child's wishes and feelings sought or expressed.
- Prepare an overview that summarises what relevant information was known to the agencies and professionals involved about the parents/carers, any perpetrator and the home circumstances of the children.

Analysis

This part of the overview should look at how and why events occurred, decisions were made and actions taken or not taken. This is the part of the report where reviewers can consider, with the benefit of hindsight, whether different decisions or actions may have led to an alternative course of events. The analysis section is also where any examples of good practice should be highlighted.

Conclusions and recommendations

This part of the report should summarise, in the opinion of the Review Panel, what lessons are to be drawn from the case, and how those lessons should be translated into recommendations for action. Recommendations should include, but should not simply be limited to, the recommendations made in individual reports from each organisation. Recommendations should be few in number, focused and specific, and capable of being implemented. If there are lessons for national as well as local policy and practice, these should also be highlighted.

LSCB action on receiving reports

8.29 On receiving an overview report the LSCB should:

- ensure that contributing organisations and individuals are satisfied that their information is fully and fairly represented in the overview report

- translate recommendations into an action plan that should be signed up to at a senior level by each of the organisations that need to be involved. The plan should set out who will do what, by when, and with what intended outcome. The plan should set out by what means improvements in practice/systems will be monitored and reviewed
- clarify to whom the report, or any part of it, should be made available
- disseminate report or key findings to interests as agreed. Make arrangements to provide feedback and debriefing to staff, family members of the subject child and the media as appropriate
- provide a copy of the overview report, action plan and individual management reports to the CSCI and DfES.

Reviewing institutional abuse

8.30 When serious abuse takes place in an institution, or multiple abusers are involved, the same principles of review apply, but reviews are likely to be more complex, on a larger scale, and may require more time. Terms of reference need to be carefully constructed to explore the issues relevant to the specific case. For example, if children are abused in a residential school, it is important to explore whether and how the school has taken steps to create a safe environment for children, and to respond to specific concerns raised.

8.31 There needs to be clarity over the interface between the different processes of investigation (including criminal investigations); case management, including help for abused children and immediate measures to ensure that other children are safe; and review – i.e. learning lessons from the case to reduce the chance of such events happening again. The three different processes should inform each other. Any proposals for review should be agreed with those leading criminal investigations, to make sure that they do not prejudice possible criminal proceedings.

Accountability and disclosure

8.32 LSCBs should consider carefully who might have an interest in reviews – e.g. elected and appointed members of authorities, staff, members of the child's family, the public, the media – and what information should be made available to each of these interests. There are difficult interests to balance, including:

- the need to maintain confidentiality in respect of personal information contained within reports on the child, family members and others
- the accountability of public services and the importance of maintaining public confidence in the process of internal review
- the need to secure full and open participation from the different agencies and professionals involved
- the responsibility to provide relevant information to those with a legitimate interest

- constraints on public information-sharing when criminal proceedings are outstanding, in that providing access to information may not be within the control of the LSCB.

8.33 It is important to anticipate requests for information and plan in advance how they should be met. For example, a lead agency may take responsibility for debriefing family members, or for responding to media interest about a case, in liaison with contributing agencies and professionals. In all cases, the LSCB overview report should contain an executive summary that will be made public and that includes, as a minimum, information about the review process, key issues arising from the case and the recommendations that have been made. The publication of the executive summary needs to be timed in accordance with the conclusion of any related court proceedings. The content needs to be suitably anonymised in order to protect the confidentiality of relevant family members and others. The LSCB should ensure that the SHA and the CSCI are briefed, so that they can work jointly to ensure that the Department of Health and the Department for Education and Skills, respectively, are fully briefed in advance about the publication of the executive summary.

Learning lessons locally

8.34 Reviews are of little value unless lessons are learnt from them. At least as much effort should be spent on acting on recommendations as on conducting the review. The following may help in getting maximum benefit from the review process:

- as far as possible, conduct the review in such a way that the process is a learning exercise in itself, rather than a trial or ordeal
- consider what information needs to be disseminated, how and to whom, in the light of a review. Be prepared to communicate both examples of good practice and areas where change is required
- focus recommendations on a small number of key areas, with specific and achievable proposals for change and intended outcomes. PCTs should seek feedback from SHAs, who should use it to inform their performance-management role
- the LSCB should put in place a means of auditing action against recommendations and intended outcomes
- seek feedback on review reports from the Commission for Social Care Inspection, who should use reports to inform inspections and performance management.

8.35 Day-to-day good practice can help ensure that reviews are conducted successfully and in a way most likely to maximise learning:

- establish a culture of audit and review. Make sure that tragedies are not the only reason inter-agency work is reviewed
- have in place clear, systematic case-recording and record-keeping systems

- develop good communication and mutual understanding between different disciplines and different LSCB members
- communicate with the local community and media to raise awareness of the positive and 'helping' work of statutory services with children, so that attention is not focused disproportionately on tragedies
- make sure staff and their representatives understand what can be expected in the event of a child death/serious case review.

Learning lessons nationally

8.36 Taken together, child death and serious case reviews should be an important source of information to inform national policy and practice. The Department for Education and Skills is responsible for identifying and disseminating common themes and trends across review reports, and acting on lessons for policy and practice. The Department for Education and Skills commissions overview reports at least every two years, drawing out key findings of serious case reviews and their implications for policy and practice. It is considering how best to disseminate the findings from the work of the local child death overview teams.

Part 2: Non-statutory practice guidance

Chapter 9 – Lessons from research and inspection

Introduction

9.1 Our knowledge and understanding of children's welfare – and how to respond in the best interests of a child to concerns about maltreatment (abuse and neglect) – develops over time, informed by research, experience and the critical scrutiny of practice. Sound professional practice involves making judgements supported by evidence: evidence derived from research and experience about the nature and impact of maltreatment, and when and how to intervene to improve outcomes for children; and evidence derived from a thorough assessment of a specific child's health, development and welfare, and his or her family circumstances.

9.2 This chapter summarises what is known about the impact of maltreatment on children's health and development, and sources of stress in families that may also have an impact on children's developmental progress (see also *The Developing World of the Child*, 2005).

The impact of maltreatment on children

9.3 The sustained maltreatment of children – physically, emotionally, sexually or through neglect – can have major long-term effects on all aspects of a child's health, development and wellbeing. **The immediate and longer-term impact can include anxiety, depression, substance misuse, eating disorders and self-destructive behaviours**. Sustained maltreatment is likely to have a deep impact on the child's self-image and self-esteem, and on his or her future life. Difficulties may extend into adulthood: the experience of long-term abuse may lead to difficulties in forming or sustaining close relationships, establishing oneself in work, and to extra difficulties in developing the attitudes and skills necessary to be an effective parent.

9.4 It is not only the stressful events of maltreatment that have an impact, but also the context in which they take place. Any potentially abusive incident has to be seen in context to assess the extent of harm to a child and decide on the most appropriate intervention. Often, it is the interaction between a number of factors that increases the likelihood or level of significant harm.

9.5 For every child and family, there may be factors that aggravate the harm caused to the child, and those that protect against harm. Relevant factors include the individual child's means of coping and adapting, support from a family and social network, and the impact of any interventions. The effects on a child are also influenced by the quality of the family environment at the time of maltreatment, and subsequent life events. The way in which professionals respond also has a significant bearing on subsequent outcomes.

Physical abuse

9.6 Physical abuse can lead directly to neurological damage, physical injuries, disability or, at the extreme, death. Harm may be caused to children both by the abuse itself and by the abuse taking place in a wider family or institutional context of conflict and aggression, including inappropriate or inexpert use of physical restraint. Physical abuse has been linked to aggressive behaviour in children, emotional and behavioural problems and educational difficulties. Violence is pervasive and the physical abuse of children frequently coexists with domestic violence.

Emotional abuse

9.7 There is increasing evidence of the adverse long-term consequences for children's development where they have been subject to sustained emotional abuse, including the impact of serious bullying. Emotional abuse has an important impact on a developing child's mental health, behaviour and self-esteem. It can be especially damaging in infancy. Underlying emotional abuse may be as important, if not more so, than other more visible forms of abuse in terms of its impact on the child. Domestic violence is abusive in itself. Adult mental health problems and parental substance misuse may be features in families where children are exposed to such abuse.

Sexual abuse

9.8 Disturbed behaviour – including self-harm, inappropriate sexualised behaviour, depression and a loss of self-esteem – have all been linked to sexual abuse. Its adverse effects may endure into adulthood. The severity of impact on a child is believed to increase the longer the abuse continues, the more extensive the abuse, and the older the child. A number of features of sexual abuse have also been linked with severity of impact, including the relationship of the abuser to the child, the extent of premeditation, the degree of threat and coercion, sadism, and bizarre or unusual elements. A child's ability to cope with the experience of sexual abuse, once recognised or disclosed, is strengthened by the support of a non-abusive adult carer who believes the child, helps the child understand the abuse, and is able to offer help and protection. The reactions of practitioners also have an impact on the child's ability to cope with what has happened, and his or her feelings of self worth. (See also *Child Sexual Abuse: Informing Practice from Research*, 1999.)

9.9 A proportion of adults who sexually abuse children have themselves been sexually abused as children. They may also have been exposed as children to domestic violence and discontinuity of care. However, it would be quite wrong to suggest that most children who are sexually abused inevitably go on to become abusers themselves.

Neglect

9.10 Severe neglect of young children has adverse effects on children's ability to form attachments and is associated with major impairment of growth and intellectual development. Persistent neglect can lead to serious impairment of health and development, and long-term difficulties with social functioning, relationships and educational progress. Neglected children may also experience low self-esteem, feelings of being unloved and isolated. Neglect can also result, in extreme cases, in death. The impact of neglect varies depending on how long children have been neglected, the children's age, and the multiplicity of neglectful behaviours children have been experiencing.

Sources of stress for children and families

9.11 Many families under great stress succeed in bringing up their children in a warm, loving and supportive environment in which each child's needs are met. Sources of stress within families may, however, have a negative impact on a child's health, development and wellbeing, either directly, or because when experienced during pregnancy it may result in delays in the physical and mental development of infants, or because they affect the capacity of parents to respond to their child's needs. This is particularly so when there is no other significant adult who is able to respond to the child's needs.

9.12 Undertaking assessments of children and families requires a thorough understanding of the factors that influence children's development: the developmental needs of children; the capacities of parents or caregivers to respond appropriately to those needs; and the impact of wider family and environmental factors on both children's development and parenting capacity. An analysis of how these three domains of children's lives interact enables practitioners to understand the child's developmental needs within the context of the family and to provide appropriate services to respond to those needs. (See the *Framework for the Assessment of Children in Need and their Families*.)

9.13 The following sections summarise some of the key research findings[33] that should be drawn on when assessing children and families, providing services to meet their identified needs and reviewing whether the planned outcomes for each child have been achieved.

Social exclusion

9.14 Many of the families who seek help for their children, or about whom others raise concerns about a child's welfare, are multiply disadvantaged. These families may face chronic poverty, social isolation, racism, and the problems associated with living in disadvantaged areas, such as high crime rates, poor housing, childcare, transport and

[33] Cleaver, H. *et al.* (1999). *Children's Needs – Parenting Capacity: The impact of parental mental illness, problem alcohol and drug use and domestic violence on children's development*. London: The Stationery Office.

education services, and limited employment opportunities. Many lack a wage earner. Poverty may mean that children live in crowded or unsuitable accommodation, have poor diets, health problems or disability, are vulnerable to accidents, and lack ready access to good educational and leisure opportunities. Racism and racial harassment are an additional source of stress for some families and children. Social exclusion can also have an indirect effect on children, through its association with parental depression, learning disability, and long-term physical health problems.

Domestic violence

9.15 Prolonged and/or regular exposure to domestic violence can have a serious impact on a child's development and emotional wellbeing, despite the best efforts of the victim's parent to protect the child. Domestic violence has an impact in a number of ways. It can pose a threat to an unborn child, because assaults on pregnant women frequently involve punches or kicks directed at the abdomen, risking injury to both mother and foetus. Older children may also suffer blows during episodes of violence. Children may be greatly distressed by witnessing the physical and emotional suffering of a parent. Both the physical assaults and psychological abuse suffered by adult victims who experience domestic violence can have a negative impact on their ability to look after their children. The negative impact of domestic violence is exacerbated when the violence is combined with drink or drug misuse; children witness the violence; children are drawn into the violence or are pressurised into concealing the assaults. Children's exposure to parental conflict, even where violence is not present, can lead to serious anxiety and distress.

The mental illness of a parent or carer

9.16 Mental illness in a parent or carer does not necessarily have an adverse impact on a child's developmental needs, but it is essential always to assess its implications for each child in the family. Parental illness may markedly restrict children's social and recreational activities. With both mental and physical illness in a parent, children may have caring responsibilities placed on them inappropriate to their years, leading them to be worried and anxious. If they are depressed, parents may neglect their own and their children's physical and emotional needs. In some circumstances, some forms of mental illness may blunt parents' emotions and feelings, or cause them to behave towards their children in bizarre or violent ways. Unusually, but at the extreme, a child may be at risk of severe injury, profound neglect, or even death. A study of 100 reviews of child deaths where abuse and neglect had been a factor in the death showed clear evidence of parental mental illness in one-third of cases.[34] In addition, postnatal depression can be linked to both behavioural and physiological problems in the infants of such mothers.

9.17 The adverse effects on children of parental mental illness are less likely when parental problems are mild, last only a short time, are not associated with family

34 Falkov, A. (1996) *A Study of Working Together 'Part 8' Reports: Fatal child abuse and parental psychiatric disorder*. London: DOH-ACPC Series, 1.

disharmony, and do not result in the family breaking up. Children may also be protected from harm when the other parent or a family member can help respond to the child's needs. Children most at risk of significant harm are those who feature within parental delusions, and children who become targets for parental aggression or rejection, or who are neglected as a result of parental mental illness.

Drug and alcohol misuse

9.18 As with mental illness in a parent, it is important not to generalise or make assumptions about the impact on a child of parental drug and alcohol misuse. Their effects on children are complex and require a thorough assessment. Maternal substance misuse in pregnancy can have serious effects on the health and development of an unborn child, often because of the mother's poor nutrition and lifestyle. Newborn babies may experience withdrawal symptoms that may interfere with the baby's attachment to their parents or caregivers. Babies may experience a lack of basic healthcare and poor stimulation, and older children may experience poor school attendance, anxiety about their parents' health and taking on caring roles for siblings. Substance misuse can affect a parent's practical caring skills: perceptions, attention to basic physical needs, control of emotion, judgement and attachment to or separation from the child. Some substance misuse may give rise to mental states or behaviour that put children at risk of injury, psychological distress or neglect. Children are particularly vulnerable when parents are withdrawing from drugs. The risk is greater when the adult's substance misuse is chaotic or otherwise out of control, and when both parents are involved. The risk is also greater where there is a dual diagnosis of mental health problems and substance misuse.

9.19 Some substance-misusing parents may find it difficult to give priority to the needs of their children, and finding money for drugs and/or alcohol may reduce the money available to the household to meet basic needs, or may draw families into criminal activities. Children may be at risk of physical harm if drugs and paraphernalia (e.g. needles) are not kept safely out of reach. Some children have been killed through inadvertent access to drugs (e.g. methadone stored in a fridge). In addition, children may be in danger if they are passengers in a car while a drug/alcohol-misusing carer is driving. The children of substance-misusing parents are at increased risk of developing alcohol and drug use problems themselves, and of being separated from their parents. Children who start drinking at an early age are at greater risk of unwanted sexual encounters, and injuries through accidents and fighting.

Parental learning disability

9.20 Where a parent has a learning disability it is important not to generalise or make assumptions about their parental capacity. Learning disabled parents may need support to develop the understanding, resources, skills and experience to meet the needs of their children. Such support is particularly needed where they experience additional stressors such as having a disabled child, domestic violence, poor physical and mental health, substance misuse, social isolation, poor housing, poverty and a history of growing up in care. It is these additional stressors, when combined with a learning disability, that are most likely to lead to concerns about the care a child or children may receive.

9.21 Children of parents with learning disabilities are at increased risk from inherited learning disability and are more vulnerable to psychiatric disorders and behavioural problems. From an early age, children may assume the responsibility of looking after their parent, and in many cases other siblings, one or more of whom may be learning disabled. Unless parents with learning disabilities are comprehensively supported – e.g. by a capable non-abusive relative, such as their own parent or partner – their children's health and development is likely to be impaired. A further risk of harm to children arises because mothers with learning disabilities may be attractive targets for men who wish to gain access to children for the purpose of sexually abusing them.

9.22 A specialist assessment is often needed and is recommended.[35] Where specialist assessments have not been carried out and/or learning disability support services have not been involved, evidence from inspections has shown that crucial decisions could be made on inadequate information.[36]

9.23 Adult learning disability services, particularly community nurses, can provide valuable input to core assessments, and there are also validated assessment tools available.[37] However, most parents with learning disabilities do not meet eligibility criteria for adult services, and lack of co-operation between children and adult services can create great difficulties.

9.24 A comparative study of children and families with learning disabled parents referred to LA children's social care services showed twice as many children had severe developmental needs, and five times as many had parents who were experiencing severe difficulties in meeting their children's needs.[38] The research found that parents with learning disabilities are more likely to need long-term support.

9.25 A comparative study of methods of supporting parents with learning disabilities found that group education, combined with home-based support, increases parenting capacity.[39] In some areas, services provide accessible information, advocacy, peer support, multi-agency and multi-disciplinary assessments, and on-going home-based and other support. This 'parenting with support' appears to yield good results for both parents and children.[40]

35 *Framework for the Assessment of Children in Need and their Families*, paragraphs 6.18–6.21.

36 Social Services Inspectorate. *A Jigsaw of Services: Supporting disabled adults in their parenting role*. London: Department of Health, paragraph 1.29.

37 McGaw, S. and Newman, T. (2005). *What Works for Parents with Learning Disabilities*. Barnardo's.

38 Cleaver, H. and Nicholson, D. (2005). *Children Living with Learning Disabled Parents*. Report submitted to Department for Education and Skills.

39 McGaw, S., Ball, K. and Clark, A. (2002). 'The effect of group intervention on the relationships of parents with intellectual disabilities'. *Journal of Applied Research in Intellectual Disabilities*, 15 (4), 354–366.

40 Tarleton, B., Ward, L. and Howarth, J. (2006). *Finding the Right Support? A review of issues and positive practice to support parents with learning difficulties and their children*. London: The Baring Foundation.

Chapter 10 – Implementing the principles on working with children and their families

Introduction

10.1 The general principles set out in Chapter 5 draw on findings from research. They underpin work with children and their families to safeguard and promote the welfare of children (see also paragraph 2.18 in the guidance issued under s11 of the Children Act 2004, *Making Arrangements to Safeguard and Promote the Welfare of Children* 2005). This chapter sets out in more detail specific aspects of working with children and their families.

Family group conferences

10.2 Family group conferences (FGCs) may be appropriate in a number of contexts where there is a plan or decision to be made. FGCs do not replace or remove the need for child protection conferences, which should always be held when the relevant criteria are met. FGCs may be valuable, for example:

- for children in need, in a range of circumstances where a plan is required for the child's future welfare
- where s47 enquiries do not substantiate concerns about significant harm, but where support and services are required
- where s47 enquiries progress to a child protection conference, the conference may agree that an FGC is an appropriate vehicle for the core group to use to develop the outline child protection plan into a fully worked-up plan.

10.3 It is essential that all parties are provided with clear and accurate information, which will make effective planning possible. The family is the primary planning group in the process. Family members need to be able to understand what the issues are from the perspective of the professionals. The family and involved professionals should be clear about:

- what the professional findings are from any core assessment of the child and family
- what the family understands about their current situation

- what decisions are required
- what decisions have already been taken
- the family's scope for decision-making, and whether there are any issues/decisions that are not negotiable
- what resources are, or might be, available to implement any plan. Within this framework, agencies and professionals should agree to support the plan if it does not place the child at risk of significant harm, and if the resources requested can be provided.

10.4 Where there are plans to use FGCs in situations where there are concerns about possible harm to a child, they should be developed and implemented under the auspices of the LSCB. This work should involve all relevant organisations and individuals, and ensure that their use is applicable to other relevant LSCB policies and procedures. Inter-agency training is necessary to build the relevant skills required to work with children and families in this way, and to promote confidence in, and develop a shared understanding of, the process.

Support, advice and advocacy to children and families

10.5 Children and families may be supported through their involvement in safeguarding processes by advice and advocacy services, and they should always be informed of services that exist locally and nationally. Independent Advocates provide independent and confidential information, advice, representation and support, and can play a vital role in ensuring children have appropriate information and support to communicate their views in formal settings, such as child protection conferences and court proceedings.

10.6 Where children and families are involved as witnesses in criminal proceedings, the police, witness support services and other services, such as those provided by Victim Support, can do a great deal to explain the process, make it feel less daunting, and ensure that children are prepared for and supported in the court process. The practice guidance *Provision of Therapy for Child Witnesses prior to a Criminal Trial* (2001) makes it clear that the best interests of a child are paramount when deciding whether, and in what form, therapeutic help is given to child witnesses. Information about the Criminal Injuries Compensation Scheme should also be provided in relevant cases.

Communication and information

10.7 The local authority has a responsibility to make sure children and adults have all the information they require to help them understand the processes that are followed when there are concerns about a child's welfare. Information should be clear and accessible and available in the family's preferred language.

10.8 Family members or friends should not be used as interpreters, since the majority of domestic and child abuse is perpetrated by family members or adults known to the child. Children should not be used as interpreters.

Race, ethnicity and culture

10.9 Children from all cultures are subject to abuse and neglect. All children have a right to grow up safe from harm. In order to make sensitive and informed professional judgements about a child's needs, and parents' capacity to respond to their child's needs, it is important that professionals are sensitive to differing family patterns and lifestyles and to child-rearing patterns that vary across different racial, ethnic and cultural groups. **At the same time they must be clear that child abuse cannot be condoned for religious or cultural reasons.**

10.10 Professionals should also be aware of the broader social factors that serve to discriminate against black and minority ethnic people. Working in a multi-racial and multi-cultural society requires professionals and organisations to be committed to equality in meeting the needs of all children and families, and to understand the effects of racial harassment, racial discrimination and institutional racism, as well as cultural misunderstanding or misinterpretation.

10.11 The assessment process should maintain a focus on the needs of the individual child. It should always include consideration of the way religious beliefs and cultural traditions in different racial, ethnic and cultural groups influence their values, attitudes and behaviour, and the way in which family and community life is structured and organised. Cultural and religious factors should not be regarded as acceptable explanations for child abuse or neglect, and are not acceptable grounds for inaction when a child is at risk of significant harm. Professionals should be aware of, and work with, the strengths and support systems available within families, ethnic groups and communities, which can be built on to help safeguard children and promote their welfare.

10.12 Professionals should guard against myths and stereotypes – both positive and negative – of black and minority ethnic families. Anxiety about being accused of racist practice should not prevent the necessary action being taken to safeguard and promote a child's welfare. Careful assessment – based on evidence – of a child's needs, and a family's strengths and difficulties, understood in the context of the wider social environment, will help to avoid any distorting effect of these influences on professional judgements.

10.13 All children, whatever their religious or cultural background, must receive the same care and safeguards with regard to abuse and neglect.

Chapter 11 – Safeguarding and promoting the welfare of children who may be particularly vulnerable

Introduction

11.1 This chapter outlines the circumstances of children who may be particularly vulnerable. The purpose of this chapter is to help inform the procedures in Chapter 5, which sets out the basic framework of action to be taken in **all** circumstances when a parent, professional, or any other person has concerns about the welfare of a child.

Children living away from home

General

11.2 Revelations of the widespread abuse and neglect of children living away from home have done much to raise awareness of the particular vulnerability of such children living away from home. Many of these revelations have focused on sexual abuse, but physical and emotional abuse and neglect – including peer abuse, bullying and substance misuse – are equally a threat in institutional settings. There should never be complacency that these are problems of the past – there is a need for continuing vigilance. The second joint Chief Inspectors' Report on Arrangements to Safeguard Children, published in July 2005, continued to highlight the safeguarding of children living away from home.

11.3 Concern for the safety of children living away from home has to be put in the context of attention to the overall developmental needs of such children, and a concern for the best possible outcomes for their health and development. Every setting in which children live away from home should provide the same basic safeguards against abuse, founded on an approach that promotes their general welfare, protects them from harm of all kinds, and treats them with dignity and respect. These values are reflected in regulations and in the National Minimum Standards, which contain specific requirements on safeguarding and child protection for each particular regulated setting where children live away from home.

11.4 LSCB procedures should include a clear policy statement that local procedures for safeguarding and promoting the welfare of children apply in every situation, and apply to all settings, including where children are living away from home. Individual agencies that provide care for children living away from home should have clear and unambiguous procedures to respond to potential matters of concern about children's welfare in line with the LSCB's arrangements.

Essential safeguards

11.5 There are a number of essential safeguards that should be observed in all settings in which children live away from home, including foster care, residential care, private fostering, armed forces bases, healthcare, boarding schools (including residential special schools), prisons, Young Offenders' Institutions, Secure Training Centres and secure units. Where services are not directly provided, essential safeguards should be explicitly addressed in contracts with external providers. These safeguards should ensure that:

- children feel valued and respected and their self-esteem is promoted
- there is an openness on the part of the institution to the external world and to external scrutiny, including contact with families and the wider community
- staff and foster carers are trained in all aspects of safeguarding children, alert to children's vulnerabilities and risks of harm, and knowledgeable about how to implement safeguarding children procedures
- children who live away from home are listened to, and their views and concerns responded to
- children have ready access to a trusted adult outside the institution – e.g. a family member, the child's social worker, independent visitor or children's advocate. Children should be made aware of the help they could receive from independent advocacy services, external mentors and ChildLine
- staff recognise the importance of ascertaining the wishes and feelings of children and understand how individual children communicate by verbal or non-verbal means
- there are clear procedures for referring safeguarding concerns about a child to the relevant local authority (LA)
- complaints procedures are clear, effective, user-friendly and are readily accessible to children and young people, including those with disabilities and those for whom English is not their preferred language. Procedures should address informal as well as formal complaints. Systems that do not promote open communication about 'minor' complaints will not be responsive to major ones, and a pattern of 'minor' complaints may indicate more deeply seated problems in management and culture that need to be addressed. Records of complaints should be kept by providers of children's services – e.g. there should be a complaints register in every children's home that records all representations or complaints, the action taken to address them and the outcomes. Children should genuinely be able to raise concerns and make suggestions for changes and improvements, which should be taken seriously

- bullying is effectively countered
- recruitment and selection procedures are rigorous and create a high threshold of entry to deter abusers
- there is effective supervision and support that extends to temporary staff and volunteers
- contractor staff are effectively checked and supervised when on site or in contact with children
- clear procedures and support systems are in place for dealing with expressions of concern by staff and carers about other staff or carers. Organisations should have a code of conduct, instructing staff on their duty to their employer and their professional obligation to raise legitimate concerns about the conduct of colleagues or managers. There should be a guarantee that procedures can be invoked in ways that do not prejudice the 'whistle-blower's' own position and prospects
- there is respect for diversity, and sensitivity to race, culture, religion, gender, sexuality and disability
- staff and carers are alert to the risks of harm to children in the external environment from people prepared to exploit the additional vulnerability of children living away from home.

Foster care

11.6 Foster care is undertaken in the private domain of carers' own homes. It is important that children have a voice outside the family. Social workers are required to see children in foster care on their own (taking appropriate account of the child's wishes and feelings), and evidence of this should be recorded.

11.7 Foster carers should be provided with full information about the foster child and his/her family, including details of abuse or possible abuse, both in the interests of the child and of the foster family.

11.8 Foster carers should monitor the whereabouts of their foster children, their patterns of absence and contacts. Foster carers should follow the recognised procedure of their agency whenever a foster child is missing from their home.[41] This involves notifying the placing authority – and, where necessary, the police – of any unauthorised absence by a child.

11.9 The LA's duty to undertake s47 enquiries, when there are concerns about significant harm to a child, applies on the same basis to children in foster care as it does to children who live with their own families. Enquiries should consider the safety of any other children living in the household, including the foster carers' own children. The LA in which the child

41 Fostering Services: National Minimum Standards – 9.8.

is living has the responsibility to convene a strategy discussion, which should include representatives from the responsible LA that placed the child. At the strategy discussion it should be decided which LA should take responsibility for the next steps, which may include a s47 enquiry. For further details on this see Chapter 5 on 'Managing individual cases'.

Private fostering

11.10 A private fostering arrangement is essentially one that is made privately (i.e. without the involvement of a LA) for the care of a child under the age of 16 (under 18 if disabled) by someone other than a parent or close relative for 28 days or more.

11.11 Privately fostered children are a diverse and sometimes vulnerable group. They include:

- children sent from abroad to stay with another family, usually to improve their educational opportunities
- asylum-seeking and refugee children
- teenagers who, having broken ties with their parents, are staying in short-term arrangements with friends or other non-relatives
- language students living with host families.

11.12 Under the Children Act 1989, private foster carers and those with parental responsibility are required to notify the LA of their intention to privately foster or to have a child privately fostered, or where a child is privately fostered in an emergency. Teachers, health and other professionals should notify the LA of a private fostering arrangement that comes to their attention, where they are not satisfied that the LA has been, or will be, notified of the arrangement.

11.13 It is the duty of every LA to satisfy itself that the welfare of children who are privately fostered within its area is being satisfactorily safeguarded and promoted, and to ensure that such advice as appears to be required is given to private foster carers. In order to do so, LA officers must visit privately fostered children at regular intervals. The minimum visiting requirements are set out in the Regulations. The LA officer should visit a child alone, unless the officer considers it inappropriate. LAs must also arrange for visits to be made to the privately fostered child, the private foster carer, or parent of the child when reasonably requested to do so. Children should be given contact details of the social worker who will be visiting them while they are being privately fostered.

11.14 LAs must satisfy themselves as to such matters as the suitability of the private foster carer and the private foster carer's household and accommodation. They have the power to impose requirements on the private foster carer or, if there are serious concerns about an arrangement, to prohibit it.

11.15 The Children Act 1989 creates a number of offences in connection with private fostering, including for failure to notify an arrangement or to comply with any requirement or prohibition imposed by the authority. Certain people are disqualified from being private foster carers.

11.16 With effect from July 2005, amendments to s67 of, and schedule 8 to, the Children Act 1989 (made by s44 of the Children Act 2004) require LAs to promote awareness in their area of notification requirements, and to ensure that such advice as appears to be required is given to those concerned with children who are, or are proposed to be, privately fostered. This includes private foster carers (proposed and actual) **and** parents.

11.17 Also with effect from July 2005, the Children (Private Arrangements for Fostering) Regulations 2005 require LAs to satisfy themselves of the suitability of a proposed arrangement **before** it commences (where advance notice is given).

11.18 The private fostering regulations require LAs to monitor their compliance with **all** their duties and functions in relation to private fostering, and place a duty on them to appoint an officer for this purpose.

11.19 In addition, LAs are inspected against the National Minimum Standards for private fostering.

11.20 The new measures in the Children Act 2004 and in the Regulations strengthen and enhance the private fostering notification scheme, and provide additional safeguards for privately fostered children. These measures, along with new National Minimum Standards and the new role for LSCBs in looking at private fostering, focus LAs' attention on private fostering and require them to take a more proactive approach to identifying arrangements in their area. The measures are expected to improve notification rates and compliance with the existing legislative framework for private fostering, and to increase significantly the number of arrangements checked out before a child is privately fostered – and, therefore, to address the key problems identified with the scheme.

11.21 Children Act 1989 guidance on private fostering, issued in July 2005, reflects the new measures on private fostering in the Children Act 2004 and in the Regulations. This guidance, along with the National Minimum Standards and guidance for LAs on promoting awareness within their areas, is available at: www.everychildmatters.gov.uk/socialcare/safeguarding/privatefostering/.

Children in hospital

11.22 The *National Service Framework for Children, Young People and Maternity Services* (NSF) (2004) sets out standards for hospital services. Standard 6 of the NSF is to be taken alongside the hospital standard, which was published in 2003 to meet the commitment made in the Government's response to the report of the Public Inquiry into Children's Heart Surgery at the Bristol Royal Infirmary 1984–1995: Learning from Bristol. The Healthcare

Commission has undertaken an improvement review of the NHS implementation of the hospital standard.

11.23 When children are in hospital, this should not in itself jeopardise the health of the child or young person further. The NSF requires hospitals to ensure that their facilities are secure and regularly reviewed. There should be policies relating to breaches of security and involving the police. The LA where the hospital is located is responsible for the welfare of children in its hospitals.

11.24 Children should not be cared for on an adult ward. The NSF Standard for Hospital Services requires care to be provided in an appropriate location, and in an environment that is safe and well suited to the age and stage of development of the child or young person. Hospitals should be child-friendly, safe and healthy places for children. Wherever possible, children should be consulted about where they would prefer to stay in hospital, and their views should be taken into account and respected. Hospital admission data should include the age of children, so that hospitals can monitor whether children are being given appropriate care in appropriate wards.

11.25 Additionally, s85 of the Children Act 1989 requires PCTs to notify the 'Responsible Authority' – i.e. the LA for the area where the child is ordinarily resident, or where the child is accommodated if this is unclear – when a child has been, or will be, accommodated by the PCT for three months or more (e.g. in hospital). This is so that the LA can assess the child's needs and decide whether services are required under the Children Act 1989.

Children in custody

11.26 The LA has the same responsibilities towards children in custody as it does towards other children in the authority area. Following the judgement of Munby, J. in November 2002[42] – which found that LAs continue to have obligations to children held in custody – it has been agreed that the Youth Justice Boards (YJB) will fund, for two years, approximately 25 LA staff across all the juvenile Young Offenders' Institutions (YOI), to undertake Children Act 1989 duties. A significant part of these duties relates to safeguarding and promoting the welfare of children. In particular, these staff are responsible for overseeing procedures to safeguard and promote the welfare of children within the secure estate, and helping to ensure that appropriate links are made between the YOI and its LSCB. *Local Authority Circular (LAC) 2004(26)* sets out LAs' responsibilities to children in custody. It can be found at: www.dh.gov.uk/PublicationsAndStatistics/LettersAndCirculars/LocalAuthorityCirculars/AllLocalAuthorityCirculars/LocalAuthorityCircularsArticle.

42 R v Secretary of State for the Home Department, ex parte Howard League for Penal Reform (2002) EWHC 2497.

Abuse of disabled children

11.27 The available UK evidence on the extent of abuse among disabled children suggests that disabled children are at increased risk of abuse, and that the presence of multiple disabilities appears to increase the risk of both abuse and neglect (see Standards 5, 7 and 8 of the *National Service Framework for Children, Young People and Maternity Services*). Disabled children may be especially vulnerable to abuse for a number of reasons. Some disabled children may:

- have fewer outside contacts than other children
- receive intimate personal care, possibly from a number of carers, which may both increase the risk of exposure to abusive behaviour and make it more difficult to set and maintain physical boundaries
- have an impaired capacity to resist or avoid abuse
- have communication difficulties that may make it difficult to tell others what is happening
- be inhibited about complaining because of a fear of losing services
- be especially vulnerable to bullying and intimidation and/or
- be more vulnerable than other children to abuse by their peers.

11.28 Safeguards for disabled children are essentially the same as for non-disabled children. Particular attention should be paid to promoting high standards of practice and a high level of awareness of the risks of harm, and strengthening the capacity of children and families to help themselves. Measures should include:

- making it common practice to help disabled children make their wishes and feelings known in respect of their care and treatment
- ensuring that disabled children receive appropriate personal, health and social education (including sex education)
- making sure that all disabled children know how to raise concerns, and giving them access to a range of adults with whom they can communicate. Those disabled children with communication impairments should have available to them at all times a means of being heard
- an explicit commitment to, and understanding of, disabled children's safety and welfare among providers of services used by disabled children
- close contact with families, and a culture of openness on the part of services
- guidelines and training for staff on good practice in intimate care; working with children of the opposite sex; handling difficult behaviour; consent to treatment; anti-bullying

strategies; and sexuality and sexual behaviour among young people, especially those living away from home.

11.29 Where there are concerns about the welfare of a disabled child, they should be acted on in accordance with the guidance in Chapter 5, in the same way as with any other child. Expertise in both safeguarding and promoting the welfare of children and in disability has to be brought together to ensure that disabled children receive the same levels of protection from harm as other children (see *Safeguarding Disabled Children* on www.everychildmatters.gov.uk/safeguarding).

11.30 Where a disabled child has communication impairments or learning disabilities, special attention should be paid to communication needs, and to ascertaining the child's perception of events, and his or her wishes and feelings. In every area, children's social care and the police should be aware of non-verbal communication systems, when they might be useful and how to access them, and should know how to contact suitable interpreters or facilitators. Agencies should not make assumptions about the inability of a disabled child to give credible evidence, or to withstand the rigours of the court process. Each child should be assessed carefully, and helped and supported to participate in the criminal justice process when this is in the child's best interest and the interests of justice.

11.31 In criminal proceedings, witnesses aged under 17 are automatically eligible for assistance with giving their evidence. The special measures they may be provided with include screens around the witness box so they do not see the defendant, video-recorded evidence in chief and live video links so that they may not have to go into the courtroom at all, and intermediaries and aids to communication to facilitate good communication. *Achieving Best Evidence* (2002) guidance for investigators includes comprehensive guidance on planning and conducting interviews with children, and a specific section about interviewing disabled children (found at: www.cps.gov.uk/publications/prosecution/bestevidencevol2.html).

Abuse by children and young people

Peer abuse

11.32 Children, particularly those living away from home, are also vulnerable to physical, sexual and emotional bullying and abuse by their peers. Such abuse should always be taken as seriously as abuse perpetrated by an adult. It should be subject to the same safeguarding children procedures as apply in respect of any child who is suffering, or at risk of suffering, significant harm from an adverse source. A significant proportion of sex offences are committed by teenagers and, on occasion, such offences are committed by younger children. Staff and carers of children living away from home need clear guidance and training to identify the difference between consenting and abusive, and between appropriate and exploitative peer relationships. Staff should not dismiss some abusive sexual behaviour as 'normal' between young people, and should not develop high thresholds before taking action.

11.33 Work with children and young people who abuse others – including those who sexually abuse/offend – should recognise that such children are likely to have considerable needs themselves, and also that they may pose a significant risk of harm to other children. Evidence suggests that children who abuse others may have suffered considerable disruption in their lives, been exposed to violence within the family, may have witnessed or been subject to physical or sexual abuse, have problems in their educational development, and may have committed other offences. Such children and young people are likely to be children in need, and some will, in addition, be suffering, or at risk of suffering, significant harm, and may themselves be in need of protection. Children and young people who abuse others should be held responsible for their abusive behaviour, while being identified and responded to in a way that meets their needs as well as protecting others.

11.34 Three key principles should guide work with children and young people who abuse others:

- there should be a co-ordinated approach on the part of youth justice, children's social care, education (including educational psychology) and health (including child and adolescent mental health) agencies
- the needs of children and young people who abuse others should be considered separately from the needs of their victims
- an assessment should be carried out in each case, appreciating that these children may have considerable unmet developmental needs, as well as specific needs arising from their behaviour.

11.35 LSCBs and Youth Offending Teams should ensure that there is a clear operational framework in place, within which assessment, decision-making and case-management take place. Neither child welfare nor criminal justice agencies should embark on a course of action that has implications for the other without appropriate consultation.

11.36 In assessing a child or young person who abuses another, relevant considerations include:

- the nature and extent of the abusive behaviours. In respect of sexual abuse, there are sometimes perceived to be difficulties in distinguishing between normal childhood sexual development and experimentation, and sexually inappropriate or aggressive behaviour. Expert professional judgement may be required, within the context of knowledge about normal child sexuality
- the context of the abusive behaviours
- the child's development, and family and social circumstances
- needs for services, specifically focusing on the child's harmful behaviour as well as other significant needs

- the risks to self and others, including other children in the household, extended family, school, peer group or wider social network. This risk is likely to be present unless the opportunity for further abuse is ended, the young person has acknowledged the abusive behaviour and accepted responsibility, and there is agreement by the young abuser and his/her family to work with relevant agencies to address the problem.

11.37 Decisions for local agencies (including the Crown Prosecution Service where relevant) according to the responsibilities of each include:

- the most appropriate course of action within the criminal justice system, if the child is above the age of criminal responsibility
- whether the young abuser should be the subject of a child protection conference
- what plan of action should be put in place to address the needs of the young abuser, detailing the involvement of all relevant agencies.

11.38 A young abuser should be the subject of a child protection conference if he or she is considered personally to be at risk of continuing significant harm. Where there is no reason to hold a child protection conference, there may still be a need for a multi-agency approach if the young abuser's needs are complex. Issues regarding suitable educational and accommodation arrangements often require skilled and careful consideration.

Bullying

11.39 Bullying may be defined as deliberately hurtful behaviour, usually repeated over a period of time, where it is difficult for those bullied to defend themselves. It can take many forms, but the three main types are:

- physical (e.g. hitting, kicking, theft)
- verbal (e.g. racist or homophobic remarks, threats, name-calling)
- emotional (e.g. isolating an individual from the activities and social acceptance of their peer group).

11.40 The damage inflicted by bullying can frequently be underestimated. It can cause considerable distress to children, to the extent that it affects their health and development or, at the extreme, causes them significant harm (including self-harm). All settings in which children are provided with services or are living away from home should have in place rigorously enforced anti-bullying strategies.

Children whose behaviour indicates a lack of parental control

11.41 When children are brought to the attention of the police or the wider community because of their behaviour, this may be an indication of vulnerability, poor supervision or neglect in its wider sense. It is important to consider whether these are children in need and to offer them assistance and services that reflect their needs. This should be done on a multi-agency basis. A range of powers should be used to engage families to improve the child's behaviour where engagement cannot be secured on a voluntary basis.

11.42 The Child Safety Order (CSO) is a compulsory intervention available below the threshold of the child being at risk of significant harm. A LA can apply for a CSO where a child has committed an act that would have been an offence if s/he were aged 10 or above, where it is necessary to prevent such an act, or where the child has caused harassment, distress or harm to others (i.e. behaved anti-socially). It is designed to help the child improve his or her behaviour, and is likely to be used alongside work with the family and others to address any underlying problems.

11.43 A Parenting Order can be made alongside a CSO or when a CSO is breached. This provides an effective means of engaging with and supporting parents, while helping them develop their ability to undertake their parental responsibilities.

Race and racism

11.44 Children from black and minority ethnic groups (and their parents) are likely to have experienced harassment, racial discrimination and institutional racism. Although racism can cause significant harm, it is not, in itself, a category of abuse. The experience of racism is likely to affect the responses of the child and family to assessment and enquiry processes. Failure to consider the effects of racism undermines efforts to protect children from other forms of significant harm. The effects of racism differ for different communities and individuals, and should not be assumed to be uniform. Attention should be given to the specific needs of children of mixed parentage and refugee children. In particular, the need for neutral, high-quality, gender-appropriate translation or interpretation services should be taken into account when working with children and families whose preferred language is not English. All organisations working with children, including those operating in areas where black and minority ethnic communities are numerically small, should address institutional racism, defined in the Macpherson Inquiry Report (2000) on Stephen Lawrence as 'the collective failure by an organisation to provide an appropriate and professional service to people on account of their race, culture and/or religion'.

Domestic violence

11.45 As outlined in Chapter 9, children may suffer both directly and indirectly if they live in households where there is domestic violence. Domestic violence is likely to have a damaging effect on the health and development of children, and it is often appropriate for such children to be regarded as children in need. Children living in families where they are exposed to domestic violence have been shown to be at risk of behavioural, emotional, physical, cognitive-functioning, attitude and long-term developmental problems. Everyone working with women and children should be alert to the frequent inter-relationship between domestic violence and the abuse and neglect of children (*National Service Framework for Children, Young People and Maternity Services*, 2004). There may be serious effects on children who witness domestic violence, which often result in behavioural issues, absenteeism, ill health, bullying, antisocial behaviour, drug and alcohol misuse, self-harm and psychosocial impacts. Where there is evidence of domestic violence, the implications for any children in the household should be considered, including the possibility that the children may themselves be subject to violence, or may be harmed by witnessing or overhearing the violence. Conversely, where it is believed that a child is being abused, those involved with the child and family should be alert to the possibility of domestic violence within the family (*Responding to Domestic Abuse: A Hand Book for Health Professionals*, 2005).

11.46 The police are often the first point of contact with families in which domestic violence takes place. When responding to incidents of violence, the police should find out whether there are any children living in the household. They should see any children present in the house to assess their immediate safety. There should be arrangements in place between the police and children's social care to enable the police to find out whether any such children are the subject of a child protection plan. The police are already required to determine whether any court orders or injunctions are in force in respect of members of the household. The police should make an assessment and, if they have specific concerns about the safety or welfare of a child, they should make a referral to children's social care. It is also important that there is clarity about whether the family is aware that a referral is to be made. Any response by children's social care to such referrals should be discreet, in terms of making contact with victims in ways that will not further endanger them or their children. In some cases, a child may be in need of immediate protection. The amendment to the Children Act 1989 made in s120 of the Adoption and Children Act 2002 clarifies the meaning of 'harm' in the Children Act, to make explicit that 'harm' includes, for example, impairment suffered from seeing or hearing the ill-treatment of another.

11.47 Normally, one serious or several lesser incidents of domestic violence where there is a child in the household indicate that children's social care should carry out an initial assessment of the child and family, including consulting existing records. It is important to include in assessments agreed arrangements for contact between children and the non-resident parent. Children who are experiencing domestic violence may benefit from a range of support and services, and some may need safeguarding from harm. Often, supporting a non-violent parent is likely to be the most effective way of promoting the child's welfare. The police and other agencies have defined powers in criminal and civil law that can be used to help those who are subject to domestic violence. Health visitors and midwives can play a key role in providing support, and need access to information shared by the police and children's social care. Safe information-sharing protocols are necessary (*Safety and Justice: Sharing Personal Information in the Context of Domestic Violence – an Overview* (2004), found at www.homeoffice.gov.uk/rds/pdfs04/dpr30.pdf).

11.48 There is an extensive range of services for women and children, delivered through refuge projects operated by Women's Aid, and probation service provision of Women's Safety Workers, for partners of male perpetrators of domestic abuse, where they are on a domestic abuse treatment programme (in custody or in the community). These services have a vital role in contributing to an inter-agency approach in child protection cases where domestic violence is an issue. In responding to situations where domestic violence may be present, considerations include:

- asking direct questions about domestic violence
- checking whether domestic violence has occurred whenever child abuse is suspected, and considering the impact of this at all stages of assessment, enquiries and intervention
- identifying those who are responsible for domestic violence, in order that relevant family law or criminal justice responses may be made
- taking into account that there may be continued or increased risk of domestic violence towards the abused parent and/or child **after separation**, especially in connection with post-separation child contact arrangements
- providing women with full information about their legal rights, and about the extent and limits of statutory duties and powers
- helping victims and children to get protection from violence, by providing relevant practical and other assistance
- supporting non-abusing parents in making safe choices for themselves and their children
- working separately with each parent where domestic violence prevents non-abusing parents from speaking freely and participating without fear of retribution.

11.49 Domestic Violence Forums have been set up in many areas, to raise awareness of domestic violence, to promote co-ordination between agencies in preventing and responding to violence, and to encourage the development of services for those who are subjected to violence or suffer its effects. Each Domestic Violence Forum and LSCB should have clearly defined links, which should include cross-membership and identifying and working together on areas of common interest. The Domestic Violence Forum and LSCB should jointly contribute – in the context of the Children and Young People's Plan – to an assessment of the incidence of children caught up in domestic violence, their needs, the adequacy of local arrangements to meet those needs, and the implications for local services. Other work might include developing joint protocols, safe information-sharing arrangements and training. Further information on domestic violence and its impact on children is included in the reading material listed at the end of this document.

11.50 In October 2005, the LGA, Association of Directors of Social Services (ADSS), Women's Aid and the Children and Family Court Advisory and Support Service (CAFCASS) published *A Vision for Services for Children and Young People affected by Domestic Violence*.[43] This

[43] LGA, ADSS, CAFCASS and Women's Aid (2005). A *Vision for Services for Children and Young People affected by Domestic Violence – guidance to local commissioners of children's service.*

commissioning guidance for Directors of Children's Services and LSCBs focuses on meeting the needs of children affected by domestic violence within the planning of integrated children's services. It provides a framework to ensure that the range of different needs that children/young people experience in relation to domestic violence are identified and addressed. It uses the now familiar tiers of intervention, and links needs and services to the five outcomes. It brings together the evidence from research, with best practice in the delivery of mainstream services, but also highlights the specialist services to which children require access. The guidance assists authorities to assure themselves that they have in place the services and responses that will satisfy the Every Child Matters Outcomes Framework target: *children affected by domestic violence are identified, protected and supported.*

Children of drug-misusing parents

11.51 The report by the Advisory Council on the Misuse of Drugs (ACMD) *Hidden Harm – Responding to the needs of children of problem drug users* estimated that there are between 200,000 and 300,000 children of problem drug users in England and Wales – i.e. 2–3 per cent of all children under the age of 16. The report also concludes that parental drug misuse can and does cause harm to children (and young people) at every age, from conception to adulthood, including physical and emotional abuse and neglect. A thorough assessment is required to determine the extent of need and level of risk of harm in every case.

11.52 It is the responsibility of LSCBs to take full account of the particular challenges and complexities of work in this area by ensuring that there are appropriate:

- LSCB policies and procedures in place
- inter-agency protocols in place for the co-ordination of assessment and support, particularly across adult drug services and children's services
- close collaboration with local DATs/CDRPs and local drug services, as well as a number of other agencies including health, maternity services, adult and children's social care, courts, prisons and probation services.

Child abuse linked to belief in 'possession' or 'witchcraft', or in other ways related to spiritual or religious belief

11.53 The belief in 'possession' and 'witchcraft' is widespread. It is not confined to particular countries, cultures or religions, nor is it confined to new immigrant communities in this country.

11.54 The number of **known** cases of child abuse linked to accusations of 'possession' or 'witchcraft' is small, but children involved can suffer damage to their physical and mental health, capacity to learn, ability to form relationships and self-esteem.

11.55 Such abuse generally occurs when a carer views a child as being 'different', attributes this difference to the child being 'possessed' or involved in 'witchcraft', and attempts to exorcise him or her. A child could be viewed as 'different' for a variety of reasons, such as disobedience, independence, bedwetting, nightmares, illness or disability. The attempt to 'exorcise' may involve severe beating, burning, starvation, cutting or stabbing, and/or isolation, and usually occurs in the household where the child lives.

11.56 Agencies should look for these indicators, be able to identify children at risk of this type of abuse and intervene to prevent it. They should apply basic safeguarding principles, including sharing information across agencies, being child-focused at all times and keeping an open mind when talking to parents and carers. They should follow the guidance set out in this document in their work with all children and families, ensure they liaise closely with colleagues, and make connections with key people in the community – especially when working with new immigrant communities – so that they can ascertain the different dimensions of a family's cultural beliefs.

11.57 Good practice guidelines for agencies that work with children in new immigrant communities will be published later in 2006.

Child abuse and information communication technology (ICT)

11.58 The range of child abuse definitions and concepts (described in Part 1 of this guidance) are now being seen in an ICT environment. As technology develops, the internet and its range of content services can be accessed through various devices.

11.59 The internet has, in particular, become a significant tool in the distribution of indecent photographs/pseudo photographs of children. Internet chat rooms, discussion forums and bulletin boards are used as a means of contacting children with a view to grooming them for inappropriate or abusive relationships, which may include requests to make and transmit pornographic images of themselves, or to perform sexual acts live in front of a webcam. Contacts made initially in a chat room are likely to be carried on via email, instant messaging services, mobile phone or text messaging. There is also growing cause for concern about the exposure of children to inappropriate material via interactive communication technology – e.g. adult pornography and/or extreme forms of obscene material. Allowing or encouraging a child to view such material over an appreciable period of time may warrant further enquiry. Children themselves can engage in text bullying and use mobile phone cameras to capture violent assaults of other children for circulation.

11.60 Where there is evidence of a child using ICT excessively, this may be a cause for concern more generally, in the sense that it may inhibit the development of real-world social relationships, or become a factor contributing to obesity. It may also indicate either a contemporary problem, or a deeper underlying issue that ought to be addressed.

11.61 There is some evidence that people found in possession of indecent photographs/pseudo photographs of children are likely to be involved directly in child abuse. Thus when somebody is discovered to have placed or accessed such material on the internet, the police should normally consider the likelihood that the individual is involved in the active abuse of children. In particular, the individual's access to children should be established, within the family, employment contexts, and in other settings (e.g. work with children as a volunteer or in other positions of trust). If there are particular concerns about one or more specific children, it may be necessary to undertake, in accordance with the guidance set out in Chapter 5, s47 enquiries. (See the Memorandum of Understanding with the police for the appropriate notification to the Internet Watch Foundation of concerns about possible child pornography and other illegal materials on the internet.)

11.62 As part of their role in preventing abuse and neglect, LSCBs should consider activities to raise awareness about the safe use of the internet. LSCBs are a key partner in the development and delivery of training and education programmes, with the Child Exploitation and Online Protection Centre[44] (CEOP). This includes building on the work of the British Educational Communications and Technology Agency (BECTA), the Home Office and the ICT industry in raising awareness about the safe use of interactive communication technologies by children.

Children and families who go missing

11.63 Local agencies and professionals should bear in mind, when working with children and families where there are outstanding concerns about the children's safety and welfare (including where the concerns are about an unborn child who may be at future risk of significant harm), that a series of missed appointments may indicate that the family has moved out of the area or overseas. Children's social care and the police should be informed as soon as such concerns arise. In the case of children taken overseas, it may be appropriate to contact the Consular Directorate at the Foreign and Commonwealth Office, which offers assistance to British nationals in distress overseas (www.fco.gov.uk, 020 7008 1500). They may be able to follow up a case through their consular post(s) in the country concerned.

11.64 Particular consideration needs to be given to appropriate legal interventions where it appears that a child for whom there are outstanding concerns about their safety and welfare may be removed from the UK by his/her family in order to evade the involvement of agencies with safeguarding responsibilities. Particular consideration should also be given to appropriate legal interventions when a child who is subject to a care order has been removed from the UK. Children's social care, the police Child Protection Unit and the Child Abduction Section at the Foreign and Commonwealth Office should be informed immediately.

11.65 Looked after children may run away or go missing from their care placement. The various agencies responsible for the care of looked-after children should understand their respective roles in these circumstances. These should be set out in standard protocols

44 The Child Exploitation and Online Protection Centre, which came into being in April 2006, is a partnership between Government, law enforcement, NGOs (including children's charities) and industry, with the common aim of protecting children. It works to protect children, families and society from paedophiles and sex offenders – in particular, those who seek to exploit children sexually online.

describing arrangements for managing missing person's investigations developed by the local police force. It is important to understand the reasons that lead children to go missing from their care placement. Where there is the possibility that this behaviour is a result of child protection concerns, the responsible LA (or others concerned for the child) must follow its procedures to safeguard and promote the welfare of children in the area where the child is living. (See also the National Minimum Standards.)

11.66 If a child or young person is receiving an education, not only do they have the opportunity to fulfil their potential, but they are also in an environment that enables local agencies to safeguard and promote their welfare. If a child goes missing from education they could be at risk of significant harm.

11.67 There are a number of reasons why children go missing from education. These can include:

- failing to start appropriate provision, and hence never entering the system
- ceasing to attend due to exclusion (e.g. illegal unofficial exclusions) or withdrawal
- failing to complete a transition between providers (e.g. being unable to find a suitable school place after moving to a new LA area).

11.68 Children's personal circumstances, or those of their families, may contribute to the withdrawal process and the failure to make a transition.

11.69 Certain groups of vulnerable children are more likely than others to go missing from education:

- young people who have committed offences
- children living in women's refuges
- children of homeless families, perhaps living in temporary accommodation
- young runaways
- children with long-term medical or emotional problems
- looked after children
- children with a gypsy/traveller background
- young carers
- children from transient families
- teenage mothers
- children who are permanently excluded from school
- migrant children, whether in families seeking asylum or economic migrants.

11.70 There is a Child Missing Education (CME) named point of contact in every LA. Every practitioner working with a child has a responsibility to inform their CME contact if they know or suspect that a child is not receiving education. To help local agencies and professionals find children who are missing from education, and identify those at risk of going missing from education, guidance was issued in July 2004, *Identifying and maintaining contact with children missing, or at risk of going missing, from education*.

Children of families living in temporary accommodation

11.71 Placement in temporary accommodation, often at a distance from previous support networks or involving frequent moves, can lead to individuals and families falling through the net and becoming disengaged from health, education, social care and welfare support systems. Some families who have experienced homelessness, and are placed in temporary accommodation by LAs under the main homeless duty, can have very transient lifestyles.

11.72 It is important that effective systems are in place to ensure that children from homeless families receive services from health and education, as well as any other specific types of services, because these families move regularly and may be at risk of becoming disengaged from services. Where there are concerns about a child or children, the procedures set out in Chapter 5 should be followed.

11.73 Statutory guidance on making arrangements under s11 of the Children Act 2004 to safeguard and promote the welfare of children sets out the LA responsibilities for homeless families (see paragraph 3.1.9).

Migrant children

11.74 In recent years the number of migrant children in the UK has increased for a variety of reasons, including the expansion of the global economy and incidence of war and conflict. Safeguarding and promoting the welfare of these children must remain paramount with agencies in their dealings with this group.

11.75 Local agencies should give particular consideration to child victims of trafficking and unaccompanied asylum-seeking children.

Child victims of trafficking

11.76 Trafficking in people involves a collection of crimes, spanning a variety of countries and involving an increasing number of victims – resulting in considerable suffering for those trafficked. It includes the exploitation of children through force, coercion, threat and the use of deception and human rights abuses such as debt bondage, deprivation of liberty and lack of control over one's labour. Exploitation occurs through prostitution and other types of sexual exploitation, and through labour exploitation. It includes the movement of people across borders and also the movement and exploitation of people within borders.

11.77 The UK is a destination country for trafficked children and young people. There is thought to be some exploitation of children in situations of domestic service or for the purpose of benefit fraud. There have been occasional instances of minors (mainly 16- and 17-year-olds) being exploited in the sex industry. Although there is no evidence of other forms of exploitation such as 'organ donation' or 'harvesting', all agencies should remain vigilant.

11.78 Such children enter the UK through various means. Some enter as unaccompanied asylum seekers, as students or as visitors. Children are also brought in by adults who state that they are their dependents, or are met at the airport by an adult who claims to be a relative. It has been suggested that children have been brought in via internet transactions, foster arrangements and contracts as domestic staff. In some cases, girls aged 16 or 17 are tricked into a bogus marriage for the purpose of forcing them into prostitution.

11.79 If it is suspected that a child is the victim of trafficking, the police or children's social care should be informed. The *Trafficking Toolkit* (details of which can be found at www.crimereduction.gov.uk/toolkits/) provides helpful guidance on dealing with trafficking. Agencies should work together to ensure a joined-up response.

11.80 The offence of trafficking for prostitution, introduced in the Nationality, Immigration and Asylum Act 2002, carries a tough maximum penalty of 14 years' imprisonment. The Sexual Offences Act 2003 introduced new wide-ranging offences, covering trafficking into, out of or within the UK for any form of sexual offence, which also carry a 14-year maximum penalty. The Act also introduced a range of new offences covering the commercial sexual exploitation of a child, protecting children up to 18 years of age. These include buying the sexual services of a child (for which the penalty ranges from seven years' to life imprisonment, depending on the age of the child); and causing or inciting, arranging or facilitating and controlling the commercial sexual exploitation of a child in prostitution or pornography, for which the maximum penalty is 14 years' imprisonment. A new offence of trafficking for exploitation, which covers trafficking for forced labour and the removal of organs, was introduced in the Asylum and Immigration (Treatment of Claimants, etc.) Act 2004. These measures also take into account the UK's international obligations under the UN Trafficking Protocol and the EU Framework Decision on Trafficking for the Purposes of Sexual and Labour Exploitation.

Unaccompanied asylum-seeking children (UASC)

11.81 A UASC is an asylum-seeking child under the age of 18 who is not living with their parent, relative or guardian in the UK.

11.82 LAs should carry out an initial assessment and, where appropriate, a care assessment of needs for every child referred to them by Immigration Services, regardless of their immigration status.

11.83 Based on this assessment, under the *Framework for the Assessment of Children in Need and their Families* (2000), LAs have a duty to provide appropriate support and services to all

UASC, as these children should be provided with the same quality of individual assessment and related services as any other child presenting as being 'in need'.

11.84 In the majority of cases, this assessment leads to them being accommodated. Once UASC become accommodated children under s20 of the Children Act 1989, they are required to be the subject of a care plan (pathway plan at 16+). The plan must be based on this comprehensive assessment of their needs, taking account of the following dimensions:

- health (including mental health, such as whether post-traumatic support and counselling is needed)
- education
- emotional and behavioural development
- identity
- family and social relationships
- social presentation
- self-care skills, including the child's understanding of the implications of their immigration status and the skills required to manage transitions.

11.85 The responsible LA should provide services for the UASC on the basis of the above assessment, irrespective of their immigration status.

Chapter 12 – Managing individuals who pose a risk of harm to children

Introduction

12.1 This section provides practice guidance and information about a range of mechanisms that are available when managing people who have been identified as presenting a risk, or potential risk, of harm to children. Areas covered include:

- collaborative working between organisations and agencies to identify and manage people who present a risk of harm to children
- the Multi Agency Public Protection Arrangements (MAPPA), which enable agencies to work together when dealing with people who require a greater degree of resources to manage the risk of harm they present to the public
- other processes and mechanisms for working with people who present a risk to children.

Collaborative working

12.2 The Children Act 1989 recognised that the identification and investigation of child abuse, together with the protection and support of victims and their families, requires multi-agency collaboration. This has rightly focussed on the child and the supporting parent/carer. As part of that protection, action has been taken, usually by the police and social services, to prosecute known offenders or control their access to vulnerable children.

12.3 This work, while successful in addressing the safety of particular victims, has not always acknowledged the ongoing risk of harm that an individual perpetrator may present to other children in the future.

Use of the term 'Schedule One offender'

12.4 The terms 'Schedule One offender' and 'Schedule One offence' have been commonly used for anyone convicted of an offence against a child listed in Schedule One of the Children and Young Person's Act 1933. However, a conviction for an offence in Schedule One does not trigger any statutory requirement in relation to child protection issues, and inclusion on the schedule was determined solely by the age of the victim and offence for which the offender was sentenced, and not by an assessment of future risk of harm to children.

12.5 **Therefore the term 'Schedule One offender' is no longer used. It has been replaced with 'Risk to children'.** This clearly indicates that the person has been identified as presenting a risk, or potential risk, of harm to children.

12.6 Interim guidance ('Guidance on offences against children', Home Office Circular 16/2005) explains how those people who present a risk, or potential risk, of harm to children should be identified. The circular explains that the present method of automatically identifying as a risk to children an offender who has been convicted of an offence listed in Schedule One of the Children and Young Person's Act 1933 fails to focus on those who **continue** to present a risk. For a copy of the circular, please access the Home Office website.

12.7 Practitioners working in this area should use the new list of offences as a 'trigger' to a further assessment to determine if an offender should be regarded as presenting a continued risk of harm to children. This allows agencies to focus resources on the correct group of individuals, and not include those who have been identified solely because a child was harmed during the offence – e.g. as in the case of a road traffic accident. An offender who has harmed a child might not continue to present a risk towards that child or other children. Practitioners should also consider that where a juvenile offender (aged under 18 years) offends against a child, it is possible that there is little or no future risk of harm to other children, and the stigma of being identified as presenting a continued risk of harm to children is potentially damaging to the development of the juvenile offender.

12.8 Once an individual has been sentenced and identified as presenting a risk to children, agencies have a responsibility to work collaboratively to monitor and manage the risk of harm to others. Where the offender is given a community sentence, Offender Managers (or Youth Offending Team workers) monitor the individual's risk to others and their behaviour, and liaise with partner agencies as appropriate.

12.9 In cases where the offender has been sentenced to a period of custody, prison establishments undertake a similar responsibility and, in addition, notify other agencies prior to any period of release.

New offences targeted at those who abuse children through prostitution

12.10 Those who abuse or exploit children through prostitution should feel the full force of the law. The Sexual Offences Act 2003 introduced a number of new offences to deal with those who abuse and exploit children in this way. The offences protect children up to the age of 18 and can attract tough penalties. They include:

- paying for the sexual services of a child
- causing or inciting child prostitution
- arranging or facilitating child prostitution
- controlling a child prostitute.

12.11 These are not the only charges that may be brought against those who use or abuse children through prostitution. Abusers and coercers often physically, sexually and emotionally abuse these children, and may effectively imprison them. If a child is a victim of serious offences, the most serious charge that the evidence will support should always be used.

MAPPA

12.12 Multi Agency Public Protection Arrangements provide a national framework in England and Wales for the assessment and management of risk posed by serious and violent offenders, including individuals who are considered to pose a risk, or potential risk, of harm to children. The arrangements impose statutory requirements on the police and probation services (the 'Responsible Authorities') to make these arrangements under s67–68 of the Criminal Justice and Court Services Act 2000. Sections 325–327 of the Criminal Justice Act 2003 extended and strengthened these public protection arrangements by:

- including the Prison Service as part of the Responsible Authorities
- placing a duty to co-operate with the Responsible Authority on a number of agencies providing services to offenders – including health, housing, social services, education, Youth Offending Teams, Jobcentre Plus and electronic monitoring providers
- increasing the public engagement with MAPPA, by appointing two lay advisers to assist the Responsible Authority in each area to monitor and review those arrangements locally.

12.13 While MAPPA does not address the concerns of further serious harm posed by all perpetrators of child abuse, its purpose is to focus on convicted sexual and violent offenders in, and returning to, the community. The development of national databases significantly enhances the capability to track offenders who move between communities and across organisational boundaries.

12.14 Practitioners, through rigorous risk assessment on an individual case basis, refer offenders to the MAPPA process. Most areas now have a co-ordinator, who can be contacted via any of the local Responsible Authorities. The Area MAPPA Strategic Management Board will be in place, and comprises lead managers from police, probation and prison services, a number of agencies with a duty to co-operate and two lay advisors.

12.15 The full MAPPA guidance and the local area annual reports, which include examples of case studies, are available at www.probation.homeoffice.gov.uk/output/page30.asp

Identification of MAPPA offenders

12.16 Offenders falling within the remit of MAPPA in each area are categorised as follows:

- **Category 1: registered sex offenders** – as defined by the Sex Offenders Act 1997, and amended by the Criminal Justice and Court Services Act 2000 and the Sexual Offences Act 2003
- **Category 2: violent and other sex offenders** – violent and sexual offenders who receive a custodial sentence of 12 months or more, those detained under hospital or guardianship orders and those who have committed specific offences against children
- **Category 3: other offenders** – offenders not in Category 1 or 2, but who are considered by the Responsible Authority to pose a serious risk to the public.

Sharing of relevant information

12.17 Exchange of information is essential for effective public protection. The MAPPA guidance clarifies how MAPPA agencies may exchange information among themselves, and with other people or organisations outside the MAPPA. Multi Agency Public Protection Panels (MAPPP) can recommend that agencies disclose information about offenders to a number of organisations, including schools and voluntary groups.

Assessment of the risk of serious harm

12.18 The National Offender Management Service (NOMS) assesses risk of harm using the Offender Assessment System (OASys). The Youth Justice Board uses ASSET for under-18-year-olds. The levels of risk are as follows:

- **low**: no significant current indicators of risk of harm
- **medium**: identifiable indicators of risk of harm. The offender has the potential to cause harm, but is unlikely to do so unless there is a change in circumstances – e.g. failure to take medication, loss of accommodation, relationship breakdown, drug or alcohol misuse
- **high**: identifiable indicators of risk of serious harm. The potential event could happen at any time, and the impact would be serious
- **very high**: an imminent risk of harm. The potential event is likely to happen imminently, and the impact to be serious.

12.19 Risk is categorised by reference to who may be the subject of that harm. This includes children who may be vulnerable to harm of various kinds, including violent or sexual behaviour, emotional harm or neglect. In this context, MAPPA works closely with

LSCBs to ensure the best local joint arrangements can be made for any individual child being considered by either setting.

Managing risk

12.20 The Responsible Authority needs to ensure that strategies to address risk are identified and plans developed, implemented and reviewed on a regular basis. Those plans must include action to monitor the behaviour and attitudes of offenders, and to intervene in their life in order to control and minimise the risk of serious harm to others.

12.21 The MAPPA framework identifies three separate but connected levels at which risk is managed:

- **level 1 – ordinary risk management.** This is where the risks posed by the offender can be managed by one agency without significantly involving other agencies
- **level 2 – local inter-agency risk management.** This is used where significant involvement from more than one agency is required, but where either the level of risk or the complexity of managing the risk is not so great as to require referral to level 3
- **level 3 – MAPPP – Multi Agency Public Protection Panels.** This relates to the 'critical few' and includes an offender who:
  - presents risks that can only be managed by a plan that requires close co-operation at a senior level, due to the complexity of the case and/or because of the unusual resource commitments it requires; **and**
  - although not assessed as being a high or very high risk, the case is exceptional because of the likelihood of a high level of media scrutiny and/or public interest in the management of the case, and there is a need to ensure that public confidence in the criminal justice system is sustained.

Other processes and mechanisms

Offending behaviour programmes

12.22 Rehabilitation of offenders is the best guarantee of long-term public protection. A range of treatment programmes, which have been developed or commissioned by the prison and probation service, have been 'tried and tested' at a national level. Examples include sex offender treatment programmes, programmes for offenders convicted of internet-related sexual offences, and programmes for perpetrators of domestic abuse.

Disqualification from working with children

12.23 The Criminal Justice and Court Services Act 2000 (CJCSA), as amended by the Criminal Justice Act 2003, provides for people to be disqualified from working with children. A person is disqualified by either:

- a disqualification order, made by the Crown Court when a person is convicted for an offence against a child (under 18) listed in schedule 4 to the CJCSA. Schedule 4 includes sexual offences, violent offences and offences of selling Class A drugs to a child
- being included in a permanent capacity on the list of people who are unsuitable to work with children, which is kept under s1 of the Protection of Children Act 1999 (see paragraph 12.29) or
- being included on DfES List 99 on the grounds of being unsuitable to work with children (see paragraph 12.33).

12.24 When making a disqualification order, the court applies different provisions, depending on the age of the offender and the sentence received:

- **adult offender who receives a qualifying sentence** (12 months or more or equivalent) or relevant order for a specified offence: a disqualification order must be made unless the court is satisfied that the individual is unlikely to commit any further offence against a child
- **juvenile offender who receives a qualifying sentence or relevant order**: a disqualification order must be made if the court is satisfied the individual is likely to commit a further offence against a child
- **adult or juvenile offender who does not receive a qualifying sentence or relevant order**: a disqualification order may be made if the court is satisfied that the offender is likely to commit a further offence against a child.

12.25 A disqualification order is of indefinite duration (i.e. for life), but application can be made for an order to be reviewed by the Care Standards Tribunal after 10 years (or five years in the case of a juvenile).

12.26 Disqualification orders are made as part of the sentence and, therefore, cannot be made on application. However, the Criminal Justice Act 2003 allows the Crown Prosecution Service to refer cases back to the courts where it appears that the court should have considered making a disqualification order but failed to do so. Therefore if an offender is identified who, it seems, should have been made subject to a disqualification order, the case should be discussed with other MAPPA agencies and the Crown Prosecution Service.

12.27 People who are disqualified from working with children are prohibited from applying for, offering to do, accepting or doing any work in a 'regulated position'. The positions covered are specified in s36 of the CJCSA and are broadly defined. They include working with children in paid or unpaid positions whose normal duties involve caring for, training, supervising or being in sole charge of children. They also include positions whose normal duties involve unsupervised contact with children under arrangements made by a responsible person – e.g. a parent – and include a broad range of work with children, from babysitting to working as a schoolteacher, and from working in a local authority education or social services department to voluntary work at a boys' football club. School governor is a regulated position, as are other positions whose normal duties include the supervision or management of another individual who works in a regulated position.

12.28 A person who is disqualified commits an offence if he/she knowingly applies for, offers to do, accepts or does any work with children. It is also an offence for an individual knowingly to offer work with children to, or procure work with children for, an individual who is disqualified from working with children, or to allow such an individual to continue in such work. The police should be contacted if such an offence is committed. The maximum penalty for breach is five years' imprisonment.

The Protection of Children Act List

12.29 The Protection of Children Act 1999 gives the Secretary of State power to keep a list of people who are unsuitable to work with children in childcare positions. Childcare organisations in the regulated sector are required to make a report to the Secretary of State in specified circumstances, principally if they dismiss a person for misconduct that has harmed a child, or put a child at risk of harm, or if a person resigns in circumstances where s/he might have been dismissed for that reason. Other organisations that employ childcare workers can also make reports in those circumstances, but do not have to.

12.30 If there appear to be grounds for including the person on the list, his/her name is added provisionally while further enquiries are made, and the person is given the opportunity to make written observations about the case. If at the end of that process the Secretary of State is of the opinion that:

- the referring organisation reasonably believed that the person was guilty of misconduct that harmed a child, or put a child at risk of harm; and
- the person is unsuitable to work with children

the person will be added to the list on a permanent basis.

12.31 Anyone who is included on the list on a permanent basis can appeal to an independent tribunal, the Care Standards Tribunal, within three months of the decision.

12.32 Childcare organisations must check the list (and List 99) before employing someone in a childcare position.

DfES List 99

12.33 List 99 is a confidential list of people whom the Secretary of State has directed may not be employed by local education authorities (LEAs), schools (including independent schools) or further education (FE) institutions as a teacher, or in work involving regular contact with children under 18 years of age. The list also includes details of people the Secretary of State has directed can only be employed subject to specific conditions.

Employers in the education sector are under a duty not to use a person who is subject to a direction in contravention of that direction.

12.34 LEAs, schools, FE institutions and other employers have a statutory duty to make reports to DfES if they cease to use a person's services on grounds of misconduct or unsuitability to work with children, or if someone leaves in circumstances where the employer might have ceased to use their services on one of those grounds. The police also make reports to DfES if a teacher or other member of staff at a school is convicted of a criminal offence.

12.35 People who are convicted of one of a number of sexual or violent offences against a child under 16 years of age, or in some cases against an adult, are automatically deemed unsuitable to work with children and are included on List 99. Those subject to a disqualification order, and those permanently included on the Protection of Children Act List, are also included on List 99 automatically. In other cases the Secretary of State, advised by a panel of experts who must consider the circumstances of the individual case and give the person concerned an opportunity to make representations before reaching a decision, has the power to direct that a person be prohibited from employment and added to the list.

12.36 People included on List 99, other than those included automatically, can appeal to the Care Standards Tribunal within three months of the decision.

Criminal Records Bureau (CRB)

12.37 The Criminal Records Bureau (CRB) is an executive agency of the Home Office. The CRB's Disclosure Service aims to help employers make safer recruitment decisions by identifying candidates who may be unsuitable for certain types of work. Employers should ask successful candidates to apply to the CRB for a Standard or Enhanced Disclosure, depending on the duties of the particular position or job involved. In addition to information about a person's criminal record, Disclosures supplied in connection with work with children contain details of whether a person is included on List 99, the Protection of Children Act List, or is disqualified by the courts from all work with children. Enhanced Disclosures may contain details of acquittals or other non-conviction information held on local police records, relevant to the position or post for which the person has been selected, and the police may also provide additional information to employers in a separate letter. Further information, including details of how to apply for Disclosures, is available at www.crb.gov.uk.

The Sex Offenders Register

12.38 The notification requirements of Part 2 of the Sexual Offences Act 2003 (known as the Sex Offenders Register) are an automatic requirement on offenders who receive a conviction or caution for certain sexual offences. The notification requirements are intended to ensure that the police are informed of the whereabouts of offenders in the community. The notification requirements do not bar offenders from certain types of employment, from being alone with children, etc.

12.39 Offenders must notify the police of certain personal details within three days of their conviction or caution for a relevant sexual offence (or, if they are in prison on this date, within three days of their release).

12.40 Such an offender must then notify the police, within three days, of any change to the notified details and whenever they spend seven days or more at another address.

12.41 All offenders must reconfirm their details at least once every 12 months, and notify the police seven days in advance of any travel overseas for a period of three days or more.

12.42 The period of time for which an offender must comply with these requirements depends on whether they received a conviction or caution for their offence and, where appropriate, the sentence they received.

12.43 Failure to comply with these requirements is a criminal offence, with a maximum penalty of five years' imprisonment. The police should be contacted if such an offence is committed.

Notification Orders

12.44 Notification Orders are intended to ensure that British citizens or residents, as well as foreign nationals, can be made subject to the notification requirements (the Sex Offenders Register) in the UK if they receive convictions or cautions for sexual offences overseas.

12.45 Notification Orders are made on application from the police to a magistrates' court. Therefore, if an offender is identified who has received a conviction or caution for a sexual offence overseas, the case should be referred to the local police for action.

12.46 If a Notification Order is in force, the offender becomes subject to the requirements of sex offender registration (see above).

12.47 For example, a Notification Order could ensure that the notification requirements apply to a British man who, while on holiday in Southeast Asia, received a caution for a sexual offence on a child.

12.48 Any information that an individual has received a conviction or caution for a sexual offence overseas should, where appropriate, be shared with the police.

Sexual Offences Prevention Orders (SOPOs)

12.49 Introduced by the Sexual Offences Act 2003, SOPOs are civil preventative orders designed to protect the public from serious sexual harm. A court may make a SOPO when it deals with an offender who has received a conviction for an offence listed at Schedule 3 (sexual offences) or Schedule 5 (violent and other offences) to the Act and is assessed as posing a risk of serious sexual harm. The police can also apply for a SOPO to a magistrates' court in respect of an offender who has a previous conviction or caution for a Schedule 3 or 5 offence and who poses a risk of serious sexual harm.

12.50 SOPOs include such prohibitions as the court considers appropriate. For example, a child sex offender who poses a risk of serious sexual harm could be prohibited from loitering near schools or playgrounds. The offender will also, if s/he is not already, become subject to the notification requirements for the duration of the order.

12.51 SOPOs can be made on application from the police, so any violent or sex offender who poses a risk of serious sexual harm should be referred to MAPPA agencies, and the police in particular. In an application for an order, the police can set out the prohibitions they would like the court to consider.

12.52 Breach of any of the prohibitions in a SOPO is a criminal offence, with a maximum punishment of five years' imprisonment. Therefore the police should be contacted whenever a SOPO is breached.

12.53 SOPOs can be particularly helpful in the management of sex offenders who are assessed as continuing to pose a high risk of harm, but are no longer subject to statutory supervision.

Risk of Sexual Harm Orders (RSHOs)

12.54 Introduced by the Sexual Offences Act 2003, RSHOs are civil preventative orders. They are used to protect children from the risks posed by individuals who do not necessarily have a previous conviction for a sexual or violent offence but who have, on at least two occasions, engaged in sexually explicit conduct or communication with a child or children, and who pose a risk of further such harm. For a RSHO to be made, it is not necessary for there to be a risk that the defendant will commit a sexual offence against a child – the risk may be that s/he intends to communicate with children in a sexually explicit way. The RSHO can contain such prohibitions as the court considers necessary. For example, in the case of an adult found regularly communicating with young children in a sexual way in internet chat rooms, a RSHO could be used to prohibit the person from using the internet in order to stop him/her from such harmful activity.

12.55 RSHOs are made on application from the police, so any person who is thought to pose a risk of sexual harm to children should be referred to the police. In an application for an order, the police can set out the prohibitions they would like the court to consider.

12.56 Breach of any of the prohibitions in a RSHO is a criminal offence, with a maximum punishment of five years' imprisonment. It is also an offence that makes the offender subject to the notification requirements (see above). The police should be contacted whenever a RSHO is breached.

Appendix 1 – Statutory Framework

1. All organisations that work with children and families share a commitment to safeguard and promote their welfare, and for many agencies that is underpinned by a statutory duty or duties.

2. This appendix briefly explains the legislation most relevant to work to safeguard and promote the welfare of children.

Children Act 2004

3. **Section 10** requires each local authority (LA)[45] to make arrangements to promote co-operation between the authority, each of the authority's relevant partners (see Table A below) and such other persons or bodies working with children in the LA's area as the authority considers appropriate. The arrangements are to be made with a view to improving the wellbeing of children in the authority's area – which includes protection from harm or neglect alongside other outcomes. This section of the Children Act 2004 is the legislative basis for children's trust arrangements.

4. **Section 11** requires a range of organisations (see Table A) to make arrangements for ensuring that their functions, and services provided on their behalf, are discharged with regard to the need to safeguard and promote the welfare of children.

5. **Section 12** enables the Secretary of State to require LAs to establish and operate databases relating to the s10 or s11 duties (above) or the s175 duty (below), or to establish and operate databases nationally. This section limits the information that may be included in those databases, and sets out which organisations can be required to, and which can be enabled to, disclose information to be included in the databases.

6. **Section 13** requires each children's services authority to establish a LSCB. It also requires a range of organisations (see Table A) to take part in LSCBs. Sections 13–16 set out the framework for LSCBs, and the LSCB Regulations set out the requirements in more detail, in particular on LSCB functions.

[45] See Glossary.

Table A: Bodies covered by key duties

Body (in addition to LAs)	**CA 2004 Section 10 (duty to co-operate)**	**CA 2004 Section 11 (duty to safeguard and promote welfare)**	**Ed Act 2002 Section 175 and regulations under Section 157 (duty to safeguard and promote welfare)**	**CA 2004 Section 13 (statutory partners in LSCBs)**	**CA 1989 Section 27 (help with children in need)**	**CA 1989 Section 47 (help with enquiries about significant harm)**
District councils	X	X		X	X	X
Police authority	X	X				
Chief officer of police	X	X		X		
Local probation board	X	X		X		
Youth Offending Team	X	X		X		
Strategic Health Authority	X	X		X	X	X
Primary Care Trust	X	X		X	X	X
Connexions service	X	X		X		
Learning and Skills Council	X					
Special Health Authority		X (as designated by the Secretary of State)			X	X
NHS Trust		X		X	X	X
NHS Foundation Trust		X		X	X	X
British Transport Police		X				
Prison or secure training centre		X		X (which detains children)		
CAFCASS				X		
Maintained schools			X			
FE colleges			X			
Independent schools			X			
Contracted services		X	X			

Education Act 2002

7. **Section 175** puts a duty on local education authorities, maintained (state) schools and further education institutions, including sixth-form colleges, to exercise their functions with a view to safeguarding and promoting the welfare of children – children who are pupils, and students under 18 years of age in the case of schools and colleges.

8. The same duty is put on independent schools, including academies, by Regulations made under s157 of that Act.

Children Act 1989

9. The Children Act 1989 places a duty on LAs to promote and safeguard the welfare of children in need in their area.

Section 17(1) of the Children Act 1989 states that:

It shall be the general duty of every local authority:

- To safeguard and promote the welfare of children within their area who are in need; and
- So far as is consistent with that duty, to promote the upbringing of such children by their families, by providing a range and level of services appropriate to those children's needs.

Section 17(10) states that a child shall be taken to be in need if:

a) he is unlikely to achieve or maintain, or to have the opportunity of achieving or maintaining, a reasonable standard of health or development without the provision for him of services by a local authority under this Part

b) his heath or development is likely to be significantly impaired, or further impaired, without the provision for him of such services, or

c) he is disabled.

(Children Act 1989, s17)

10. The primary focus of legislation about children in need is on how well they are progressing and whether their development will be impaired without the provision of services.

11. It also places a specific duty on other LA services and health bodies to co-operate in the interests of children in need in s27. Section 322 of the Education Act 1996 places a duty on social services to assist the local education authority where any child has special educational needs.

> Where it appears to a local authority that any authority mentioned in sub-section (3) could, by taking any specified action, help in the exercise of any of their functions under this Part, they may request the help of that other authority, specifying the action in question. An authority whose help is so requested shall comply with the request if it is compatible with their own statutory or other duties and obligations and does not unduly prejudice the discharge of any of their functions.
>
> The authorities are:
>
> *a. Any local authority;*
>
> *b. Any local education authority;*
>
> *c. Any local housing authority;*
>
> *d. Any health authority, special health authority, Primary Care Trust, National Health Service Trust or NHS Foundation Trust; and*
>
> *e. Any person authorised by the Secretary of State for the purpose of this section.*
>
> (Children Act 1989, s27)

12. Under s47 of the Children Act 1989, the same agencies are placed under a similar duty to assist LAs in carrying out enquiries into whether or not a child is at risk of significant harm.

13. Section 47 also sets out duties for the LA itself, around making enquiries in certain circumstances to decide whether they should take any action to safeguard or promote the welfare of a child.

Section 47(1) of the Children Act 1989 states that:

Where a local authority:

a. are informed that a child who lives, or is found, in their area (i) is the subject of an emergency protection order, or (ii) is in police protection, or (iii) has contravened a ban imposed by a curfew notice imposed within the meaning of Chapter I of Part I of the Crime and Disorder Act 1998; or

b. have reasonable cause to suspect that a child who lives, or is found, in their area is suffering, or is likely to suffer, significant harm:

The authority shall make, or cause to be made, such enquiries as they consider necessary to enable them to decide whether they should take any action to safeguard or promote the child's welfare.

In the case of a child falling within paragraph (a) (iii) above, the enquiries shall be commenced as soon as practicable and, in any event, within 48 hours of the authority receiving the information.

(Children Act 1989, s47)

14. Under s17 of the Children Act 1989, LAs carry lead responsibility for establishing whether a child is in need and for ensuring that services are provided to that child as appropriate. This does not necessarily require LAs themselves to be the provider of such services.

15. Section 17(5) of the Children Act 1989 enables the LA to make arrangements with others to provide services on their behalf.

Every local authority:

a. Shall facilitate the provision by others (including in particular voluntary organisations) of services which the authority have power to provide by virtue of this section, or section 18, 20, 23, 23B to 23D, 24A or 24B; and

b. May make such arrangements as they see fit for any person to act on their behalf in the provision of any such service.

(Children Act 1989, s17(5))

16. Section 53 of the Children Act 2004 amends both s17 and s47 of the Children Act 1989, to require in each case that before determining what services to provide or what action to take, the LA shall, so far as is reasonably practicable and consistent with the child's welfare:

- ascertain the child's wishes and feelings regarding the provision of those services or the action to be taken
- give due consideration (with regard to the child's age and understanding) to such wishes and feelings of the child as they have been able to ascertain.

Emergency protection powers

17. There is a range of powers available to LAs and others such as the NSPCC and the police to take emergency action to safeguard children.

Emergency protection orders

The court may make an emergency protection order under s44 of the Children Act 1989, if it is satisfied that there is reasonable cause to believe that a child is likely to suffer significant harm if:

- s/he is not removed to different accommodation; or
- s/he does not remain in the place in which s/he is then being accommodated.

An emergency protection order may also be made if enquiries (e.g. made under s47) are being frustrated by access to the child being unreasonably refused to a person authorised to seek access, and the applicant has reasonable cause to believe that access is needed as a matter of urgency.

An emergency protection order gives authority to remove a child, and places the child under the protection of the applicant.

Exclusion requirement

The court may include an exclusion requirement in an interim care order or emergency protection order (Sections 38A and 44A of the Children Act 1989). This allows a perpetrator to be removed from the home instead of having to remove the child. The court must be satisfied that:

- there is reasonable cause to believe that if the person is excluded from the home in which the child lives, the child will cease to suffer, or cease to be likely to suffer, significant harm, or that enquires will cease to be frustrated; and
- another person living in the home is able and willing to give the child the care that it would be reasonable to expect a parent to give, and consents to the exclusion requirement.

Continued

Police protection powers

Under s46 of the Children Act 1989, where a police officer has reasonable cause to believe that a child would otherwise be likely to suffer significant harm, s/he may:

- remove the child to suitable accommodation and keep him or her there; or
- take reasonable steps to ensure that the child's removal from any hospital, or other place in which the child is then being accommodated is prevented.

No child may be kept in police protection for more than 72 hours.

Homelessness Act 2002

18. Under s12 (which inserts s213A of the Housing Act 1996), housing authorities are required to refer to social services homeless persons with dependent children who are ineligible for homelessness assistance, or are intentionally homeless, as long as the person consents. If homelessness persists, any child in the family could be in need. In such cases, if social services decide the child's needs would be best met by helping the family to obtain accommodation, they can ask the housing authority for reasonable assistance in this, and the housing authority must give reasonable assistance.

Appendix 2 – Framework for the Assessment of Children in Need

1. The *Framework for the Assessment of Children in Need and their Families* (outlined in Figure 2) provides a systematic basis for collecting and analysing information to support professional judgements about how to help children and families in the best interests of the child. Practitioners should use the framework to gain an understanding of:

- a child's developmental needs
- the capacity of parents or caregivers to respond appropriately to those needs, including their capacity to keep the child safe from harm
- the impact of wider family and environmental factors on the parents and child.

Each of these three main aspects of the framework is outlined in more detail in Boxes 1, 2 and 3, respectively.

2. The framework is to be used for the assessment of all children in need, including cases where there are concerns that a child may be suffering significant harm. The process of engaging in an assessment should be viewed as being part of the range of services offered to children and families. Use of the framework should provide evidence to help, guide and inform judgements about children's welfare and safety, from the first point of contact, through the processes of initial and more detailed core assessments, according to the nature and extent of the child's needs. The provision of appropriate services need not, and should not, wait until the end of the assessment process, but should be determined according to what is required, and when, to promote the welfare and safety of the child.

3. Evidence about children's developmental progress – and their parents' capacity to respond appropriately to the child's needs within the wider family and environmental context – should underpin judgements about:

- the child's welfare and safety
- whether – and, if so, how – to provide help to children and family members
- what form of intervention will bring about the best possible outcomes for the child
- the intended outcomes of intervention.

Box 1: Dimensions of children's developmental needs

Health

Includes growth and development, as well as physical and mental wellbeing. The impact of genetic factors and of any impairment needs to be considered. Involves receiving appropriate healthcare when ill, an adequate and nutritious diet, exercise, immunisations (where appropriate) and developmental checks, dental and optical care and, for older children, appropriate advice and information on issues that have an impact on health, including sex education and substance misuse.

Education

Covers all areas of a child's cognitive development, which begins from birth. Includes opportunities:

- for play and interaction with other children
- to have access to books
- to acquire a range of skills and interests
- to experience success and achievement.

Involves an adult interested in educational activities, progress and achievements, who takes account of the child's starting point and any special educational needs.

Emotional and behavioural development

Concerns the appropriateness of response demonstrated in feelings and actions by a child, initially to parents and caregivers and, as the child grows older, to others beyond the family. Includes nature and quality of early attachments, characteristics of temperament, adaptation to change, response to stress and degree of appropriate self-control.

Identity

Concerns the child's growing sense of self as a separate and valued person. Includes the child's view of self and abilities, self-image and self-esteem, and having a positive sense of individuality. Race, religion, age, gender, sexuality and disability may all contribute to this. Feelings of belonging and acceptance by family, peer group and wider society, including other cultural groups.

Family and social relationships

Development of empathy and the capacity to place self in someone else's shoes. Includes a stable and affectionate relationship with parents or caregivers, good relationships with siblings, increasing importance of age-appropriate friendships with peers and other significant people in the child's life, and response of family to these relationships.

Social presentation

Concerns the child's growing understanding of the way in which appearance, behaviour and any impairment are perceived by the outside world and the impression being created. Includes appropriateness of dress for age, gender, culture and religion; cleanliness and personal hygiene; and availability of advice from parents or caregivers about presentation in different settings.

Self care skills

Concerns the acquisition by a child of practical, emotional and communication competencies required for increasing independence. Includes early practical skills of dressing and feeding, opportunities to gain confidence and practical skills to undertake activities away from the family, and independent living skills as older children. Includes encouragement to acquire social problem-solving approaches. Special attention should be given to the impact of a child's impairment and other vulnerabilities, and on social circumstances affecting these in the development of self care skills.

Box 2: Dimensions of parenting capacity

Basic care

Providing for the child's physical needs, and appropriate medical and dental care. Includes provision of food, drink, warmth, shelter, clean and appropriate clothing and adequate personal hygiene.

Ensuring safety

Ensuring the child is adequately protected from harm or danger. Includes protection from significant harm or danger, and from contact with unsafe adults/other children and from self-harm. Recognition of hazards and danger both in the home and elsewhere.

Emotional warmth

Ensuring the child's emotional needs are met, giving the child a sense of being specially valued and a positive sense of their own racial and cultural identity. Includes ensuring the child's requirements for secure, stable and affectionate relationships with significant adults, with appropriate sensitivity and responsiveness to the child's needs. Appropriate physical contact, comfort and cuddling sufficient to demonstrate warm regard, praise and encouragement.

Stimulation

Promoting the child's learning and intellectual development through encouragement and cognitive stimulation and promoting social opportunities. Includes facilitating the child's cognitive development and potential through interaction, communication, talking and responding to the child's language and questions, encouraging and joining the child's play, and promoting educational opportunities. Enabling the child to experience success and ensuring school attendance or equivalent opportunity. Facilitating the child to meet the challenges of life.

Guidance and boundaries

Enabling the child to regulate their own emotions and behaviour. The key parental tasks are demonstrating and modelling appropriate behaviour and control of emotions and interactions with others, and guidance that involves setting boundaries, so that the child is able to develop an internal model of moral values and conscience, and social behaviour appropriate for the society within which they will grow up. The aim is to enable the child to grow into an autonomous adult, holding their own values, and able to demonstrate appropriate behaviour with others rather than having to be dependent on rules outside themselves. This includes not over-protecting children from exploratory and learning experiences. Includes social problem-solving, anger management, consideration for others, and effective discipline and shaping of behaviour.

Stability

Providing a sufficiently stable family environment to enable a child to develop and maintain a secure attachment to the primary caregiver(s) in order to ensure optimal development. Includes ensuring secure attachments are not disrupted, providing consistency of emotional warmth over time and responding in a similar manner to the same behaviour. Parental responses change and develop according to the child's developmental progress. In addition, ensuring children keep in contact with important family members and significant others.

Box 3: Family and environmental factors

Family history and functioning

Family history includes both genetic and psycho-social factors. Family functioning is influenced by:

- who is living in the household and how they are related to the child
- significant changes in family/household composition
- history of childhood experiences of parents
- chronology of significant life events and their meaning to family members
- nature of family functioning, including sibling relationships, and its impact on the child
- parental strengths and difficulties, including those of an absent parent
- the relationship between separated parents.

Wider family

Who are considered to be members of the wider family by the child and the parents? This includes related and non-related persons and absent wider family. What is their role and importance to the child and parents, and in precisely what way?

Housing

Does the accommodation have basic amenities and facilities appropriate to the age and development of the child and other resident members? Is the housing accessible and suitable to the needs of disabled family members? Includes the interior and exterior of the accommodation and immediate surroundings. Basic amenities include water, heating, sanitation, cooking facilities, sleeping arrangements and cleanliness, hygiene and safety and their impact on the child's upbringing.

Employment

Who is working in the household, their pattern of work and any changes? What impact does this have on the child? How is work or absence of work viewed by family members? How does it affect their relationship with the child? Includes children's experience of work and its impact on them.

Income

Income available over a sustained period of time. Is the family in receipt of all its benefit entitlements? Sufficiency of income to meet the family's needs. The way resources available to the family are used. Are there financial difficulties that affect the child?

Family's social integration

Exploration of the wider context of the local neighbourhood and community and its impact on the child and parents. Includes the degree of the family's integration or isolation, its peer groups, friendship and social networks and the importance attached to them.

Community resources

Describes all facilities and services in a neighbourhood, including universal services of primary health care, day care and schools, places of worship, transport, shops and leisure activities. Includes availability, accessibility and standard of resources and impact on the family, including disabled members.

Appendix 3 – Use of questionnaires and scales to evidence assessment and decision-making

1. **The Strengths and Difficulties Questionnaires** (Goodman *et al.,* 1997; Goodman *et al.*, 1998). These scales are a modification of the very widely used instruments to screen for emotional and behavioural problems in children and adolescents – the Rutter A + B scales for parents and teachers. Although similar to Rutter's scales, the wording of the Strengths and Difficulties Questionnaire was reframed to focus on a child's emotional and behavioural strengths as well as difficulties. The actual questionnaire incorporates five scales: pro-social, hyperactivity, emotional problems, conduct (behavioural) problems and peer problems. In the pack, there are versions of the scale to be completed by adult caregivers or teachers for children aged three to 16, and for children aged 11 to 16. These questionnaires have been used with disabled children and their teachers and carers. They are available in 40 languages on the following website: http://chp.iop.kcl.ac.uk/sdq/b3.html.

2. **The Parenting Daily Hassles Scale** (Crinic and Greenberg, 1990; Crinic and Booth, 1991). This scale aims to assess the frequency and intensity/impact of 20 potential parenting 'daily' hassles experienced by adults caring for children. It has been used in a wide variety of research studies concerned with children and families – particularly families with young children. Parents (or caregivers) generally like filling it out, because it touches on many aspects of being a parent that are important to them.

3. **The Recent Life Events Questionnaire** (taken from Brugha *et al.*, 1985) helps to define negative life events over the last 12 months, but could be used over a longer timescale, and significantly whether the respondent thought they have a continuing influence. Respondents are asked to identify which of the events still affect them. It is hoped that use of the scale will:

    - result in a fuller picture of a family's history and contribute to greater contextual understanding of the family's current situation
    - help practitioners explore how particular recent life events have affected the carer and the family

- in some situations, identify life events that family members have not reported earlier.

4. **The Home Conditions Assessment** (Davie *et al.,* 1984) helps make judgements about the context in which the child is living, dealing with questions of safety, order and cleanliness that have an important bearing where issues of neglect are the focus of concern. The total score has been found to correlate highly with indices of the development of children.

5. **The Family Activity Scale** (derived from the Child-Centredness Scale – Smith, 1985) gives practitioners an opportunity to explore with carers the environment provided for their children, through joint activities and support for independent activities. This includes information about the cultural and ideological environment in which children live, as well as how their carers respond to their children's actions (e.g. concerning play and independence). They aim to be independent of socio-economic resources. There are two separate scales – one for children aged two to six, and one for children aged seven to 12.

6. **The Alcohol Scale** (developed by Piccinelli *et al.,* 1997). Alcohol abuse is estimated to be present in about six per cent of primary carers, ranking it third in frequency behind major depression and generalised anxiety. Higher rates are found in certain localities, and particularly among those parents known to social care. Drinking alcohol affects different individuals in different ways. For example, some people may be relatively unaffected by the same amount of alcohol that incapacitates others. The primary concern, therefore, is not the amount of alcohol consumed, but how it impacts on the individual and, more particularly, on their role as a parent. This questionnaire has been found to be effective in detecting individuals with alcohol disorders and those with hazardous drinking habits.

7. **Adult Wellbeing Scale** (based on the Irritability, Depression, Anxiety – IDA scale – Snaith *et al.,* 1978). This scale was devised by a social worker involved in the pilot. The questions are framed in a 'personal' fashion (i.e. I feel, my appetite is…). The scale looks at how an adult is feeling in terms of their depression, anxiety and irritability. It allows adults to respond from four possible answers, which gives them some choice, and therefore less restriction. This could enable adults to feel more empowered.

8. **The Adolescent Wellbeing Scale** (Self-rating Scale for Depression in Young People – Birleson, 1980). This was originally validated for children aged between seven and 16. It involves 18 questions, each relating to different aspects of a child or adolescent's life and how they feel about these. As a result of the pilot, the wording of some questions was altered in order to be more appropriate to adolescents. Although children as young as seven and eight have used it, older children's thoughts and beliefs about themselves are more stable. The scale is intended to enable practitioners to gain more insight and understanding into how adolescents feel about their life.

9. **The HOME Inventory** (Cox and Walker, 2002). This assessment provides, through interview and observation, an extensive profile of the context of care provided for the child, and is a reliable approach to assessment of parenting. It gives a reliable account of the parents' capacities to provide learning materials, language stimulation and an appropriate physical environment; to be responsive, stimulating, providing adequate modelling variety and acceptance. A profile of needs can be constructed in these areas, as well as an analysis of how considerable the changes would need to be to meet the specific needs of the significantly harmed child, and the contribution of the environment provided by the parents to the harm suffered. The HOME Inventory has been used extensively to demonstrate change in the family context as a result of intervention, and can be used to assess whether intervention has been successful.

10. **The Family Assessment** (Bentovim and Bingley Miller, 2001). The various modules of the Family Assessment include an exploration of family and professional views of the current situation, the adaptability to the child's needs, quality of parenting, various aspects of family relationships and the impact of history. The Family Assessment provides a standardised evidence-based approach to assessing current family strengths and difficulties that have played a role in the significant harm of the child. It also provides a means of assessing the capacity for change, resources in the family to achieve a safe context for the child, and the reversal of family factors that may have played a role in significant harm, and aiding the recovery and future health of the child. The Family Assessment profile achieves this by its qualitative and quantitative information on the parents' understanding of the child's state, the level of responsibility they take for the significant harm, their capacity to adapt to the children's changing needs in the past and future, their ability to promote development, provide adequate guidance and care, manage conflict, make decisions and relate to the wider family and community. Strengths and difficulties in all these areas are delineated, as well as the influence of history, areas of change to be achieved, and the capacities of the family to make such changes.

Appendix 4 – MOD child protection contacts

1. Appendix 4 offers points of contact for the relevant service agencies in child protection matters.

Royal Navy

2. All child protection matters within the Royal Navy are managed by the Naval Personal and Family Service (NPFS) – the Royal Navy's social work department. This provides a confidential and professional social work service to all naval personnel and their families, liaising as appropriate with local authority (LA) social services departments. Child protection issues involving the family of a member of the Royal Navy should be referred to the relevant Area Officer, NPFS.

NPFS Eastern Area Portsmouth
(02392) 722712 Fax: 725803

NPFS Northern Area Helensburgh
(01436) 672798 Fax: 674965

NPFS Western Area Plymouth
(01752) 555041 Fax: 555647

Royal Marines

3. The Royal Marines Welfare Service is staffed by trained but unqualified Royal Marine senior non-commissioned officers (NCOs). They are accountable to a qualified social work manager at Headquarters Royal Marines, Portsmouth. For child protection matters involving Royal Marines families, social services departments should notify SO3 (WFS) at Portsmouth. Tel: (02392) 547542.

Army

4. Staffed by qualified civilian social workers and trained and supervised army welfare workers, the Army Welfare Service (AWS) provides professional welfare support to army personnel and their families. AWS also liaises with LAs where appropriate, particularly where a child is subject to child protection concerns. LAs who have any enquiries or concerns regarding safeguarding or promoting the welfare of a child from an army family should contact the Senior Army Welfare Worker in the nearest AWS team location or:

Chief Personal Support Officer
HQ AWS
HQ Land Command
Erskine Barracks
Wilton
Salisbury
SP2 0AG

Tel: 01722 436564
Fax: 01722 436307
e-mail christine.blagbrough576@land.mod.uk

Royal Air Force

5. Welfare support for families in the RAF is managed as a normal function of Command and co-ordinated by each station's Personnel Officer, the Officer Commanding Personnel Management Squadron (OCPMS) or the Officer Commanding Administrative Squadron (OCA), depending on the size of the station.

6. A number of qualified SSAFA Forces Help Social Workers and trained professionally supervised Personal and Family Support Workers are located throughout the UK to assist the chain of Command in providing welfare support.

7. Any LA that has any enquiries or concerns regarding safeguarding or promoting the welfare of a child from an RAF family should contact the parent's unit or, if this is not known, the OC PMS/OCA of the nearest RAF unit. Additionally, the SSAFA Forces Help Head of Service RAF can be contacted at:

Head of Service
SSAFA-Forces Help Social Work Service RAF
HQ Personnel and Training Command
RAF Innsworth
Gloucester
GL3 1 EZ

Tel: 01452 712612 ext 5815/5840
Fax: 01452 510875

or

Director of Social Work SSAFA-Forces Help
19 Queen Elizabeth Street
London
SE1 2LP

Tel: 020 7403 8783
Fax: 020 7403 8815

Overseas

8. The following should be consulted:

Royal Navy

Area Officer (NPFS) Eastern
HMS Nelson
Queen Street
Portsmouth
PO1 3HH

Tel: (02392) 722712
Fax: (02392) 725083

Army and Royal Air Force

Director of Social Work SSAFA-Forces Help
Contact details as shown above.

*For **any** child being taken abroad and subject to child protection procedures or a child protection plan, the Director of Social Work SSAFA-Forces Help **must** be consulted, using the same contact details shown above.*

Appendix 5 – Procedures for managing allegations against people who work with children

Scope

1. The framework for managing cases set out in this guidance applies to a wider range of allegations than those in which there is reasonable cause to believe a child is suffering, or is likely to suffer, significant harm. It also caters for cases of allegations that might indicate that the alleged perpetrator is unsuitable to continue to work with children in his or her present position, or in any capacity. It should be used in respect of all cases in which it is alleged that a person who works with children has:

- behaved in a way that has harmed, or may have harmed, a child
- possibly committed a criminal offence against, or related to, a child; or
- behaved towards a child or children in a way that indicates s/he is unsuitable to work with children.

2. There may be up to three strands in the consideration of an allegation:

- a police investigation of a possible criminal offence
- enquiries and assessment by children's social care about whether a child is in need of protection or in need of services
- consideration by an employer[46] of disciplinary action in respect of the individual.

[46] For convenience, the term 'employer' is used throughout this guidance to refer to organisations that have a working relationship with the individual against whom the allegation is made. This includes organisations that use the services of volunteers or people who are self-employed, as well as service providers, voluntary organisations, employment agencies or businesses, contractors, fostering services, regulatory bodies such as Ofsted in the case of childminders, and others that may not have a direct employment relationship with the individual, but will need to consider whether to continue to use the person's services, or to provide the person for work with children in future, or to deregister the individual. Note: in some circumstances, the term 'employer' for these purposes encompasses more than one organisation – e.g. where staff providing services for children in an organisation are employed by a contractor, or where temporary staff are provided by an agency. In those circumstances, both the contractor or agency and the organisation in which the accused individual worked need to be involved in dealing with the allegation.

Supporting those involved

3. Parents or carers of a child or children involved should be told about the allegation as soon as possible if they do not already know of it (subject to paragraph 14 below). They should also be kept informed about the progress of the case, and told the outcome where there is not a criminal prosecution. That includes the outcome of any disciplinary process. Note: the deliberations of a disciplinary hearing, and the information taken into account in reaching a decision, cannot normally be disclosed, but those concerned should be told the outcome.[47]

4. In cases where a child may have suffered significant harm, or there may be a criminal prosecution, children's social care or the police, as appropriate, should consider what support the child or children involved may need.

5. The employer should also keep the person who is the subject of the allegations informed of the progress of the case, and arrange to provide appropriate support to the individual while the case is ongoing. (That support may be provided via occupational health or employee welfare arrangements where those exist.) If the person is suspended, the employer should also make arrangements to keep the individual informed about developments in the workplace. As noted in paragraph 15, if the person is a member of a union or professional association, they should be advised to contact that body at the outset.

Confidentiality

6. Every effort should be made to maintain confidentiality and guard against publicity while an allegation is being investigated/considered. In accordance with ACPO guidance, the police do not normally provide any information to the press or media that might identify an individual who is under investigation, unless and until the person is charged with a criminal offence. (In exceptional cases, where the police might depart from that rule – e.g. an appeal to trace a suspect – the reasons should be documented and partner agencies consulted beforehand.) The system of self-regulation, overseen by the Press Complaints Commission, also provides safeguards against the publication of inaccurate or misleading information.

Resignations and 'compromise agreements'

7. The fact that a person tenders his or her resignation, or ceases to provide their services, must not prevent an allegation being followed up in accordance with these procedures. It is important that every effort is made to reach a conclusion in all cases of allegations bearing on the safety or welfare of children, including any in which the person concerned refuses to co-operate with the process. Wherever possible, the person should be given a full opportunity to answer the allegation and make representations about it. The

[47] In deciding what information to disclose, careful consideration should be given to duties under the Data Protection Act 1998, the law of confidence and, where relevant, the Human Rights Act 1998.

process of recording the allegation and any supporting evidence, and reaching a judgement about whether it can be regarded as substantiated on the basis of all the information available, should continue, even if that cannot be done or the person does not co-operate. It may be difficult to reach a conclusion in those circumstances, and it may not be possible to apply any disciplinary sanctions if a person's period of notice expires before the process is complete, but it is important to reach and record a conclusion wherever possible.

8. By the same token, so-called 'compromise agreements' – by which a person agrees to resign, the employer agrees not to pursue disciplinary action, and both parties agree a form of words to be used in any future reference – must not be used in these cases. In any event, such an agreement will not prevent a thorough police investigation where appropriate, nor can it override an employer's statutory duty to make a referral to the Protection of Children Act List or DfES List 99 where circumstances require that (see paragraphs 12.29 and 12.33 respectively).

Record-keeping

9. It is important that employers keep a clear and comprehensive summary of any allegations made, details of how the allegations were followed up and resolved, and of any action taken and decisions reached. These should be kept in a person's confidential personnel file and a copy should be given to the individual. Such information should be retained on file, including for people who leave the organisation, at least until the person reaches normal retirement age, or for 10 years if that is longer. The purpose of the record is to enable accurate information to be given in response to any future request for a reference. It will provide clarification in cases where a future CRB Disclosure reveals information from the police that an allegation was made but did not result in a prosecution or a conviction. It will also prevent unnecessary re-investigation if, as sometimes happens, allegations resurface after a period of time.

Timescales

10. It is in everyone's interest to resolve cases as quickly as possible, consistent with a fair and thorough investigation. Every effort should be made to manage cases to avoid any unnecessary delay. Indicative target timescales are shown for different actions in the summary description of the process. These are not performance indicators: the time taken to investigate and resolve individual cases depends on a variety of factors, including the nature, seriousness and complexity of the allegations, but they provide useful targets to aim for that are achievable in many cases.

Oversight and monitoring

11. LSCB member organisations, county-level and unitary local authorities and police forces should each have officers who fill the roles described in paragraphs 6.23 and 6.24.

12. Other employers' procedures should identify a senior manager within the organisation to whom allegations or concerns that a member of staff or volunteer may have abused a child should be reported. Procedures should make sure that all staff and volunteers know who that person is. The procedures should also identify an alternative person to whom reports should be made in the absence of the named senior manager, or in cases where that person is the subject of the allegation or concern. The procedures should include contact details for the LA designated officer responsible for providing advice and liaison and monitoring the progress of cases, to ensure that cases are dealt with as quickly as possible, consistent with a fair and thorough process.

Initial considerations

13. Procedures need to be applied with common sense and judgement. Some allegations are so serious as to require immediate referral to social care and the police for investigation. Others are much less serious, and at first sight may not seem to warrant consideration of a police investigation or enquiries by children's social care. However, it is important to ensure that even apparently less serious allegations are seen to be followed up, and that they are examined objectively by someone independent of the organisation concerned. Consequently, the LA designated officer should be informed of all allegations that come to the employer's attention and appear to meet the criteria in paragraph 1, so that s/he can consult police and social care colleagues as appropriate. The LA designated officer should also be informed of any allegations that are made directly to the police (which should be communicated via the police force's designated officer) or to children's social care.

14. The LA designated officer should first establish, in discussion with the employer, that the allegation is within the scope of these procedures (see paragraph 1) and may have some foundation. If the parents/carers of the child concerned are not already aware of the allegation, the designated officer will also discuss how and by whom they should be informed. In circumstances in which the police or social care may need to be involved, the LA officer should consult those colleagues about how best to inform parents. However, in some circumstances an employer may need to advise parents of an incident involving their child straight away – e.g. if the child has been injured while in the organisation's care and requires medical treatment.

15. The employer should inform the accused person about the allegation as soon as possible after consulting the LA designated officer. However, where a strategy discussion is needed, or it is clear that police or children's social care may need to be involved, that should not be done until those agencies have been consulted and have agreed what information can be disclosed to the person. If the person is a member of a union or professional association, s/he should be advised to seek support from that organisation.

16. If there is cause to suspect a child is suffering, or is likely to suffer, significant harm, a strategy discussion should be convened in accordance with paragraph 5.54. Note: in these

cases the strategy discussion should include a representative of the employer (unless there are good reasons not to do that) and should take account of any information the employer can provide about the circumstances or context of the allegation.

17. In cases where a formal strategy discussion is not considered appropriate – because the threshold of 'significant harm' is not reached – but a police investigation might be needed, the LA designated officer should nevertheless conduct a similar discussion with the police, the employer, and any other agencies involved with the child to evaluate the allegation and decide how it should be dealt with. (Note: the police must be consulted about any case in which a criminal offence may have been committed.) Like a strategy discussion, that initial evaluation may not need to be a face-to-face meeting. It should share available information about the allegation, the child and the person against whom the allegation has been made, consider whether a police investigation is needed and, if so, agree the timing and conduct of that. In cases where a police investigation is necessary, the joint evaluation should also consider whether there are matters that can be taken forward in a disciplinary process in parallel with the criminal process, or whether any disciplinary action needs to wait for completion of the police enquiries and/or prosecution.

18. If the complaint or allegation is such that it is clear that investigations by police and/or enquiries by social care are not necessary, or the strategy discussion or initial evaluation decides that this is the case, the LA designated officer should discuss next steps with the employer. In such circumstances, options open to the employer range from taking no further action, to summary dismissal or a decision not to use the person's services in future. The nature and circumstances of the allegation and the evidence and information available determine which of the range of possible options is most appropriate.

19. In some cases, further investigation is needed to enable a decision about how to proceed. If so, the LA designated officer should discuss with the person's employer how and by whom the investigation will be undertaken. The investigation should normally be undertaken by the employer. However, in some circumstances appropriate resources may not be available in the employer's organisation, or the nature and complexity of the allegation might point to the employer commissioning an independent investigation.

Suspension

20. The possible risk of harm to children posed by an accused person needs to be evaluated and managed effectively – in respect of the child(ren) involved in the allegations, and any other children in the individual's home, work or community life. In some cases this requires the employer to consider suspending the person. Suspension should be considered in any case where there is cause to suspect a child is at risk of significant harm, or the allegation warrants investigation by the police, or is so serious that it might be grounds for dismissal. People must not be suspended automatically or without careful thought. Employers must consider carefully whether the circumstances of a case warrant a person being suspended from contact with children until the allegation is resolved. Note:

neither the LA, nor the police, nor children's social care can require an employer to suspend a member of staff or a volunteer. The power to suspend is vested in the employer alone. However, where a strategy discussion or initial evaluation discussion concludes that there should be enquiries by social care and/or an investigation by the police, the LA designated officer should canvass police/social care views about whether the accused member of staff needs to be suspended from contact with children, to inform the employer's consideration of suspension.

Monitoring progress

21. The LA designated officer should regularly monitor the progress of cases, either via review strategy discussions, or by liaising with the police and/or children's social care colleagues or the employer, as appropriate. Reviews should be conducted at fortnightly or monthly intervals, depending on the complexity of the case.

22. If the strategy discussion or initial evaluation decides that a police investigation is required, the police should set a target date for reviewing the progress of the investigation and consulting the Crown Prosecution Service (CPS) to consider whether to charge the individual, continue to investigate, or close the investigation. Wherever possible, that review should take place **no later than four weeks** after the initial action meeting. Dates for subsequent reviews, at fortnightly or monthly intervals, should be set at the meeting if the investigation continues.

Information sharing

23. In the initial consideration at a strategy discussion or joint evaluation, the agencies concerned – including the employer – should share all relevant information they have about the person who is the subject of the allegation and about the alleged victim.

24. Wherever possible, the police should obtain consent from the individuals concerned to share the statements and evidence they obtain with the employer, and/or regulatory body, for disciplinary purposes. This should be done as the investigation proceeds rather than after it is concluded, to enable the police and CPS to share relevant information without delay at the conclusion of their investigation or any court case.

25. Children's social care should adopt a similar procedure when making enquiries to determine whether the child or children named in the allegation are in need of protection or services, so that any information obtained in the course of those enquiries that is relevant to a disciplinary case can be passed to the employer or regulatory body without delay.

Action following a criminal investigation or a prosecution

26. The police or the CPS should inform the employer and LA designated officer straightaway when a criminal investigation and any subsequent trial is complete, or if it is decided to close an investigation without charge, or not to prosecute after the person has been charged. In those circumstances, the LA designated officer should discuss with the

employer whether any further action is appropriate and, if so, how to proceed. The information provided by the police and/or children's social care should inform that decision. Action by the employer, including dismissal, is not ruled out in any of those circumstances. The range of options open depends on the circumstances of the case, and the consideration needs to take into account the result of the police investigation or trial, as well as the different standard of proof required in disciplinary and criminal proceedings.

Action on conclusion of a case

27. If the allegation is substantiated and the person is dismissed or the employer ceases to use the person's services, or the person resigns or otherwise ceases to provide his/her services, the LA designated officer should discuss with the employer whether a referral to the Protection of Children Act List or DfES List 99 is required or advisable, along with the form and content of a referral. Also, if the person is subject to registration or regulation by a professional body or regulator – e.g. by the General Social Care Council, General Medical Council, OFSTED, etc. – the designated officer should advise on whether a referral to that body is appropriate.

28. If it is decided on conclusion of the case that a person who has been suspended can return to work, the employer should consider how best to facilitate that. Most people will benefit from some help and support to return to work after a very stressful experience. Depending on the individual's circumstances, a phased return and/or the provision of a mentor to provide assistance and support in the short term may be appropriate. The employer should also consider how the person's contact with the child or children who made the allegation can best be managed if they are still in the workplace.

Learning lessons

29. At the conclusion of a case in which an allegation is substantiated, the employer should review the circumstances of the case to determine whether there are any improvements to be made to the organisation's procedures or practice to help prevent similar events in the future.

Action in respect of false or unfounded allegations

30. If an allegation is determined to be unfounded, the employer should refer the matter to children's social care to determine whether the child concerned is in need of services, or may have been abused by someone else. In the rare event that an allegation is shown to have been deliberately invented or malicious, the police should be asked to consider whether any action might be appropriate against the person responsible.

Summary of process

Allegation made to employer

31. The allegation should be reported to the senior manager identified in the employer's procedure immediately, unless that person is the subject of the allegation, in which case it should be reported to the designated alternative.

32. If the allegation meets any of the criteria set out in paragraph 1, the employer should report it to the LA designated officer within one working day.

Allegation made to the police or children's social care

33. If an allegation is made to the police, the officer who receives it should report it to the force's designated liaison officer without delay, and the designated liaison officer should, in turn, inform the LA designated officer straightaway. Similarly, if the allegation is made to children's social care, the person who receives it should report it to the LA designated officer without delay.

Initial consideration

34. The LA designated officer will discuss the matter with the employer and, where necessary, obtain further details of the allegation and the circumstances in which it was made. The discussion should also consider whether there is evidence/information that establishes that the allegation is false or unfounded.

35. If the allegation is not patently false and there is cause to suspect that a child is suffering, or is likely to suffer, significant harm, the LA designated officer will immediately refer to children's social care and ask for a strategy discussion to be convened straightaway. In those circumstances, the strategy discussion should include the LA designated officer and a representative of the employer.

36. If there is no cause to suspect that 'significant harm' is an issue, but a criminal offence might have been committed, the LA designated officer should immediately inform the police and convene a similar discussion to decide whether a police investigation is needed. That discussion should also involve the employer.

Action following initial consideration

37. Where the initial evaluation decides that the allegation does not involve a possible criminal offence, it is dealt with by the employer. In such cases, if the nature of the allegation does not require formal disciplinary action, appropriate action should be instituted **within three working days**. If a disciplinary hearing is required and can be held without further investigation, the hearing should be held **within 15 working days**.

38. Where further investigation is required to inform consideration of disciplinary action, the employer should discuss who will undertake that with the LA designated officer. In some settings and circumstances, it may be appropriate for the disciplinary investigation to

be conducted by a person who is independent of the employer or the person's line management to ensure objectivity. In any case, the investigating officer should aim to provide a report to the employer **within 10 working days**.

39. On receipt of the report of the disciplinary investigation, the employer should decide whether a disciplinary hearing is needed **within two working days**, and if a hearing is needed it should be held **within 15 working days.**

40. In any case in which children's social care has undertaken enquiries to determine whether the child or children are in need of protection, the employer should take account of any relevant information obtained in the course of those enquiries when considering disciplinary action.

41. The LA designated officer should continue to liaise with the employer to monitor progress of the case and provide advice/support when required or requested.

Case subject to police investigation

42. If a criminal investigation is required, the police will aim to complete their enquiries as quickly as possible, consistent with a fair and thorough investigation, and will keep the progress of the case under review. They should, at the outset, set a target date for reviewing progress of the investigation and consulting the CPS about whether to proceed with the investigation, charge the individual with an offence, or close the case. Wherever possible that review should take place **no later than four weeks** after the initial evaluation, and if the decision is to continue to investigate the allegation, dates for subsequent reviews should be set at that point. (It is open to the police to consult the CPS about the evidence that will need to be obtained in order to charge a person with an offence at any stage.)

43. If the police and/or CPS decide not to charge the individual with an offence, or decide to administer a caution, or the person is acquitted by a court, the police should pass all information they have which may be relevant to a disciplinary case to the employer without delay. In those circumstances the employer and the LA designated officer should proceed as described in paragraphs 37–41.

44. If the person is convicted of an offence, the police should also inform the employer straightaway so that appropriate action can be taken.

Referral to PoCA list or regulatory body

45. If the allegation is substantiated, and on conclusion of the case the employer dismisses the person or ceases to use the person's services, or the person ceases to provide his/her services, the employer should consult the LA designated officer about whether a referral to the PoCA list and/or to a professional or regulatory body is required. If a referral is appropriate, the report should be made within one month.

Appendix 6 – A guide to the acronyms in the document

ACPO	Association of Chief Police Officers
APA	Annual Performance Assessment
CAIU	Child Abuse Investigation Units
CAFCASS	Children and Family Court Advisory and Support Service
CAMHS	Child and Adolescent Mental Health Services
CCPAS	Churches Child Protection Advisory Service
CPS	The Crown Prosecution Service
CPSU	Child Protection in Sport Unit
CYPP	Children and Young People's Plan
DATs	Drug Action Teams
DCS	Director of Children's Services
FGM	Female Genital Mutilation
ICS	Integrated Children's System
ICT	Information Communication Technology
INI	IMPACT National Index
IROs	Independent Reviewing Officers
JAR	Joint Area Review
LA	Local Authority
LSCB	Local Safeguarding Children Board
MAPPA	Multi Agency Public Protection Arrangements

NSF	National Service Framework
ONS	Office for National Statistics
PCTs	Primary Care Trust
PHCT	Primary Health Care Team
PSHE	Personal Social and Health Education
RSL	Registered Social Landlord
SHA	Strategic Health Authorities
STC	Secure Training Centre
VISOR	Violent and Sexual Offenders Register
YCW	Youth and Community Worker
YJB	Youth Justice Board
Yot	Youth Offending Team

References and internet links

Academy of Medical Royal Colleges (2005). *Medical Expert Witness: Guidance from the Academy of Medical Royal Colleges.* Website: www.aomrc.org.uk

The Advisory Council on the Misuse of Drugs (ACMD) (2003). *Hidden Harm – Responding to the needs of children of problem drug users.* London: Home Office. Website: www.drugs.gov.uk

Aldgate, J., Jones, D., Rose, W. and Jeffery, C. (eds) (2006). *The Developing World of the Child.* London: Jessica Kingsley Publishers.

Association of Chief Police Officers (2005). *Investigating Child Abuse and Safeguarding Children.* Website: www.acpo.police.uk/policies.asp

Association of Directors of Social Services, Department for Education and Skills, Department of Heath, Home Office, Foreign And Commonwealth Office (2004). *Young People and Vulnerable Adults Facing Forced Marriage. Practice Guidance for Social Workers.* Website: www.adss.org.uk/publications/guidance/marriage.pdf

Bentovim, A. and Bingley Miller, L. (2001) *The Family Assessment: Assessment of Family Competence, Strengths and Difficulties.* Brighton: Pavilion Publishing.

Chief Inspector of Social Services, Commission for Health Improvement, Her Majesty's Chief Inspector of Constabulary, Her Majesty's Chief inspector of the Crown Prosecution Service, Her Majesty's Chief inspector of the Magistrates' Courts Service, Her Majesty's Chief inspector of Schools, Her Majesty's Chief Inspector of Prisons, Her Majesty's Chief Inspector of Probation (2002). *Safeguarding Children – A joint Chief Inspectors' Report on Arrangements to Safeguard Children.* London: Department of Health.

Children Act 1989. London: HMSO.

Children Act 2004. London: HMSO.

The Children (Private Arrangement for Fostering) Regulations (2005) S.I. No. 1533. Website: www.everychildmatters.gov.uk/socialcare/safeguarding/privatefostering

Cleaver, H., Wattam, C. and Cawson, P. (1998). *Assessing Risk in Child Protection*. London: NSPCC.

Cm 5730 (2003). *The Victoria Climbié Inquiry. Report of an Inquiry by Lord Laming*. London: The Stationery Office. Website: www.victoria-climbie-inquiry.org.uk/finreport/finreport.htm

Cm 5860 (2003). *Every Child Matters*. London: The Stationery Office. Website: www.everychildmatters.gov.uk/

Cm 5861 (2003). *Keeping Children Safe – the Government's response to the Victoria Climbié Inquiry Report and joint Chief Inspectors' Report: Safeguarding Children*. London: The Stationery Office.

Commission for Social Care Inspection (CSCI), HM Inspectorate of Court Administration, The Healthcare Commission, HM inspectorate of Constabulary, HM Inspectorate of Probation, HM Inspectorate of Prisons, HM Crown Prosecution Service Inspectorate, The Office for Standards in Education (2005). *Safeguarding Children: The second joint Chief Inspectors' Report on Arrangements to Safeguard Children*. Website: www.safeguardingchildren.org.uk

Cox, A. and Walker, S. (2002). *The HOME Inventory – Home Observation and Measurement of the Environment*. Brighton: Pavilion Publishing.

Crime and Disorder Act 1998. London: HMSO. Website: www.opsi.gov.uk/acts/acts1998/19980037.htm

Criminal Justice Act 2003. London: HMSO. Website: www.opsi.gov.uk/acts/acts2003/20030044.htm

Criminal Justice and Court Services Act 2000. London: HMSO. Website: www.opsi.gov.uk/acts/acts2000/20000043.htm

Crown Prosecution Service, Department of Health and Home Office (2001). *Provision of Therapy for Child Witnesses prior to a Criminal Trial. Practice Guidance*. London: CPS Website: www.cps.gov.uk/publications/docs/therapychild.pdf

Data Protection Act 1998. London: HMSO. Website: www.opsi.gov.uk/ACTS/acts1998/19980029.htm

Department for Education and Skills (2004a). *Safeguarding Children in Education*. London: Department for Education and Skills. Website: www.teachernet.gov.uk/wholeschool/familyandcommunity/childprotection/guidance/

Department for Education and Skills (2004b). *Identifying and maintaining contact with children missing, or at risk of going missing, from education*. The guidance can be found on the *Every Child Matters* website: http://www.everychildmatters.gov.uk/ete/?asset=document&id=15394

Department for Education and Skills (2005). *Children Act 1989 Guidance on Private Fostering*. London: Department of Education and Skills.
Website: www.everychildmatters.gov.uk/socialcare/safeguarding/privatefostering/

Department for Education and Skills (2005). National Minimum Standards for Private Fostering. London: Department of Education and Skills.
Website: www.everychildmatters.gov.uk/socialcare/safeguarding/privatefostering/

Department for Education and Skills (2005). *Safeguarding Children in Education: Dealing with Allegations of Abuse against Teachers and Other Staff*. London: Department for Education and Skills. Website:
www.teachernet.gov.uk/wholeschool/familyandcommunity/childprotection/guidance/

Department for Education and Skills (2005). *Safeguarding Children: Safer Recruitment and Selection in Education Settings*. London: Department for Education and Skills.
Website:
www.teachernet.gov.uk/wholeschool/familyandcommunity/childprotection/guidance/

Department of Health (1999). *Guidance on the Visiting of Psychiatric Patients by Children* (HSC 1999/222: LAC (99)32). Website:
www.dh.gov.uk/PublicationsAndStatistics/Publications/PublicationsPolicyAndGuidance/fs/en)

Department of Health (2000). *Assessing Children in Need and their Families: Practice Guidance*. London: The Stationery Office

Department of Health (2002). *The Integrated Children's System*.
Website: www.everychildmatters.gov.uk/ics

Department of Health (2003). *Children and Young People in Hospital*. London: Department of Health. Website:
www.dh.gov.uk/PolicyAndGuidance/HealthAndSocialCareTopics/ChildrenServices/ChildrenServicesInformation/fs/en

Department of Health (2005). *Responding to Domestic Abuse: A Hand Book for Health Professionals*. London: Department of Health. Website:
www.dh.gov.uk/PolicyAndGuidance/HealthAndSocialCareTopics/ChildrenServices/ChildrenServicesInformation/fs/en

Department of Health, Cox, A. and Bentovim, A. (2000). *The Family Assessment Pack of Questionnaires and Scales*. London: The Stationery Office.

Department of Health and Department for Education and Skills (2004). *National Service Framework for Children, Young People and Maternity Services*. London: Department of Health.
Website:
www.dh.gov.uk/PolicyAndGuidance/HealthAndSocialCareTopics/ChildrenServices/ChildrenServicesInformation/fs/en.

Department of Health, Department for Education and Employment and Home Office (2000). *Framework for the Assessment of Children in Need and their Families*. London: The Stationery Office. Website: www.dh.gov.uk/PolicyAndGuidance/HealthAndSocialCareTopics/ChildrenServices/ChildrenServicesInformation/fs/en.

Department of Health, Home Office, Department for Education and Employment and the National Assembly for Wales (2000). *Safeguarding Children Involved in Prostitution*. London: Department of Health. Website: www.dh.gov.uk/PublicationsAndStatistics/Publications/fs/en

Department of Health, Home Office, Department for Education and Skills, Welsh Assembly Government (2002). *Safeguarding Children in whom Illness is Fabricated or Induced*. London: Department of Health. Website: www.dh.gov.uk/PublicationsAndStatistics/Publications/fs/en

Domestic Violence, Crime and Victims Act 2005. London: HMSO. Website: http://www.crimereduction.gov.uk/legislation37.htm

Education Act 1996. London: HMSO. Website: www.opsi.gov.uk/acts/acts1996/1996056.htm

Education Act 2002. London: HMSO. Website: www.opsi.gov.uk/ACTS/acts2002/20020032.htm

Health Act 1999. London: HMSO. Website: www.opsi.gov.uk/acts/acts1999/19990008.htm

HM Government (2004). *Every Child Matters: Change for Children Programme*. Nottingham: Department for Education and Skills. Website: www.everychildmatters.gov.uk/

HM Government (2005a). *Statutory Guidance on Inter-agency co-operation to improve the well-being of children: Children's Trusts*. London: Department for Education and Skills. Website: www.everychildmatters.gov.uk/strategy/guidance/

HM Government (2005b). *Guidance on the Children and Young People's Plan*. London: Department for Education and Skills. Website: www.everychildmatters.gov.uk/resources-and-practice/search/?cat=29978

HM Government (2005c). *Common Core of Skills and Knowledge for the Children's Workforce*. London: Department for Education and Skills. Website: www.everychildmatters.gov.uk/commoncore/

HM Government (2005d). *Statutory guidance on making arrangements to safeguard and promote the welfare of children under section 11 of the Children Act 2004*. London: Department for Education and Skills.

HM Government (2006a). *Making Safeguarding Everyone's Business – Response to the second joint Chief Inspectors' Report on Safeguarding Children*. London: Department for Education and Skills. Website: www.everychildmatters.gov.uk/socialcare/safeguarding/

HM Government (2006b). *The Common Assessment Framework for children and young people: practitioners' guide*. London: Department for Education and Skills. Website: www.everychildmatters.gov.uk/caf

HM Government (2006c). *Information Sharing: Practitioners' guide*. London: Department for Education and Skills. Website: www.everychildmatters.gov.uk/information sharing

HM Government (2006d). *What To Do If You're Worried A Child Is Being Abused*. London: Department for Education and Skills. Website: www.everychildmatters.gov.uk/safeguarding

HM Prison Service (2003). Prison Service Order 2855 – *Prisoners with physical, sensory and mental disabilities*. London: HM Prison Service.

HM Prison Service (2004). *Public Protection Manual*. London: HM Prison Service. Website: www.adss.org.uk/publications/guidance/protection/welcome.shtml

HM Prison Service (2004). *National Security Framework*. London: HM Prison Service. Website: pso.hmprisonservice.gov.uk/pso1600/home.htm

HM Prison Service (2004). Prison Order 4950 – *Juvenile Regimes*. London: HM Prison Service. Website: pso.hmprisonservice.gov.uk/PSO_4950_regimes_for_juveniles.doc.

HM Treasury, Department for Education and Skills, Department for Work and Pensions, Department for Trade and Industry (2004). *Choice for parents, the best start for children: a ten year strategy for childcare*. London: The Stationery Office. Website: www.hmtreasury.gov.uk/pre_budget_report/prebud_pbr04/assoc_docs/prebud_pbr04_adchildcare.cfm

Home Office (1993). *Safe from Harm: a Code of Practice for Safeguarding the Welfare of Children in Voluntary Organisations in England and Wales.*

Home Office (2004). *Safety and Justice: sharing personal information in the context of domestic violence – an overview.* Website: www.homeoffice.gov.uk/rds/pdfs04/dpr30.pdf

Home Office. Female Circumcision Act 1985. Female Genital Mutilation Act 2003. *Home Office Circular 10/2004.* Website: www.knowledgenetwork.gov.uk/HO/circular.nsf/ViewTemplate%20For%20HOCircularsWeb?OpenForm&Start=1&Count=1000&ExpandView&Seq=1

Home Office Circular 16/2005 *Guidance on offences against children.* Website: www.knowledgenetwork.gov.uk/HO/circular.nsf/79755433dd36a66980256d4f004d1514/1b6d4af0fe8c4d4780256fcc00414639?OpenDocument)

Home Office and Department of Health (2002). *Complex Child Abuse Investigations: Inter-agency Issues*. Website: www.dh.gov.uk/PublicationsAndStatistics/PressReleases/

Home Office, Lord Chancellor's Department, Crown Prosecution Service, Department of Health and National Assembly for Wales (2002). *Achieving Best Evidence in Criminal Proceedings: Guidance for vulnerable or intimidated witnesses, including children*. London, Home Office. Website: www.homeoffice.gov.uk/justice/legalprocess/witnesses/index.html.

Housing Act 1996. London: HMSO. Website: www.opsi.gov.uk/ACTS/acts1996/1996052.htm

Housing Act 2004. London: HMSO. Website: www.opsi.gov.uk/ACTS/acts2004/20040034.htm

Human Rights Act 1998. London: HMSO.
Website: www.opsi.gov.uk/ACTS/acts1998/19980042.htm

Learning and Skills Act 2000. London: HMSO.
Website: www.opsi.gov.uk/acts/acts2000/20000021.htm

Licensing Act 2003. London: HMSO.
Website: www.opsi.gov.uk/ACTS/acts2003/20030017.htm

Local Authority Social Services Act 1970.
Website: www.dfes.gov.uk/childrenandfamilies/cfcirculars.shtml

Local Government Act 2000. London: HMSO.
Website: www.opsi.gov.uk/Acts/acts2000/20000022.htm

LGA, ADSS, CAFCASS and Women's Aid (2005). *Vision for services for children and young people affected by domestic violence – guidance to local commissioners of children's service*
Website: www.adss.org.uk/publications/guidance/domestic.pdf

The Local Safeguarding Children Boards Regulations 2006, Statutory Instrument No. 2006/90. Website: www.opsi.gov.uk/si/si2006/20060090.htm

National Centre for Policing Excellence (2005). *Guidance on Investigating Child Abuse and Safeguarding Children*. Hampshire: National Centre for Policing Excellence. Website: www.probation.homeoffice.gov.uk/files/pdf/PC63%202005.pdf

National Probation Service (2003). *Probation Circular 69/2003*.

Police Act 1996. London: HMSO. Website: www.opsi.gov.uk/acts/acts1996/1996016.htm

Police and Criminal Evidence Act 1984. London: HMSO.
Website: www.opsi.gov.uk/si/si2001/20012254.htm

Prisons Act 1952. London: HMSO.

Protection of Children Act 1999. London: HMSO.
Website: www.opsi.gov.uk/acts/acts1999/19990014.htm

Railways and Transport Safety Act 2003. London: HMSO.
Website: www.opsi.gov.uk/ACTS/acts2003/20030020.htm

Royal College of Psychiatrists (2004). *Child Abuse and Neglect: the role of Mental Health Services.* Website: www.rcpsych.ac.uk/publications/collegereports/cr/cr120.aspx

Royal College of Psychiatrists (2002). *Patients as Parents.*
Website: www.rcpsych.ac.uk/publications/collegereports/cr/cr105.aspx

Sexual Offences Act 2003. London: HMSO.
Website: www.opsi.gov.uk/ACTS/acts2003/20030042.htm

The Trafficking Toolkit. Website: www.crimereduction.gov.uk/toolkits/

Youth Justice Board. *Key Elements of Effective Practice: Assessment, Planning Interventions and Supervision.* London: Youth Justice Board (2002). Website: www.youth-justiceboard.gov.uk/Publications/Scripts/prodView.asp?idproduct=106&eP=

Youth Justice Board (2002). *National Specification for Learning and Skills for Young People on a Detention and Training Order in Prison Service Accommodation.* London: Youth Justice Board. Website:
www.youth-justiceboard.gov.uk/Publications/Scripts/prodView.asp?idproduct=106&eP=

Youth Justice Board (2004a). *National Standards for Youth Justice Services.* London: Youth Justice Board. Website:
www.youth-justiceboard.gov.uk/Publications/Scripts/prodView.asp?idproduct=106&eP=

Youth Justice Board (2004b). *Sustaining the Success: Extending the Guidance; Establishing Youth Offending Teams.* London: Youth Justice Board. Website:
www.youth-justiceboard.gov.uk/Publications/Scripts/prodView.asp?idproduct=106&eP=